AGROFUELS IN THE AMERICAS

Food First Books
398 60th Street
Oakland, CA 94618
510-654-4400
www.foodfirst.org

T0272927

Cover, text design, and interior design by Richard Jonasse
Cover Photo, Composite:
"Cane Burn": Shanna Riley Creative Commons License share (details: http://creativecommons.org/licenses/by-sa/2.0/deed.en) Photo URL: http://www.flickr.com/photos/skatoolaki/2308050201/
"Grasslands": Richard Jonasse

ACKNOWLEDGEMENTS

This project began a little over a year ago with five of the authors sitting around a table at Food First in Oakland, CA. They included Annie Shattuck, Isabella Kenfield, Jessica Aguirre, Gretchen Gordon, Ellen Tarby, and myself. Beyond the wonderful work of the authors herein, we would like to thank Eric Holt-Giménez for providing his insights and many key paragraphs to most of the pieces herein. Annie Shattuck, had a hand in every article. Marilyn Borchardt provided tremendous support, humor, feedback, and commentary. Martha and Rowena shared their kindness and mung beans. There have been a number of people here who have stepped in to help with research, fact checking, translation, proofreading, citation hunting, fact-finding, and general commentary. These include: Annie, Marilyn, Martha, Jessica Aguirre, Jody Zaitlin, Karla Pena, Tamara Wattnem, Leonora Hurtado, Loren Peabody, Zack Zimbalist, Matt Dintenfass, Angie Rodriguez, Maria Barrera, Ellen Tyler, Amanda El-Khoury, Mihir Mankad, Jasmine Tilley, William Wroblewski, and Matt King.

About the Editor:

Richard Jonasse is currently a Research Fellow at Food First in Oakland, CA. His research interests lie in development issues, including International Finance Institutions, food sovereignty, labor/human rights, and environmental sustainability. He has a Masters in Telecommunication and Film from University of Oregon, and a Ph.D. in Communication (Science and Technology) from U. C. San Diego.

TABLE OF CONTENTS:

PREFACE:

THE AGROFUELS TRANSITION

BY ANNIE SHATTUCK

Steven Roemerman

CARGILL PROCESSING PLANT, EDDYVILLE IOWA

Biofuels evoke an image of a green future, one with prosperous farmers and secure homegrown energy, but the term masks a much darker reality. Industrial monocultures of crops destined for American and European gas tanks are spreading into virgin forests, displacing small farmers, and driving up the price of food. These "agrofuels" have very little to do with environmental quality or rural development.

Driven by mandates and subsidies, the world has seen a boom in the production of agrofuels over the past four years that has prompted massive changes in the global food system. Far from being a grass roots tool for development, agrofuels have become another extractive industry. Monocultures mine soil and water. "Land grabs" for farmland in the Global South are on the rise. Raw materials are shipped, largely from the Global South to consumers in the Global North, following the same extractive patterns of our fossil fuel economy.

But the agrofuels industry is much more than an extractive industry. It reaches into the food system to rearrange the ways food and fuel are produced, owned, distributed, and accessed around the world. The agrofuels boom is changing the structure of the food system, concentrating ownership of land, genetic resources, and market power, and changing the structure of trade, patterns of investment, and the nature of agribusiness in favor of large multi-nationals. While International Finance Institutions like the World Bank and the International Monetary Fund use loan conditions to restructure finance and trade rules, ministries, and regulatory frameworks; agribusinesses are concentrating land ownership and market power to ensure the efficient extraction of surplus.

The Corporate Capture of Agricultural Profits:

This restructuring is largely a continuation of the past 200 years of increasing industrialization of agriculture. In a process that Goodman, Sorj, and Wilkinson[1] refer to as appropriation and substitution; capital investment in agriculture engages with food production by substituting seed, fertility, pest control, cultivation, etc.—which were once on-farm products—with GMO's, synthetic nitrogen, agrochemicals, combines, and so on. On the consumer end, agricultural corporations substitute industrial products for farm products by turning them into basic elements (sugars, starch, oil, etc) for "value added" processed food and feedstock. By capturing the inputs and processing markets, the agri-foods industry profits from off-farm activities rather than engaging in the risks inherent to farming.

By controlling inputs and processing; along with importation, distribution, and retailing; capital consolidates market power over agricultural production.[2] As consumers of expensive industrial inputs and producers of cheap raw materials, farmers are at a structural disadvantage, capturing less than 20% of the food dollar (from which they still must pay for inputs). This has led to the expansion of large, industrialized farms that operate on ever-shrinking profit margins.

Despite a twenty-year trend in falling farm-gate prices and cheap food, global purchasing power has not kept up with production capacity, leading to ever declining margins for agribusiness corporations. Despite capital's structural advantages; grain has remained cheap and, other than the "food crises" of 1970 and 2008, returns to industrial capital in agriculture have been declining as a whole.[3]

Because they add value to otherwise cheap grain, agrofuels are an industrial one-stop-shop to solve the problem of falling rates of profit. The transformation of food into fuel: a) opens up new market space for overproduced commodities like corn, soy and sugar cane; b) inflates the value of those commodities in both food and fuel markets, and; c) creates more processing steps that allow corporations to add and capture more value. This "added value" also helped spark the food price inflation in 2006-7, inviting the speculative bubble in grain futures in 2008.

The Agrofuels Transition:

Because the agrofuels industry confers these benefits to the agri-foods (and petrochemical) industries, the structure of the food system is changing. The restructuring taking place under the agrofuels transition is of grave concern for indigenous peoples, small farmers, and broader movements for food sovereignty. The long-term effects of the agrofuels transition on the global food system are still yet to be seen.

Agrofuels in the Americas is the first book to take a close look at the changes being affected on the ground as s result of the agrofuels boom; examining the consequences of the industry, from Brazil to Guatemala and the United States; looking at changes in global trade and international finance; and examining the push for acceptance of genetically engineered fuel crops. This book is an opportunity to take a step back, and look at just what the effects of the agrofuels boom have been. It also provides a basis for re-examining public support for the agrofuels industry.

Photo and Image Credits:

Cargill Ethanol: Steven Roemerman, Creative Commons License (details: http://creativecommons.org/licenses/by-nc-nd/2.0/deed.en) Photo URL: http://www.flickr.com/photos/roemerman/234274194/

References:

1. Goodman, David, Bernardo Sorj, and John Wilkenson. (1987). From Farming to Biotechnology: a theory of agro-industrial development, Blackwell, Oxford.

2. Walker, Richard. (2004). The Conquest of Bread: 150 years of agribusiness in California. The New Press, London

3. Moore, Jason (2008). Ecological Crises and the Agrarian Question in World – Historical Perspective. Monthly Review, November 60(6).

Agrofuels
in the
Americas

INTRODUCTION:
AGROFUELS AND OUR ENDANGERED WORLD

BY RICHARD JONASSE

INDUSTRIAL SOYBEAN PLANTATION, BRAZIL

In the midst of the current economic and financial crises many have forgotten "food bubble" in commodity futures that preceded the meltdown. The sudden rise in food prices was sparked by a jump in grain prices due mostly to low reserves and the expansion of agrofuels, followed by unregulated financial speculation in global food commodities. Governments and International Financial Institutions (IFIs), now scrambling to halt the global economic free-fall, appear unshaken in their belief that the solution to just about everything is to repeat the irrational growth strategies that got us into this mess in the first place: opening vulnerable economies to global investment capital, technological responses to every problem,[I] and the North's monopolization of the world's resources.

This planetary strategy has a guiding imperial logic. The hundreds of billions of stimulus dollars lavished on the industrial North's banks, financial houses, key industries and public works, all give the countries in the Organization for Economic Cooperation and Development (OECD) a tremendous advantage in the global marketplace. The countries of the Global South, unable to subsidize their own economic recoveries, will once again fall prey to the economic expansion of the industrial North. They will be called upon to provide access to their extensive markets and natural resources to temporarily bail out the affluent countries.

While the rise of agrofuels cannot be explained based on their dubious social,

---

I. For example, organizations such as the Gates Foundation in Africa are turning to biotechnology and industrial agriculture as solutions to food shortages, which are profitable for Northern corporations like Monsanto, Cargill, and ADM, but harm rural communities' ability to earn money and feed themselves.

energetic and environmental merits, it *can* be explained as a product of an economic system that continually generates false "solutions" that require large infusions of investment capital. The documented drawbacks of agrofuels —in terms of energy balance, food security, poor climate change mitigation, hunger and human rights—are all trumped by their tremendous utility to global finance capital that is hungry for investment opportunities: to biotech companies desperate for returns on their massive investments in genetic engineering, to grain traders looking for a hedge in volatile commodity markets, and to politicians searching to provide the public with a magic bullet for the systemic problems of overconsumption.

While the financial sector has exploded over the past third of a century, the real economy (that produces actual *things*) has largely remained stagnant.[1] This has led to an ongoing *crisis of accumulation* in which tremendous concentrations of wealth and financial capital have difficulty finding investment outlets in the real economy. This is reflected in the unprecedented concentration of global wealth (the world now has over 500 billionaires) alongside growing poverty and flat global economic growth.[2]

The International Monetary Fund, the World Trade Organization and other International Financial Institutions were designed to continually provide escape valves for this excess capital. They have done so by deregulating global trade and finance, allowing (primarily Northern and emerging economy) investments to speed around the globe to wherever they can squeeze out profits (for example, by providing an international framework for biotech corporations to enclose, patent, and license the genetic commons for private profit). Market "logic" has thus come to replace informed policy as the default arbiter of global interaction, giving rise to a series of financial bubbles—and to unprecedented corporate monopoly power.

Among the more irrational aspects of this strategy has been the application of this neoliberal economic model to agricultural production. It has produced a volatile and vulnerable global food system that benefits financiers and large agribusinesses, while putting much of the world at risk of hunger and food insecurity. It has led to a "race to the bottom" as corporations extract (and export) as much as they can from the land, water, and labor of developing countries that often find it difficult to feed themselves. According to the UN, this free market in agriculture has recently pushed 110 million people into poverty, and added

44 million to the swelling ranks of the undernourished.[3] At the other end of the world's hunger spectrum, corporations have found ways to squeeze more "value" into processed foods in order to squeeze more profits out of agriculture—leaving the developed world with wonders such as high fructose corn syrup, a plethora of chemical additives, and growing obesity and diabetes epidemics.[4]

Agrofuels are a new and different type of value-added agricultural product—one for which the world has unlimited appetite. As Gordon and Aguirre (this volume[II]) point out, agrofuels are leading to a renewed push for monocrop industrial agriculture, genetically modified crops, and infrastructure projects that provide access to thus far untouched resources. They have led to a new 'gold rush' in the Global South as agribusiness, biotech, and energy corporations seek to capitalize on new captive agro-energy markets that are sustained by blending mandates in the U.S. and EU. They are expanding their hold on agricultural resources; and further concentrating wealth and land holdings in poor countries with high levels of hunger and food insecurity—though the industry has *nothing* to do with feeding people. By competing with food production for land, water and financial resources; agrofuels have contributed to higher food prices, lower food security, and increased hunger—leading the former UN Rapporteur on the Right to Food to call them "a crime against humanity."[5]

Cellulosic Fuels

"Second generation" cellulosic agrofuel promoters are trying to side-step the food versus fuel debate by projecting a boundless energy future through "underutilized" "waste" materials from "marginal lands."[6] These projections are invariably short on details, they seem to sidestep the laws of thermodynamics, and they distort the logic of

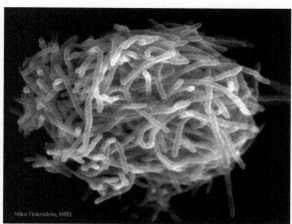

PATENTED *THERMOPHYLLUS CELLULOLYTICUS*, ISOLATED FROM YELLOWSTONE THERMAL SPRINGS. PRODUCES ENZYMES THAT HELP BREAK DOWN CELLULOSE

ecology.[7] Corporations are marketing this cellulosic future as a logical next step with no down side. Under the threat of energy shortages, and as a faux solution to climate change, they insist that we let biotechnology go directly from the lab to the field in order to save the planet. But as British Petroleum's own marketing materials warn: *"Such statements are only predictions, and actual events or results may differ materially from those projected in such forward-looking statements."* [8]

The OECD's International Energy Agency has said that cellulosic biofuels are most likely at least 10 years from viability.[9] Furthermore, as Smolker and Tokar (this volume[III]) argue with great detail, genetic engineering must still contend with the laws of physics. One cannot expect to continually remove energy; AKA grasses from the prairies, and agricultural and logging "waste" from forests, etc.; without adding energy (such as chemical fertilizers) back into the system.

Smolker and Tokar also demonstrate that biotechnology corporations, in their search for profits, are playing a dangerous game of roulette with our global ecology:

> The synthetic biology industry envisions thousands of bio-refineries dotting the landscape efficiently turning plant matter into plastics, fuels and drugs. In such a scenario environmental escape of synthetic microorganisms through waste streams or human error is inevitable, with largely unpredictable consequences.

Cellulosic fuels could lead to catastrophic ecological disasters; as genetically modified, freeze-tolerant, weedy eucalyptus trees invade natural forests, or wholly-synthetic lignin-digesting microorganisms designed to break down cellulose escape into fields and forests.[10, 11] And, as Annie Shattuck (this volume[IV]) demonstrates, these corporations have become very adept at using bribes and coercion, along with international courts, to break down political barriers to genetically modified crops in the Global South.

Corporate Capture

While agrofuels may do little to benefit rural communities or the environment, they have been a bonanza for investors, agribusinesses, and industrial agriculture. Agribusinesses do not normally invest directly in production, preferring instead to capture profits associated with the agricultural value chain (inputs and processing), and leaving risk to farmers. The agrofuels boom is another example

III Magical, Myth-Illogical, Biological Fuels??
IV. The Agrofuels Trojan Horse: Biotechnology and the Corporate Domination of Agriculture

of the way that these corporations keep farmers in a precarious position.

In 2002, when the market was still uncertain, U.S. farmers began pooling their resources to form local cooperatives for ethanol production. By 2006 these co-ops made 45% of all the ethanol produced in the United States.[12] With the firming up of the ethanol market via the Renewable Fuel Standards in the 2008 U.S. Farm Bill, the agrofuels industry quickly morphed into a large-scale industrial enterprise[13] to the extent that the two largest corporate ethanol producers, ADM and POET, soon controlled 33.7% of U.S. production (see Holt-Giménez and Kenfield, this volume[V]). Bunge, Cargill, and Monsanto moved in to capture the profits via the processing and input markets; and a host of investment firms, oil companies, food conglomerates, and forestry companies have shifted their investment strategies to capitalize on agrofuels and biofuels.[14]

While many farmers in the U.S. have benefitted from higher corn and soy prices due to the diversion of crops into fuel production, the majority of the benefits of the agrofuels boom have gone to the powerful corporations and large landowners that already benefitted from the global commodities market.[15]

Between 2006 and 2007 corn prices rose nearly 50%, soybean prices were up 60%, and wheat rose 50%. But small farmers did not reap a proportional share of the benefits because input providers raised the price of fuel, fertilizer, seed, feed, and equipment.[16] Agrofuels may be a short-term benefit to farmers, but this artificial scarcity does nothing to change the balance of power within the agriculture industry. Indeed, these new agrofuel profits are increasing the inequity in the system by leading to an influx of financial capital that will lead to further concentration and price instability, and squeeze all small farmers in the long term.

The current economic downturn appears to bear this out. Valero Oil recently made a bid for U.S.-based Verasun, which filed for bankruptcy in October, 2008 (leaving contract farmers sitting on their crops).[17] At the time of this writing, ADM is preparing to lease 18 grain warehouses and purchase assets in the state of Sao Paolo, Brazil from the 4,000 member Cooagri Cooperative, which is struggling due to the downturn in the credit markets. ADM is also using the crisis to squeeze more profits out of producers in the Global South by striking deals that are more to its advantage.[18]

V. When Renewable Isn't Sustainable: Agrofuels and the Inconvenient Truth behind the 2007 U.S. Energy Independence and Security Act.

Legislation

Agrofuels have been embraced by the U.S. and EU in part because they do not require significant infrastructural, economic, or lifestyle changes. Against the warnings of food advocates, agrofuel demand has been codified in U.S. and EU fuel mandates. They are essential to meeting the U.S.'s "Twenty in Ten" goals of reducing the country's dependence on foreign oil by 20% in 10 years.[19] While the actual figures have yet to emerge, the U.S.'s 2008 ethanol subsidies could potentially amount to a $13 billion giveaway to the industry.[20, 21]

The EU has mandates for a 5% conversion to liquid biofuels by 2015, increasing to 10% by 2020.[22] The Obama administration is backing the agrofuel industry (and higher food prices) by subsidizing inefficient corn ethanol and promoting the "Holy Grail" of cellulosic fuels. President Obama's appointments of former Iowa Governor, Tom Vilsack (Biotechnology Industry Organization's "Governor of the Year") as Secretary of Agriculture and Steven Chu as Energy Secretary have pleased the National Biodiesel Board because it means that agrofuels will remain a significant part of any new energy mosaic—although the details have yet to be seen.

With the current economic downturn affecting energy prices, the U.S. agrofuels industry is lobbying for its own financial "bailout" package in the form of:

- Cellulosic ethanol, biobutanol, and synthetic petroleum fuel requirements,

- A new Renewable Fuels Standard mandating 60 billion gallons of "advanced biofuels" by 2030,

- A mandate for ethanol blends above what they call the EPA's "arbitrary"[23] 10% figure (ethanol blends above 10-15% harm current engines), and

- An E85 (85% ethanol) Flexible Fuel Vehicles mandate for all new vehicles by 2010 for automakers that receive federal funds.

While Mr. Vilsack has endorsed a 12%-13% ethanol blend,[24] the industry is not going to get all they ask for. This wish list does however provide a picture of the industry's plans for dramatic expansion. When the production of agrofuels again becomes more profitable than growing food, the market will favor the obvious choice. But in the final analysis, growing our way out of the energy crisis is fraught with too many uncertainties and produces too many undesirable externalities.

Looking back at what the last several years have wrought, it is clear that a dramatic expansion of agrofuels will increase the release of greenhouse gases, while simultaneously forcing more people into starvation and leading to weather changes that negatively affect their ability to grow their own food. Tinkering with the details of production, therefore, is not enough. We ultimately need to turn away from these false solutions to climate change towards genuinely sustainable ways to meet energy needs.

Effects in Latin America

Agrofuels are spreading throughout Latin America due to free trade agreements, Brazil's desire to become an energy superpower, and the IMF's neoliberal policy prescriptions. As Jonasse (this volume[VI]) shows, the Inter-American Development Bank (IDB) has also been very supportive. For 2008, it pledged US$3 billion in loans and guarantees for Latin American agrofuels, US$570 million in Brazil alone.[25] The IDB has also backed large export infrastructure projects for agrofuels and is currently conducting studies that promote agribusiness and monocrop agrofuels plantations as a trickle down "rural development" strategy.[26,27,28] The IDB's promotion of agrofuels comes on top of the influx financial capital—a phenomenon that the current downturn will likely exacerbate.

The results of this concerted push have been predictable. In 2007 the state of São Paulo, Brazil saw sugar cane plantations increase by more than 300,000 hectares, as land available for food crops shrank by around 170,000 hectares.[29] The following year, Brazilian ethanol exports rose 45.7% to a record-high 5.16 billion liters.[30] Ecuador has an estimated 200,000 hectares of oil palm plantations, with plans for as much as 450,000 hectares; which will replace biodiverse native forests, and rural and indigenous populations in the Amazon and elsewhere.[31] Argentina planted 16 million hectares of soybeans for the 2006/2007 season;[32] 90 percent of which is GM "Roundup ready" soy that encourages increased use of the herbicide, requires fewer workers to cultivate, and introduces herbicides into rivers and aquifers, harming wildlife and causing illness in rural villages.[33]

All of this land and labor for monocrop export-oriented agriculture comes at the expense of poor rural communities. In this volume, both Hurtado[VII] (in Guatemala) and Mendonça[VIII] (in Brazil) catalogue the effects of the agrofuels explosion. The expansion has exaggerated the impacts of an agricultural

VI. Field of Dreams: IFIs and the Latin American Agrofuels Expansion
VII. Agrofuel Plantations and the Loss of Land for Food Production in Guatemala
VIII. The Environmental and Social Consequences of "Green Capitalism" in Brazil

model that has devastated rural communities. It has resulted in evictions and land grabs, and the concentration of numerous old landholdings under new corporate ownership.[34,35] It has disrupted indigenous communities; increased social problems; and encouraged a whole catalogue of human atrocities, including slavery, committed to meet the energy needs of industrialized countries.[36,37,38] Despite the rhetoric that says agrofuels create jobs, local smallholders find it difficult to jump on the value chain at all—except under exploitative conditions.[39] Hurtado describes how many people lease their lands to companies for extended periods and watch as the soil becomes degraded due to exploitative industrial farming practices. Altieri[IX] explains that in Brazil, soybean cultivation displaces eleven workers for every one it employs.

On top of the human tragedy comes a poor environmental record (catalogued by both Altieri and Shattuck[X] this volume). The record includes habitat destruction, the rapid spread of genetically modified organisms (GMOs),[40] water depletion, oceanic dead zones; and deforestation in rainforests, peat lands, savannas, and grasslands.[41,42] Studies have shown that, depending on crops and conditions, agrofuel land use changes produce between 17 and 420 times more CO_2 than the displaced fossil fuels.[43]

"Sustainable" Agrofuels

All of the above makes it clear that in a world with growing populations and finite agricultural resources, there is no room left to promote such a destructive industry. But as the negative effects of agrofuels come to light, oil companies and agricultural corporations continually 'greenwash' their images by public relations campaigns promoting their "sustainable" fuels.

One current example of this is the Roundtable on Sustainable Biofuels (RSB), discussed by Annie Shattuck in this volume.[XI] The goal is to create a certification system for sustainably produced agrofuels that will include labor and environmental considerations. Environmental groups have joined the RSB in an effort to prevent some of the more egregious agricultural practices and human rights violations; and this may lead to some welcome modifications. But there are numerous complicated pitfalls to account for in such a scheme—and other attempts at less complicated certification schemes have shown cracks. As Shattuck cautions, "if sustainability initiatives merely provide enough cover to

IX. The Ecological and Social Tragedy of Crop-Based Biofuel Production in the Americas
X. The Agrofuels Trojan Horse: Biotechnology and the Corporate Domination of Agriculture
XI. Will Sustainability Certifications Work? A Look at the Roundtable on Sustainable Biofuels

convince the public that agrofuels are an efficient and socially valuable energy source, they will do so at the expense of real solutions to both the food and energy crises."

Even if smallholder provisions, and labor and environmental standards remain conditions for certification, at the end of the day agrofuels will still be produced by the profit-seeking corporations that are funding the Roundtable. Agrofuels will thus remain a capital-intensive enterprise that seeks continual expansion— and the corporate bottom line will ensure that they will at best 'balance' the costs of complying with the standards against the profits derived from externalizing harmful environmental and social costs.

Next?

While the global recession and a reprieve in oil prices have temporarily slowed the agrofuels boom we have an opportunity to review the changes to the global agricultural system that have already been wrought. Oil prices will eventually rise and "green" fuels will again be cost-competitive. While the world's attention is diverted by the economic crisis, agrofuel interests continue to improve their positions. Land is cheap in the Global South, and corporations and wealthy countries are working to secure their access to this limited and shrinking resource.[44]

Truly sustainable agrofuels—those that do not increase greenhouse gas emissions; that do not displace or impact rural and/or indigenous communities; that do not threaten food sovereignty and food security; and do not destroy or degrade farmland, waterways, or ecosystems—simply *cannot* be produced on a scale that will deflect a significant degree of the roughly 50 million barrels of oil consumed by the OECD countries every day.[45] The development of truly sustainable agrofuels will require significant structural changes, rather than regulations and certifications plied on top of a market-driven agroindustrial model that is addicted to growth. At best, we may advance sustainable **biofuels**—by which we mean local production for cooking and other energy need—as opposed to **agrofuels** that displace food production and food security to ship the finite agricultural resources of the Global South out of region and around the globe.

The application of large capital growth requirements and industrial practices to agriculture is an intrusion on a social model that has sustained human communities for thousands of years. A more socially and environmentally

LOCAL, DIVERSE AGRICULTURE: QUETZALTENANGO, GUATEMALA

sustainable form of agriculture would entail treating food and agriculture differently from industrial products. Changing the way we produce food cannot be a return to some mythical Arcadian past however. As Eric Holt-Giménez explains, it will require new social networks and modern broad-based political movements:

> The transition to sustainable agriculture ultimately depends on a combination of efforts between farmers and economic and social institutions; the markets, banks, government ministries, agricultural research institutions, farmers' organizations, churches, and nongovernmental/nonprofit organizations (NGOs). Each of these institutions—including the market—has its own strengths and weaknesses; and each responds to the political agendas of the actors who are able to use it. Scaling up the successes of any experience in sustainable agriculture ... is therefore not simply farmers teaching other farmers to farm sustainably, but a political project that engages the power of these institutions to permit, facilitate, and support sustainable farming.[47]

Anyone concerned about the future of food needs to take stock of what the last several years of agrofuels production have wrought, and look toward policies, actions, and broad-based environmental and social networks that can resist the next wave of the agrofuels boom. A coherent strategy needs to begin *before* the establishment of agrofuels policies, trade agreements, and infrastructures blindside us again; and make it difficult or impossible to turn back.

Agrofuels in the Americas looks at the ways in which agribusiness and energy corporations are taking advantage of peak oil, climate concerns, and global free trade rules to shape the future of agriculture to their profitable advantage. The following articles illuminate the dynamics of trade relations, global capital flows, and their symbiotic relationship with international financial institutions such as the World Trade Organization, the World Bank, and the International Monetary Fund. They open the black box of biotechnology strategies, the corporate cooptation of the genetic commons, and the voracious land and resource consumption of the agrofuels industry. Finally, these pieces discuss the human tragedy of agrofuels' affects on peasant farmers, rural labor, indigenous peoples, and the environment—and the corporate externalization of their social and environmental costs. They provide a picture of the future of agriculture, labor, and the biosphere if the forces capitalizing on the current global crises can push their plans through. It touches on these key concerns with the aim of informing the current debate on food and fuel production. The essays that follow examine overlapping aspects of agrofuels production.

This book is organized in three major sections:

Part One: *Regulation and Institutional Support for Agrofuels*;

Part Two: *The Social and Environmental Consequences of Agrofuels*; and

Part Three: *The Future: "Next Generation" Agrofuels and the Transformation of Life*.

Part One, **Regulation and Institutional Support for Agrofuels,** looks at governmental and International Finance Institutional (IFI) support for agrofuel production, as well as the up-hill battle faced by those attempting to instill sustainability standards. It covers government subsidies, the World Trade Organization the General Agreement on Tariffs and Trade, the International Monetary Fund, the World Bank, the InterAmerican Development Bank, and the Roundtable on Sustainable Biofuels.

- In *When Renewable Isn't Sustainable: Agrofuels and the Inconvenient Truth behind the 2007 U.S. Energy Independence and Security Act,* Eric Holt-Giménez and Isabella Kenfield look at the far-reaching direct and indirect effects of the 2007 U.S. Farm Bill. The Renewable Fuel Standards that were mandated in the bill will not help climate change, but they will accelerate hunger, poverty and ecological destruction. These standards will enrich agribusinesses including ADM, Bunge, and Cargill, who are using global crises as an excuse to increase their control over food systems. There is a *frisson* of inter-activity between agribusinesses, biotech, automobile, and oil interests. Cargill has moved into Brazil and Paraguay, and biotech companies are using climate change and the food crisis as a Trojan horse to get their products into the field. In order to advance truly sustainable agricultural development at home and abroad, we need to challenge the dominance of the industrial food complex. There are many good alternatives to industrial agrofuels, but we will never know if they are feasible until we challenge and change the current context.

- In *The Free Market in Agrofuels: Regulation and Trade in the Americas*, Gretchen Gordon and Jessica Aguirre look at the World Trade Organization and General Agreement on Tariffs and Trade (GATT), and the global trade rules that promote the agrofuels industry. While the EU is looking for ways to ensure sustainable production, agribusiness companies are looking to expand an unsustainable global free trade in agrofuels—with dire social and environmental consequences. These corporations are pursuing their agendas on many fronts, so efforts to mitigate these impacts through narrow regulation, without regulating the agricultural and financial markets will be ineffective. As things stand, it is almost impossible to promote sustainable agrofuels or local small-scale biofuels producers without violating GATT—and it is very difficult to devise certification programs that aren't vulnerable to trade challenges from agribusiness corporations.

- In Agribusiness' *Field of Dreams: IFIs and the Latin American Agrofuels Expansion*, Rick Jonasse points out that the agrofuels boom in Latin America is a natural consequence of the Structural Adjustment Policies (SAPs) imposed by the International Monetary Fund, the World Trade Organization's global trade rules, and the development philosophy of the World Bank and the Inter-American Development Bank (IDB). SAPs have primarily benefitted corporations and large landowners. They have encouraged monocrop plantations and the flows of international investment capital that are turning the Global South into a vast plantation to feed the North's hunger for energy. Large infrastructure projects and trade agreements have provided a route between South America's resources and the global economy. In order to compete with the private capital pouring into the region, the IDB and the World Bank have lowered their already anemic labor and environmental standards, channeling and legitimizing private capital flows, with destructive consequences.

• In *Will Sustainability Certifications work? A look at the Roundtable on Sustainable Biofuels,* Annie Shattuck looks at this current joint industry-nongovernmental organization effort to create, and enforce, a set of sustainability standards for agrofuel production. This detailed analysis asks hard questions, while delving into the details of the language and logic of this evolving program. Shattuck examines similar initiatives dealing with soy, palm oil, and forest products for past precedent. While noting the program may be able to curb some of the worst abuses of the industry, the article concludes that the process is highly contentious, and is likely to *greenwash* the industry without substantially reforming its destructive, monoculture production model. This is all the more dangerous because the industry receives the bulk of renewable energy funding; funding that could go to building truly sustainable food and energy systems. Corporations are using climate change fears and global trade rules to reshape the future of agriculture, and the very future of life on this planet.

*Part Two, **The Social and Environmental Consequences of Agrofuels**,* shows how the regulatory (and deregulatory) policies described in *Section One* have lead to the exacerbation of inequality between the wealthy and powerful, who have access to infrastructural advantages and economies of scale, and the rural poor in the Global South who have often tenuous access to agricultural resources of their own. This section also describes the environmental devastation that is a consequence of the captive markets created by U.S. (and others') agrofuel blending mandates and the global economy's addiction to cheap energy.

• In *The Environmental and Social Consequences of "Green Capitalism" in Brazil,* Maria Luisa Mendonça adds details to the Brazilian situation described in *Section One* by looking at the fallout from the 2007 Bush-Lula biofuels accord. Mendonça catalogues the problems that have arisen with the new push for ethanol and biodiesel production. These problems include the expansion of agriculture into the biodiverse Cerrado region, destruction in the Amazon basin due to sugar and soy production, land evictions and land grabs ("grilagem"), the harmful health affects on laborers in the agrofuels industry, and other human rights violations, including slavery.

She ends with a call for a more diverse, small-scale agriculture: peasant agriculture, diverse ecosystems, and stronger rural social organizations that support food sovereignty.

- Laura Hurtado's piece, *Agrofuel Plantations and the Loss of Land for Food Production in Guatemala* looks at the loss of food sovereignty due to the increase in agrofuel plantations. The Guatemalan government and International Financial Institutions have supported this process since 1983, without regard for the rural agriculture, and the people's right to food and well-being. Currently, these agrofuel corporations are growing stronger and taking over land previously used for peasant production, food production for local markets, and the diverse uses of forested land. There is also increasing industry consolidation. The 1996 Peace Accords were supposed to guarantee access to land for indigenous and peasant farmers. But due to corruption, the difficult application process, and "market-based" guidelines, peasant farmers are being tricked out of their land and otherwise pushed to marginal lands, where it is difficult to grow enough food to survive and into migrant seasonal labor.

- In *The Ecological and Social Tragedy of Crop-based Biofuel Production in the Americas,* Miguel Altieri and Elizabeth Bravo look at the direct effects of agrofuels on land, farming, and labor. Corn, sugar cane, soybean, oil palm and other crops pushed by the agrofuels industry will not reduce greenhouse gas emissions but they will displace tens of thousands of farmers, decrease food security in many countries, and accelerate deforestation and environmental destruction in the Global South. Food sovereignty movements recognize the threat that this expansion poses for access to food and agricultural land to grow food.

*Part Three, **The Future: "Next Generation" Agrofuels and the Transformation of Life*** projects a disconcerting future if the biotechnology industry and their allies have their way. Promoters of these biotechnologies claim that, since they are not food, they won't increase hunger. But these fuel crops will vie for precisely the same resources as food. The effects on agriculture and food security will be direct and immediate. It is not hyperbole to suggest that their plans; which include wholly synthetic life forms and the enhancement of already-weedy, invasive species; will affect the entire biosphere and all life within it.

- Annie Shattuck looks at biotechnology, and the present/future of agriculture and global ecology in *The Agrofuels Trojan Horse: Biotechnology and the Corporate Domination of Agriculture*. She discusses the ways in which seed companies are using the threat of global warming to gain legitimacy for their genetically engineered agrofuels crops, and consolidate their market shares—which has contributed to a catalogue of ecological consequences. She describes the strong-arm tactics they have used to break down laws against GMOs and get their crops in the ground. These companies are now espousing the futuristic promise of second-generation cellulosic biofuels, which are designed to increase profits by: engineering invasive plants for increased range, drought and herbicide tolerance; and making them easier to process into fuels.

- Rachel Smolker and Brian Tokar give "second generation" agrofuel promoters a dose of reality in *Magical, Myth-Illogical, Biological Fuels?* This piece tackles a number of the myths behind the 'something-for-nothing,' greenhouse-gas-busting hype that has been coming from corporations and governments promoting this dubious energy future. The authors describe the science behind cellulosic fuels: what is currently feasible, where the industry is looking to go, and which industry claims are science-fiction. They then look at the consequences that will ensue—for climate, ecology, land, water, forests, food, and labor—if this vision becomes reality. While promoters often repeat the mantra that these new scientific fuels will allow us to grow fuels on "marginal lands," these authors 1) question the very notion of marginal lands in the first place, and 2) point out that when the price is right, farmers will use prime agricultural lands to produce these same crops—leading to hunger and food insecurity.

These articles provide a glimpse into what corporations, governments, and International Financial Institutions are currently doing; and what they are planning for the future. We hope that they spur a renewed understanding of the global impacts of the current agrofuels boom. It is time we return to agriculture for society and culture—for a sustainable future for humanity and the planet—rather than for the short-sighted goals of a handful of governments and the bottom-lines of global corporations.

Photo and Image Credits:

1. Amazon Soybean Farm, Mato Grosso, Brazil. Leonardo F. Freitas Creative Commons License (details: http://creativecommons.org/licenses/by-nc-sa/2.0/) Photo URL: http://www.flickr.com/photos/leoffreitas/789138111/in/photostream/

2. Acidothermus Cellulolyticus: Mark Finkelstein, National Renewable Energy Laboratory Photo at: http://www.nrel.gov/data/pix/Jpegs/01727.jpg

3. Local, diverse, agriculture, Quetzaltenango, Guatemala. Seth Pipkin, Creative Commons License: http://creativecommons.org/licenses/by-sa/2.0/deed.en Photo at: http://www.flickr.com/photos/thepinksip/54493118/

References:

1   Foster, J.B., and Fred Magdoff. 2009. The Great Financial Crisis: Causes and Consequences. Monthly Review Press.

2   Harvey, David. 2003. The New Imperialsim. Oxford; Oxford University Press.

3   United Nations Environment Programme. 2009. The Environmental Food Crisis: The Environment's Role in Averting Future Food Crises, A UNEP Rapid Response Assessment.Nellemann, C., MacDevette, M., Manders, T., Eickhout, B., Svihus, B., Prins, A. G., Kaltenborn, B. P. (eds.). Accessed 03/16/09: http://www.unep.org/publications/search/pub_details_s.asp?ID=4019

4   Roberts, Paul. 2008. The End of Food. Boston: Houghton Mifflin.

5   Borger, J. 2008. UN Chief calls for Review of Biofuels Policy. The Guardian. Accessed 07/08/08: http://www.guardian.co.uk/environment/2008/apr/05/biofuels.food

6   Kleiner, K. 2007.The Backlash Against Biofuels. Nature Reports. Accessed 02/07/09: http://www.nature.com/climate/2008/0801/full/climate.2007.71.html

7   Friedemann, A. 2009. Peak Soil: Why Cellulosic ethanol and other Biofuels are Not Sustainable and a Threat to America's National Security - Part III. Cybertech Inc. Accessed 03/04/09: http://www.energypulse.net/centers/article/article_display.cfm?a_id=1482

8   British Petroleum. 2009. BP and Verenium Form Leading Cellulosic Ethanol Venture to Deliver Advanced Biofuels. Accessed 03/02/09: http://www.bp.com/genericarticle.do?categoryId=2012968&contentId=7051362

9   International Energy Agency. 2008. From 1st- to 2nd-Generation Biofuel Technologies: An overview of current industry and RD&D activities. Accessed 03/04/09: http://www.iea.org/textbase/papers/2008/2nd_Biofuel_Gen_Exec_Sum.pdf

10 Shattuck, Annie. 2008. Green Gold: Why cellulosic ethanol is a threat to farmers and the planet. Food First Institute. Accessed 10/22/08: http://www.foodfirst.org/en/node/2263

11 Pollack, A. 2006. Redesigning Crops to Harvest Fuel. New York Times. Accessed 06/09/08: http://www.nytimes.com/2006/09/08/business/08crop.html

12 Stebbins, Christine. 2006. FEATURE - U.S. Farmers Big Winners in Booming Ethanol

Business. Reuters: http://www.planetark.com/dailynewsstory.cfm/newsid/34736/story.htm

13   Holt-Giménez, Eric & Isabella Kenfield. 2008. When Renewable Isn't Sustainable: Agrofuels and the Inconvenient Truth behind the 2007 U.S. Energy Independence and Security Act. Food First Institute. Accessed 08/09/08: http://www.foodfirst.org/en/node/2064

14   ibid.

15   Holt-Giménez, E., & Isabella Kenfield. 2008.

16   Wise, T.A. and Alicia Harvie. 2009. Boom for Whom? Family Farmers Saw Lower On-Farm Income Despite High Prices. Global Development and Environment Institute, Tufts University. Accessed 03/05/09: http://www.ase.tufts.edu/gdae/Pubs/rp/PB09-02BoomForWhomFeb09.pdf

17   Etter, Lauren. 2009. Valero Bids for VeraSun Assets. Wall Street Journal Online. Accessed 02/07/09: http://online.wsj.com/article/SB123396710307859085.html?mod=googlenews_wsj

18   Reuters. 2009. ADM to lease Brazil Co-op, Wants to Buy – Report. Accessed 02/06/09: http://uk.reuters.com/article/marketsNewsUS/idUKN0645939920090206

19   U.S. Department of Agriculture. 2008. FACT SHEET: National Biofuels Action Plan. Accessed 01/22/09: http://www.usda.gov/wps/portal/!ut/p/_s.7_0_A/7_0_1OB?contentidonly=true&contentid=2008/10/0258.xml

20   Hansen-Kuhn, Karen. 2008.Flawed Biofuels Policies. Foreign Policy in Focus (FPIF). Accessed 02/09/09: http://www.fpif.org/fpiftxt/5635

21   Koplow, Doug. 2008. Biofuels-at What Cost?: Government support for ethanol and biodiesel in the United States. International Institute for Sustainable Development (IISD). Accessed 02/09/09: http://www.globalsubsidies.org/files/assets/pdf/Brochure_-_US_Report.pdf

22   Kanter, James. 2008. EU Legislators Call for more Modest Biofuels Goal. International Herald Tribune. Accessed 01/21/09: http://www.iht.com/articles/2008/09/11/business/biofuel.php

23   POET Ethanol Corp. 2008. Ethanol in the Year Ahead. Accessed 02/12/09: http://www.rhapsodyingreen.com/rhapsody_in_green/2008/12/ethanol-in-the-year-ahead.html

24   Associated Press. 2009. Vilsack: US Should Boost Ethanol Blend in Gasoline. International Herald Tribune. 03/09/09. http://www.iht.com/articles/ap/2009/03/09/america/Vilsack-Pelosi-Farmers.php

25   Ortiz, Lucia 2008. Multilateral Banks: Feeding the exportation of biofuels and the disputes over land use in Brazil. Friends of the Earth. http://ifis.choike.org/informes/790.html. Accessed 03/17/2008.

26   Inter-American Development Bank. 2008. Inter-American Development Bank Announces Partnership to Develop Sustainable Biofuels. Accessed 04/15/08: http://www.iadb.org/news/detail.cfm?language=English&id=4507

27 Sombilla, Mercedita A. 2008. Biofuels Development Initiative in the Greater Mekong Subregion. Asian Development Bank:http://www.adb.org/Documents/events/2008/ACEF/Session8-Sombilla.pdf

28 Thaindia News. 2008. African Development Bank Calls for Alternative Fuel-producing crops. Accessed 06/09/08: http://www.thaindian.com/newsportal/business/african-development-bank-calls-for-alternative-fuel- producing-crops_10080189.html

29 Kuma, Rahul. 01/20/09. Why are Food Prices Rising? ActionAid. Accessed 02/02/09: http://ipsterraviva.net/uploads/TV/wsfbrazil2009Pt/photos/HUNGER%20FREE%20jan%202009%20WEB.pdf

30 Checkbiotech 2009. Brazil Registers Record-High Ethanol Fuel Export. Accessed 02/06/09 http://bioenergy.checkbiotech.org/news/brazil_registers_record_high_ethanol_fuel_export

31 Roundtable on Sustainable Palm Oil (RSPO). 2008. International Declaration Against the 'Greenwashing' of Palm Oil by the Roundtable on Sustainable Palm Oil. Accessed 04/01/09: http://www.regenwald.org/international/englisch/news.php?id=1070

32 Harris, A. K. 2007. Record Soy Crop Ahead? Farm Chemicals International. Accessed 03/09/09: http://www.fc- international.com/globalmarkets/latinamerica/argentina/?storyid=180

33 Friends of the Earth. 2008. Fuelling Destruction in Latin America: The real price of the drive for agrofuels. Accessed 11/07/08: http://www.foei.org/en/publications/pdfs/biofuels-fuelling-destruction-latinamerica

34 Grain. 2007. Agrofuels Special Issue. Accessed 03/04/08: http://www.grain.org/seedling_files/seed-07-07-en.pdf

35 Holt-Gimenez, Eric. 2008a. Food First Backgrounder Vol 14, Number 1—From Food Rebellions to Food Sovereignty: Urgent call to fix a broken food system. Food First Institute. Accessed 11/02/08: http://www.foodfirst.org/en/node/2199

36 Brown Lester. 2006. Exploding U.S. Grain Demand for Automotive Fuel Threatens World Food Security and Political Stability. Earth Policy Institute. Accessed 11/08/09: http://www.earth-policy.org/Updates/2006/Update60.htm

37 Runge, C. Ford & Benjamin Senauer. 2008. How Ethanol Fuels the Food Crisis. Council on Foreign Relations. Accessed 01/15/09: http://www.foreignaffairs.org/20080528faupdate87376/c-ford-runge-benjamin-senauer/how-ethanol-fuels-the-food-crisis.html

38 Holt-Giménez, E. & Isabella Kenfield. 2008.

39 Via Campesina. 2008. Small farmers feed the world Industrial agrofuels fuel hunger and poverty. Accessed 09/22/08: http://www.viacampesina.org/main_en/index.php?option=com_content&task=view&id=568&Itemid=1

40 Crutzen, P. J., A. R. Mosier, K. A. Smith, & W. Winiwarter. 2008. N2O release from agro-biofuel production negates global warming reduction by replacing fossil fuels, Atmos. Chem. Phys. Discuss., 7, 11191-11205. Accessed 11/09/08: http://www.atmos-chem-phys.net/8/389/2008/acp-8-389-2008.pdf

41   Morton, D.C. et al (2006) Cropland Expansion Changes Deforestation Dynamics in the Southern Brazilian Amazon. PNAS 103(39): 14637-14641.

42   Butler, Rhett A. 2006. U.S. Biofuels Policy Drives Deforestation in Indonesia, the Amazon. Accessed 10/28/08: http://news.mongabay.com/2008/0117-biofuels.html

43   Fargione,J., Jason Hill, David Tilman, Stephen Polasky, Peter Hawthorne. 2008. Land Clearing and the Biofuel Carbon Debt. SCIENCE VOL. 319 29 FEBRUARY 2008. Accessed 03/04/09: http://climateknowledge.org/figures/Rood_Climate_Change_ AOSS480_Documents/Fargione_Land_Clearing_Biofuels_Science_2008.pdf

44   Friends of the Earth. 2008. The Great European Land Grab: The costs of Europe's appetite for animal feeds and agrofuels. Accessed 04/01/09. *www.foeeurope.org/agrofuels/FFE/ Media%20Briefing%20final.pdf*

45   British Petroleum. 2009. Oil Consumption Table: Barrels per day. Accessed 03/01/09: http://www.bp.com/liveassets/bp_internet/globalbp/globalbp_uk_english/reports_ and_publications/statistical_energy_review_2008/STAGING/local_assets/ downloads/pdf/oil_table_of_world_oil_ consumption_barrels_2008.pdf

46   Holt-Gimenez, E. 2006. Movimiento Campesino a Campesino: Linking sustainable agriculture and social change. Food First. Accessed 08/09/08: http://www.foodfirst. org/files/pdf/backgrounders/ws06v12n1.pdf

PART ONE

Regulation and Institutional Support for Agrofuels

WHEN RENEWABLE ISN'T SUSTAINABLE: AGROFUELS AND THE INCONVENIENT TRUTHS BEHIND THE 2007 U.S. ENERGY INDEPENDENCE AND SECURITY ACT

BY ERIC HOLT-GIMÉNEZ & ISABELLA KENFIELD

Randy Wick

The Fracturing of the Agrofuels Consensus

Policymakers in the United States turned up the heat on the agrofuels boom by setting ambitious targets for the nation's Renewable Fuels Standards (RFS). In December 2007, the Energy Independence and Security Act passed the House and Senate and was signed into law by President George W. Bush. The Act, legislated in the political glow of a strong bipartisan consensus, mandated the use of 36 billion gallons of agrofuels annually by 2022—a five-fold increase over then-current levels.

Politicians, both red and blue, gushing over the new green alternative, insisted that agrofuels were vital to national energy security, would curb global warming and be the next step in the nation's transition from peak oil to a renewable fuel economy. Closer analysis reveals that agrofuels provide few of these benefits. In fact, they have exacerbated problems of hunger, poverty and

> **"Agrofuels"** are liquid fuels made from fuel crops grown on a large agro-industrial scale. Agrofuels, such as ethanol and biodiesel, are currently produced from plants such as corn, oil palm, soy, sugar cane, sugar beet, rapeseed, canola, jatropha, rice and wheat. Agrofuels are blended with gasoline or diesel, mainly to power the 800 million automobiles that consume over 50% of the world's energy. **"Biofuels,"** the term commonly used for agrofuels, refers to small-scale, non-industrial liquid fuels frequently made in owner-operated facilities for local consumption. This report concerns itself with industrial agrofuels, not small-scale biofuels.

ecological destruction. In this case, renewable does not mean "sustainable." For this reason, even in the face of the industry's breathtaking expansion, the social consensus on agrofuels is fracturing; locally, nationally and globally. The fractures are reflected in the steadily eroding support for agrofuels among farmers, scientists, activists, non-governmental organizations and many communities. They are also reflected in decreasing rates of investment and recent public relations efforts by the industry.[1] Those still strongly in favor of agrofuels range from pro-industry academics—flush with corporate research money—to hard-strapped mid-western corn farmers who are experiencing economic prosperity for the first time in decades. They are supported by a powerful phalanx of multi-billion dollar industries, venture capital investors and politicians, eager to implement the legislation that House Speaker Nancy Pelosi once heralded as "a shot heard 'round the world for energy independence."[2]

Opposition to agrofuels is coming largely from independent scientists, international food security experts, food sovereignty movements, conservationists, and, increasingly, from peri-urban communities that do not want ethanol plants in their backyards. But opposition is also growing among farmers, some oil companies, some environmentalists, and even a few politicians (albeit timidly), who are becoming increasingly uncomfortable with the industrial fuel crop model.

The fractured consensus has uncovered agrofuels' "inconvenient truths," revealing a hydra-headed industrial juggernaut driven by giant grain, genetic engineering, and petroleum companies actively speculating with food and fuel systems at taxpayers' expense. Behind the heroic corporate claims of energy independence and green energy, the agrofuels boom is violently transforming food and fuel systems in the Americas and elsewhere.

This report describes three aspects of agrofuels' inconvenient truths: food shortages, energy dependence, and environmental damage. In the face of the fracturing agrofuels' consensus, we proposed a moratorium and a broad public dialog to build a context for sound food and fuel alternatives.[1]

Food: The Canary in the Mineshaft

In 2007 Lester Brown of Earth Policy Institute shocked the environmental policy community by stating flatly: "The grain required to fill a 25-gallon SUV

I. See: http://ga3.org/campaign/agrofuelsmoratorium

gas tank with ethanol will feed one person for a year." With this statement, Brown drew the U.S. into a "food versus fuel" debate that had long since erupted in Europe. Former United Nations Special Rapporteur on the Right to Food, Jean Ziegler, was much more direct. He called agrofuels a "crime against humanity" and exhorted governments to implement a five year moratorium in order to provide time for "[a]n assessment of the potential impact on the right to food, as well as on other social, environmental and human rights, and should ensure that biofuels do not produce hunger."[3]

The food versus fuel debate is a reflection of the harsh calculus of the multinational grain corporations. Under the RFS' promise of obligatory ethanol purchases (that essentially create a captive market) Archer Daniels Midland (ADM), Bunge, and Cargill diversified their monopsonistic purchases to include corn for fuel as well as corn for food. Between 2001 and 2006, the amount of corn used in U.S. ethanol distilleries tripled; from 18 million tons to an estimated

Increase in Grain Prices

In 2006, U.S. corn prices increased by 60% and world corn prices increased by more than 50%; U.S. prices for wheat and soybeans increased by 25% and 8%, respectively, and by 21% and 7% on the world market.[1] In the early months of 2008, prices for wheat and soybeans on the Chicago Board of Trade have hit all-time highs, double what they were a year ago. In mid-January, corn was trading over $5 per bushel, close to its historic high.[2]

55 million tons.[4] Between 2006 and 2007, the increase in demand for corn from U.S. ethanol distilleries—from 54 to 81 million tons—was over twice the annual increase in global demand for the world's grain. Because U.S. corn accounts for some 40% of global production, increased demand for U.S. corn as feedstock for fuel impacts global markets for corn as food.[5] As demand for corn increases, more is planted, pushing out other food grains such as wheat and soybeans. With less land available for cultivation, the price of these products goes up. Because corn and soy are main ingredients for processed food and livestock feed, the increase in corn prices dramatically increases food prices worldwide.

In December 2007, the Economist reported that its food-price index was higher than at any time since it was created in 1845. Prices have jumped by 75% since 2005.[6] By late 2007, the price of a loaf of whole wheat bread in the U.S. was 12% higher than one year earlier, milk was up 29%, and eggs were up 36%. In Mexico, corn meal prices shot up 60%. In Pakistan, flour prices doubled, and China faced rampant food price inflation.[7] The world was down to only 54 days of grain reserves—the lowest on record.[8]

While middle-income consumers in industrialized countries spend between 10-20% of their income on groceries, many poor consumers in the Global South spend between 50-80% of their income on food. These consumers are particularly vulnerable to rising and volatile food prices because, while these countries are usually net exporters of agricultural commodities, they are still net importers of food.[9] The Food and Agriculture Organization estimates that in 2006, developing countries' food import costs increased by 10% from 2005 and in 2007, food import prices rose by 25%.[10]

As a result, in 2007, many people in the Global South took to the streets. The world saw more protests over higher food prices than over fuel hikes.[11] There were food riots in Mexico over the skyrocketing prices of tortillas, rice riots in Senegal, and street demonstrations in Italy over higher prices for pasta. Higher wheat prices in Pakistan led to smuggling and the need for troops to guard grain reserves. In January 2008, in Indonesia, police were forced to clear the streets due to food riots over rising soybean prices.[12]

The International Food Policy Research Institute (IFPRI) predicts that depending on rates of agrofuels expansion, by 2020, the global price of corn will increase by 26 to 72% and the price of oilseeds between 18 and 44%. "In both scenarios, rises in crop prices would lead to decreases in food availability and calorie consumption in all regions of the world, with Sub-Saharan Africa suffering the most."[13] Countries where corn is the major staple grain will be particularly affected by rising grain costs. One study estimates that, depending on ethanol expansion in the U.S., food basket costs in Mexico will rise between 10 to 20%, Mozambique will see food basket prices rise between 11 to 23%, and South Africa's food basket costs will rise between 9 and 19%.[14] On March 6, 2008, Josette Sheeran, the Executive Director of the UN World Food Programme announced they were facing a US$500 million shortfall just due to soaring food and fuel costs—up over 40% since June 2007, warning it would implement ration cuts unless the program received additional help.[15]

With every one percent rise in the cost of food, 16 million people are made food insecure. This has serious implications for the three billion people in the world living on less than $2 a day, and for the 36 million hungry people in the United States that the USDA also terms "food insecure." If current trends continue, some 1.2 billion people could be chronically hungry by 2025—double the current number and 600 million more than previously predicted.[16]

However, the physical substitution of fuel for food crops is only part of the reason food prices are climbing and food insecurity is increasing. The mainstream conventional wisdom claims that the food crisis is a combination of increasing global population, rising meat consumption in China and India, and rising input prices. In this quantitative view, agrofuels play only a partial role. But this reasoning ignores the driving industrial forces behind agrofuels: big grain, big biotech, and, yes, even big oil. Industrial agriculture dominated by multinational corporations is largely responsible for creating a skewed global food system in which 1 billion suffer from obesity while 840 million people go hungry.[II]As the food and financial crises worsen, these corporate interests not only profit, they increase their global control over food and the resources needed to produce it. Agrofuels play a central role in increasing the market shares and articulating the market power of the same corporations of the industrial agri-foods complex that created the crisis in the first place.

For example, the agrofuels boom turns food crises into a doubly lucrative opportunity for grain merchants and grain processors. Because corporations like ADM and Cargill both buy and sell grain, they stand to gain from either low or high prices. When grain prices drop, they buy. Because of their market power they can withhold grain from the market—hoarding supplies until the price goes up again. When grain prices rise, they sell. This speculation was at the heart of the Mexican "Tortilla Crisis" in 2007. It makes no difference that white corn is used for tortillas and yellow corn for cattle feed. As agrofuels cut into the acreage planted to yellow corn, inflating its price, white corn was fed to cattle, taking it off the tortilla market and sending its price up as well. Grain merchants, like ADM and Cargill, and corn processors, like Mexico's Maseca, raised their prices. When the Mexican government attempted to intervene with a price cap, these corporations responded by withholding grain from the market, exacerbating the problem. The incident illustrates how the agrofuels boom increases the market

---

II. In this system, food and raw materials from the Global South are exported and sold cheaply to obtain foreign exchange—largely to pay off chronic foreign debt. Many countries with hungry populations actually export food—78% of all malnourished children under five live in countries with food surpluses. See, "The Myth-Scarcity: The Reality—There IS Enough Food," Food First Backgrounder, Spring 1998, Vol. 5, No. 1, and "12 Myths about Hunger," Food First Backgrounder, Summer, 2006, www.foodfirst.org.

power of these corporations—a power summarily unchecked by governments.

Like the proverbial canary in the mineshaft, ongoing global food crisis should be seen as a dire warning that something is terribly wrong with our food system. Unleashing the worldwide expansion of agrofuels with the RFS targets of the U.S. Energy Act has made things much worse. The agrofuels boom is a dangerous strategy that consolidates the tremendous market power of the industrial agri-foods complex—precisely when it needs to be dismantled.

From Oil Dependency to Agrofuel Dependency: The hidden agenda

Despite massive increases in U.S. ethanol production, the RFS targets—36 billion gallons per year by 2022—far exceed the U.S.' current capacity for fuel crop production. Of the mandate, less than half—15 billion gallons—will come from corn ethanol. Achieving this volume will require 45 million acres—nearly 50 percent of the country's current corn acreage. (Even if all of the U.S.'s 90 million-acre corn crop were converted to ethanol, just 12-16% of our gasoline would be replaced—barely enough for current ten percent ethanol blends (E-10), much less the 98% blends suggested in the Energy Bill)[17]

The remaining 21 billion gallons in the RFS are defined as "advanced biofuels." This futuristic sounding term actually includes any fuel crop other than corn, including soy-beans, oil palm, sugarcane and jatropha. While politicians have pinned their hopes on cellulosic ethanol made from native grasses or genetically-engineered (GE) fast-growing trees, by most accounts these fuels will need years and billions of dollars in research and infrastructure development to become commercially viable.[18] The 36 billion gallon mandate only replaces some 7% of our current fuel use—about 1.5 million barrels of oil per day.[19] Regardless of the technology, the other inconvenient truth lurking in the 2007 U.S. Energy Act was that North America had no significant additional cropland available for agrofuels.[20] *Politicians had been planning all along to access the agricultural resources in the impoverished Global South to make up the shortfall.*

This is why the term "advanced agrofuels" is strategically vague. It includes imported agrofuels, coming primarily from Latin America to the U.S. According to the OECD, 84% of the world's additional land available for agrofuels is in South America and Africa.[21] This is despite the fact that in 2006, imported ethanol accounted for 13.5% of ethanol used in the U.S.. Countries that export ethanol to the U.S. make up a growing list that includes Costa Rica, El Salvador,

The North-South Connection

In the short run, many governments in the Global South are eager to oblige the U.S.'s energy appetite—even at the expense of local food security. In Colombia, where40% of the population was food insecure in 2006, the government is increasing palm-oil plantations from 2.5 to15 million acres in order to supply the U.S. agrofuels market.[1] According to an official from Colombia's Ministry of Agriculture, "Colombia cannot compete with U.S. crops, and facing the possibility of numerous free trade agreements, we decided to look for another export product. Palm was the answer. Palm is the future. The demand is expected to be very large."[2] Brazil—the world's largest exporter of ethanol—is planning to increase acreage planted to sugarcane fivefold in order to replace 10% of the world's gasoline by 2025, despite the fact that more than one-quarter of the country's population is food insecure.[3]

Jamaica, Guatemala, Trinidad-Tobago, and Brazil, our major supplier. In 2005, the U.S. imported 31 million gallons of ethanol from Brazil. Then, in 2006, Brazilian imports jumped to 434 million gallons.[22] Rather than ensuring energy independence, the RFS mandate reflected an agreement between industry and politicians to legislate the U.S.'s dependency on imported agrofuels.[23] [III]

When the Road to Energy Independence is an Expensive Dead End

The need to reduce U.S. dependence on foreign oil has led many people to embrace agrofuels as a replacement for fossil fuels. Some assert that agrofuels will help moderate high oil prices or even help conserve oil.[24] But agrofuels are an additive, not a replacement. Far from providing a transition from our dependence on petroleum to renewable energy sources, the agrofuels boom has simply extended the present petroleum-based economy and the era of peak oil—with all of its negative consequences. Why pursue this option? With agrofuels, the planet's energy crisis is potentially an $80 - $100 trillion bonanza for both Big Oil and Big Grain companies.[25] Rather than conserving, this strategy allows oil companies to pump every last drop of oil from reserves in the world's

III. Agrofuels dependency not only links our energy consumption to access to resources in other countries, it connects us to the ways those resources are produced. The sugar cane and oil palm industries in Brazil, Colombia and other agrofuel producing countries are guilty of systematic labor and human rights violations—including land dispossession and slavery. Our dependency on their feedstock serves to perpetuate, not alleviate these injustices. See Food First Backgrounder "Colombia palm oil biodiesel plantations: A "lose-lose" development strategy?" and our upcoming report "Agrofuels and Human Rights."

Paul Filmer

BRAZILIAN OIL TANKER

hard to reach, environmentally fragile areas, inviting us to consume our way out of over-consumption. There will be no renewable "transition" with agrofuels; only a longer, more expensive road to the oil economy's inevitable dead end.

Taxpayer Dollars Feeding our Other Dependency: Big Grain
The main drivers of the agrofuels boom are the multinational corporations in the agribusiness, petroleum, biotech and automotive industries seeking to extend their market power. Over the past several years, venture capital investment in agrofuels has increased by nearly 700%.[26] Private investment in agrofuels is pouring in to public research institutions, setting the agenda not only for agrofuels, but for public research in general.[27] New corporate partnerships are being formed between agribusinesses, biotechnology companies, oil companies and car manufacturers.[IV, 28] Even given the current financial crisis, millions of dollars are being invested in the agrofuel sector in a development often likened to a 'green gold rush,' in which countries are rapidly turning land over to agrofuel crops and developing infrastructure for processing and

IV. For example: October 2007 announcement of cooperation between ADM and Conoco-Philips, April 2007 cooperation between Chevron.

transporting them. While the rest of the world is in an economic recession, these corporations are expanding and profiting. How? Taxpayer dollars.

In anticipation of passage of the 2007 Energy Bill, ADM's stock surged nearly 20% from August to mid-December.[29] The company announced that it was "optimistic about the expanded role [agrofuels] will play in improving energy security, strengthening rural economies and helping to improve our environment."[30]Archer Daniels Midland, the largest U.S. (and multinational) grain processor, received 25% of its operating profit from agrofuels in 2008, including both ethanol and biodiesel.[31]

In order to establish the international agrofuels market, these corporations require extensive government subsidies, tariffs and tax breaks. Corn and soybeans are the most subsidized crops in the U.S., raking in a total of $51 billion in federal handouts between 1995 and 2005. Ethanol subsidies amount to as much as $1.38 per gallon—about half of its wholesale market price.[32] In 2006, the combined state and federal support for the U.S. ethanol industry was between $5.1 and $6.8 billion.[33] According to Don Briggs, president of the Louisiana Oil and Gas Association, the 2007 U.S. Energy Bill was "a giant ethanol subsidy."[34]

"The ethanol boondoggle is largely a tribute to the political muscle of a single company: agribusiness giant Archer Daniels Midland," states a recent Rolling Stone article. ADM has a historic and large presence in Washington DC. In the 1970s, as ADM began searching for ways to diversify profits from corn, the corporation began producing ethanol. ADM established a relationship with Sen. Bob Dole of Kansas, a.k.a. "Senator Ethanol." During the 1992 election, ADM gave $1 million to Dole and his friends in the GOP (compared with $455,000 to the Democrats). In return, Dole helped the company secure billions of dollars in subsidies and tax breaks. In 1995, the conservative Cato Institute, estimating that nearly half of ADM's profits came from products either subsidized or protected by the federal government, called the company 'the most prominent recipient of corporate welfare in recent U.S. history.' Since 2000, the company has contributed $3.7 million to state and federal politicians.[35]

The Agrofuels Industry: Concentrated growth

According to the Renewable Fuels Association (RFA) the ethanol industry's lobbying group, out of a total of 134 operational ethanol processing plants in the U.S., 49 are presently farmer-owned associations, accounting for 28% of the

Sara y Tsunki

CARGILL SOY TERMINAL: SANTAREM, BRAZIL

nation's total capacity. That is rapidly changing. The vast majority are owned by large corporations, while the farmer owned percentage of total plant capacity has fallen to less than 20% (note: RFA and the USDA have been accused of under-reporting the number of ethanol plants under construction,[36] so the degree of corporate control may well be higher). Five corporations control roughly 47% of all ethanol production in the U.S. ADM and POET, the two largest corporate ethanol producers, control 33.7% of all ethanol production. The top 10 producers together control an estimated 70 percent.[37] Because of ADM's economies of scale of its plants and the fact that it can dominate the grain market in both food and fuel crops, it is emerging as the hegemonic player in the U.S. While other ethanol companies are struggling with shrinking margins due lower fuel prices, ADM has strengthened its market share, and its profits.[V]

Concentration of ownership of global agrofuels production by U.S. agribusiness is proceeding apace. Having recently bought majority shares in Brazil's largest

---

V. "The days of cheap corn are over, and the industry's new, lower profit margins clearly favor ethanol leader Archer Daniels Midland ... over all the smaller producers like Verasun, privately-held Poet Energy and the many, many farmer-owned ethanol cooperatives. ADM's massive 200 million-gallon-a-year ethanol plants simply have better economies of scale than their 50-million-gallon-a-year rivals. And the fact some of ADM's big plants run on coal instead of natural gas makes ADM's cost advantage that much greater." The ethanol bust: The ethanol boom is running out of gas as corn prices spike. Jon Birger, senior writer, Fortune, February 28th, http://money.cnn.com/2008/02/27/magazines/fortune/ethanol.fortune/?postversi, accessed 2008-03-06

ethanol distillery, U.S.-based Cargill is now the largest shipper of both raw sugar and soybeans from Brazil—the former for ethanol feedstock, the latter either feed or biodiesel. Cargill also has the largest capacity for processing oil seeds in Paraguay.[VI]

The prospects for consolidating corporate monopolies through the agrofuels boom are staggering. New corporate partnerships and mergers are being formed at a dizzying rate: ADM with both Monsanto and Conoco-Phillips; BP with DuPont and Toyota, as well as with Monsanto and Mendel Biotechnology; Royal Dutch Shell with Cargill, Syngenta, and Goldman-Sachs, and DuPont with British Petroleum and Weyerhauser.[38] In June 2007, BP, Associated British Foods, and chemicals producer DuPont Co. announced that they will invest $400 million to build an agrofuels plant in England.[39]

Agrofuels: Renewable ... but not green

Before the advent of electricity and hydropower, much of the Western world lit their lamps with oil rendered from the blubber of whales, a "renewable" resource that the whaling industry nearly drove to extinction.[VII] Confusing the term "renewable" with the notion of a green, sustainable fuel hides yet another inconvenient truth: Agrofuels targets in the industrial North are leading to massive environmental destruction in the Global South. Millions of hectares of tropical forests, grasslands, and peat lands around the world are rapidly being cleared and burned to plant fuel crops for export.

Far from being "clean and green," agrofuels simply perpetuate the agroindustrial model—already a major contributor to greenhouse gas (GHG) emissions, pollution, and water depletion. Land use changes, agricultural production and transportation combined account for 46% of total GHG emissions.[40] In February 2008 a science journal article reported that agrofuels cause more greenhouse gas emissions than conventional fuels if the full emissions costs of producing these "green" fuels are taken into account, from land clearing to consumption.[41] Deforestation sends more carbon dioxide into the atmosphere than all the world's planes, trains, trucks and automobiles,

---

VI. With an estimated 13 silos and an illegal port facility built in the Amazon, Cargill is leading soy's invasion into the region - spurring the incursion of illegal farms and infrastructure to deliver soy to global markets. In 2005, Cargill became the majority shareholder of two palm oil plantations in Indonesia, on the islands of Sumatra and Borneo, and three more in Papua New Guinea. www.cargill.com

VII. Even after petroleum replaced oil as the fuel of choice, because the whaling industry was financially committed to whale hunting, it continued to slaughter whales for years as it attempted to develop markets in non-essential items like corsets and perfume. This should serve a grim warning to those who believe in a smooth industrial transition from corn to 2nd generation ethanol.

accounting for about 20% of anthropogenic emissions.[42] Every ton of palm oil generates 33 tons of carbon dioxide emissions—10 times more than petroleum. Because clearing releases carbon trapped in the vegetation, tropical forests cleared for sugar cane ethanol emit 50% more GHG emissions than the production and use of the same amount of gasoline.[43] Fifty percent of global GHG emissions from changes in land use are generated in Indonesia and Brazil—two global leaders of agrofuels feedstock production.[44]

The use of synthetic nitrogen fertilizers, a common practice in industrial agriculture, and one that can be expected to expand with the development of agrofuels, results in the emission of nitrous oxide ($N2O$)—a greenhouse gas 296 times more potent than CO^2. A recent study by Nobel laureate Paul Crutzen states that "production of commonly used biofuels, such as biodiesel from rapeseed and bioethanol from corn, can contribute as much or more to global warming by N2O emissions than cooling by fossil fuel savings."[45] In the U.S., corn cultivation involves intensive application of nitrogen fertilizer, which contributes to the Midwestern agricultural runoff into the Mississippi River. This flows to the Gulf of Mexico where each year it creates an oxygen-depleted "dead zone" the size of New Jersey.[46] When U.S. corn acreage reached a record high last summer, so did the size of the "dead" zone.[47]

In addition, the extensive cultivation and processing of ethanol and other agrofuels will significantly deplete and pollute water resources in the U.S. and around the world. According to Colorado State University and UNESCO, it takes anywhere from 925 to 2700 gallons of water to produce the corn for just one gallon of ethanol.[48] To process a gallon of ethanol takes three to six more gallons of water, and can produce up to 13 gallons of waste water. Simply because they are "renewable" does not mean that industrially-produced agrofuels are sustainable. The greenwashing of agrofuels hides their real environmental costs to farmers, consumers and the environment.

Big Biotechnology: The biggest agrofuel polluter
The agrofuels boom offers biotech companies, including Monsanto and Syngenta, the opportunity to irreversibly convert all agriculture to genetically engineered crops worldwide. Presently 52% of corn, 89% of soy and 50% of canola in the U.S. is genetically modified (GM). Like a Trojan horse, the expansion of GM corn and soy for special ethanol processing plants will remove geographical barriers

to the contamination of all non-GMO crops.[49] In the EU, consumer resistance has, to a large extent, kept GM crops out. Yet with agrofuels, the biotech industry has a chance to gain access through the back door by presenting GM crops as energy crops, not food crops.[50] Once in the field, GM fuel crops can pollute non-GM crops indiscriminately, forcing acceptance of GM seeds upon farmers and GM foods on consumers. According to Bill Niebur, Vice President for genetics research and development at DuPont, "Demand for ethanol means that the race is on to rapidly ramp up grain yields."[51] In the seed and chemical industry, "ramping up" means "spreading out" of GM crops.

Seed Monopolies

Seed giant Monsanto alone accounts for 20% of the world's commercial seed market, 25% of the commercial market for soybean seeds, and 41% of the corn seed market.[1] In Brazil, Monsanto controls 30% of the corn seed market and over 50% of the soybean seed market; the company expects to control 90% of the market by the end of the decade.[2] The top three seed companies—Monsanto, Dupont and Syngenta—already control 44% of the global commercial seed market.[3]

Second Generation to the Rescue?

The industry and political discourse on the U.S. Energy Bill has rested on claims that second generation agrofuels—such as cellulosic agrofuels from native plants like switchgrass and fast-growing trees such as eucalyptus—can be developed that will solve the problems posed by current agrofuels technology. The aim is for Big Biotech to profit by modifying the physiology of native plants and trees through genetic engineering (GE). Second generation agrofuels will not solve the ecological problems from the monocultures promoted by industrial agriculture, nor do they resolve the problem of resource competition between food and fuel. When and if fuel crops like switchgrass and eucalyptus trees become viable commodities, they will very likely migrate from hedgerows and woodlots into the crop field, where they will compete with food crops for land, water and resources. In addition, second generation agrofuels will not be commercially available for at least a decade (if ever), and they will require major breakthroughs in plant physiology—not simple refinements of existing technology. A recent study from Iowa State University indicates that under the RFS targets, the expansion of cellulosic feedstock for ethanol production will worsen, not lessen, the competition for land and resources between food and fuel, sending prices sky-rocketing; as Baker, et. al. explain:

If the cellulosic mandates in the act are designed to avoid the feed-versus-fuel trade-off, our results suggest it will actually exacerbate the situation by inducing even higher feedstuff costs than under the regime with only corn ethanol in production. With a fixed amount of land, it is impossible to increase the amount of each crop devoted to energy and maintain the same level of consumption of each commodity for food uses such as feeding livestock.[52]

Further, the authors determine that "In order for switchgrass ethanol to be commercially viable, it must receive a differential subsidy *over* that awarded to corn-based ethanol (emphasis ours)." In other words, subsidies to second generation fuels must be even greater than those presently propping up corn ethanol (which the authors conclude would disappear without government subsidies).

Certified Sustainable Agrofuels

One alternative to ensure the environmental and social sustainability is "sustainable regulation." Theoretically, these regulations certify that participating companies do not use slave labor, do not grow feedstock on land that has been cleared of rainforest, and that they use ecologically sound production and processing practices.

Unfortunately, as pointed out in a recent OECD study, macro-level impacts such as the relocation of production to lands outside the scope of certification cannot be addressed through these schemes. Likewise, certification cannot deal with other macro-level impacts, like the competition with food production, and access to land, water and other natural resources vital for human life. Historically, certification schemes have failed to ensure Free Prior and Informed Consent of affected communities and indigenous peoples.

The development of agrofuels is proceeding faster than certification can be implemented. Many countries lack the regulatory capacity to ensure the implementation and monitoring of safeguards and accountability mechanisms. Further, certification on a country-by-country basis leads to market segmentation rather than a significant reduction of unsustainable practices and a uniform and globally enforceable certification scheme is not likely.[1]

Under the current agrofuels context, sustainable agrofuels will likely develop into a niche market for consumers of fair trade products. An agrofuels niche market will not ensure sufficient agribusiness compliance at the global scales needed to prevent global warming, the destruction of the planet's forests and conservation lands, and food and water rights for local populations. Without changing the context, certified agrofuel plantations will be small, sustainable islands in a globally unsustainable sea. Or worse, specialty niches for an affluent, environmentally-conscious, but globally irrelevant percentage of the planet's energy market.

In April 2007, the Brazilian corporation Aracruz Celulose S.A., the world's largest producer of bleached eucalyptus pulp, was given license to conduct experiments with GM eucalyptus. The expansion of non-GM eucalyptus plantations in the South already poses serious risks to water tables, biodiversity, and livelihoods for rural communities. Because of their potential for genetic contamination, the threats from future GM eucalyptus agrofuel plantations are doubly dangerous.

The promise of second generation agrofuels is frequently invoked when corn,

LANDLESS WORKERS PROTEST ON A MONSANTO GE EUCALYPTUS PLANTATION:
"EUCALYPTUS = DROUGHT AND HUNGER, AGRARIAN REFORM = JOBS AND FOOD"

sugar, and palm-based ethanol are criticized. In the quixotic search for the "silver bullet" that will solve the food and fuel problem by technical means, these promises minimize the difficulties in making second generation feedstocks commercially viable, and ignore the problems of corporate concentration in the agrofuels industry. Faith in science is not science. Second generation agrofuels are less of a "great green hope" than a corporate smokescreen.

Alternatives: Building the next food and energy context

The fracturing of the agrofuels consensus will not necessarily portend the end of the industry, or even the boom, for that matter. When the industry's spectacular growth settles—pushing farmers' profits down and eliminating smaller corporate players from the market—big grain, big biotech and big oil will use agrofuels to maintain their grip on our economy. They are able to do so because they have created the technical, political and economic conditions for agrofuels: the food and energy context. As long as food production is technically and financially constructed to respond to the industry's commercial interest, and as long as the political will for legislation and regulation is determined by the same corporate interests, agrofuels, arguably one of the worst ideas in the history of the modern agri-foods complex, will continue to invade and transform our food and fuel systems.

In order to think about alternatives to agrofuels—biofuels, conservation, wind, or solar—and in order to advance truly sustainable agricultural development at home and abroad, we need to construct an alternative food and energy context. Without changing the context, we cannot hope to affect the tremendous power of the corporations controlling our food and fuel systems. Constructing a context for truly green and fair alternatives requires a food and energy systems approach that challenges the dominance of the industrial agri-foods complex. We must challenge the political-economic context as well as the technologies, debunk the assumptions as well as the claims, and propose new relationships between producers and consumers in our food and fuel systems. This is a big order. However, it can start simply, by removing the artificial market incentive that created the industry: the RFS targets.

The U.S. Moratorium on Agrofuels—A necessary first step
Unless the current U.S. political and economic context for the expansion of agrofuels changes significantly, there is little to stop ADM, Cargill, Monsanto, DuPont, Toyota, BP and the other agrofuels giants from transforming our food and fuel systems for their own corporate profit. We need time for an informed public debate on agrofuels. As a society, we need to weigh the evidence to date, undertake further research, and build an alternative context that favors family farmers in the North and South, and local alternatives to monopolistic, transnational industrial models.

There are many good proposals for local "bioeconomies," for an equitable, sustainable "Farm and Food Bill," and for the conservation of land, water, environment, and energy. We will never know if they are feasible until we change the current context that not only puts these alternatives at an industrial disadvantage, but almost guarantees their failure.

The targets set in the Renewable Fuel Standards of the U.S. Energy Act are the keystone of the agrofuels boom because they frame the economic context by obliging us to consume agrofuels. Without the targets, neither agrofuels' substantial subsidies nor their protective tariffs can sustain the boom. Remove the 36 billion gallon per year targets and the boom comes to a grinding halt. This is why concerned citizens in the United States are calling for a moratorium on agrofuels by suspension of agrofuel targets.

In 2008, along with a coalition of progressive environmental and social justice groups in the U.S., Food First launched a global call for a U.S. Moratorium. The call for an agrofuels moratorium in Europe forced European Commission officials to acknowledge the dangers of agrofuels expansion, leading to a re-evaluation of Europe's own agrofuels mandates.[53] These encouraging developments were the result of the mobilization of concerned citizens and civil society groups.

Building Social Movements for Food & Fuel Sovereignty

Because they undermine food systems, agrofuels are a threat to food sovereignty: the right of all people to healthy and culturally appropriate food produced through ecologically sound and sustainable methods, and their right to define their own food and agriculture systems. Food sovereignty is now joined by the concept of fuel sovereignty, a re-vindication of the right to sustainable fuel systems that do not put food systems, farmers, or consumers at risk. At the heart of these concepts is the belief that we need to democratize our food and fuel systems in order to ensure equity and sustainability.

INDIGENOUS FARMERS' PROTEST FOR LAND REFORM IN GUATEMALA

The democratization of our food and fuel systems requires a social change in the way we manage food and fuel. These changes will require immediate legislation in order to formulate the proper regulatory context for sustainable and equitable food and fuel systems. These changes depend on the degree of political will on the part of business, our legislators, and our communities. Political will results from social pressure emanating from social movements—movements for food and fuel sovereignty. These movements already exist, and are gaining force, locally, nationally and internationally. If we can change our thinking, we change the context. When we change the context, we level the playing field, allowing effective alternatives for food and fuel sovereignty to emerge.

Photo and Image Credits:

1. Corn Rows: Photo by Randy Wick, Creative Commons License (details: http://creativecommons.org/licenses/by-sa/2.0/deed.en) Photo URL: http://www.flickr.com/photos/cantchangerandy/2762050945/

2. Brazilian Tanker: Photo by Paul Filmer, Creative Commons License (TdetailsT: HThttp://creativecommons.org/licenses/by-nc-nd/2.0/deed.enTTH) Photo URL: http://www.flickr.com/photos/lynx81/578740826/

3. Cargill soya terminal Santarem, Brazil: Sara y Tzunki Creative Commons License (Tdetails: HTThttp://creativecommons.org/licenses/by-nc/2.0/TH) Photo url: HThttp://www.flickr.com/photos/sara_y_tzunki/435638435/T

4. MST Eucalyptus Protest: Roberto Vinicius Creative Commons http://creativecommons.org/licenses/by-nc-nd/2.0/deed.en Photo URL: http://www.flickr.com/photos/robvini/505756004

5. Indigenous Farmers' Protest: Photo by Surizar / Jacob Creative Commons License share (info: http://creativecommons.org/licenses/by-sa/2.0/deed.en) Photo URL: http://www.flickr.com/photos/puchica/2736813792/

References:

1   Reo Research/ F&C Investments. 2008. Biofuels and Sustainability: An investor perspective. http://www.fundnets.net/fn_filelibrary/file/co_gsi_reo_research_biofuels.pdf

2   Pelosi, Nancy. 2008. You Tube: http://www.youtube.com/watch?v=O9SRZfJAKKM. Accessed 3.6.08

3   Ziegler, Jean. August 22, 2007. The Right to Food, Report of the Special Rapporteur on the right to food. United Nations General Assembly, A/62/289. http://www.righttofood.org/A62289.pdf

4   Brown, Lester R. 2006. Supermarkets and service stations now competing for grain. Earth Policy Institute. http://www.earth-policy.org/Updates/2006/Update55.htm. July 13.

5   Elobeid, Amani & Chad Hart. 2007. Ethanol Expansion in the Food versus Fuel Debate: How will Developing Countries Fare? Journal of Agricultural & Food Industrial Organization, Special Issue: Explorations in Biofuels Economics, Policy and History. Vol. 5, Article 6.

6   The Economist. 2007. The End of Cheap Food. Dec. 6.

7   Brown, Lester R. 2006..

8   Brown, Lester R. 2008. ibid Elobeid & Hart, 2007.

9   Elobeid & Hart, 2007.Rosen, Stacey & Shahla Shapouri. 2008. Rising food prices
    Intensify food insecurity in developing countries. USDA Economic Research Service.
    Amber Waves. February. http://www.csmonitor.com/2008/0118/p08s01-comv.html

10 Rosen, Stacey & Shahla Shapouri. 2008. Rising food prices Intensify food insecurity
    in developing countries. USDA Economic Research Service. Amber Waves. February.
    http://www.csmonitor.com/2008/0118/p08s01-comv.html.

11 Christian Science Monitor. 2008. The global grain bubble. http://www.csmonitor.
    com/2008/0118/p08s01-comv.html

12 ibid.

13 Von Braun, Joachim. 2007. Rising food prices threaten the world's poor
    people. International Food Policy Research Institute. http://www.ifpri.org/
    pressrel/2007/20071204.asp. Dec. 4

14 Elobeid & Hart, 2007.

15 Testimony to the European Parliament Development Committee, March 6, 2008,
    Brussels, http://documents.wfp.org/stellent/groups/public/documents/newsroom/
    wfp17.

16 C. Ford Runge and Benjamin Senauer. 2007. How Biofuels Could Starve the Poor. Foreign
    Affairs, May/June.

17 Hill, Jason, Erik Nelson, David Tilman, Stephen Polasky, and Douglas Tiffany.
    "Environmental, economic and energetic costs of biodiesel and ethanol biofuels."
    Proceedings of the National Academy of Sciences, July 12, 2006.

18 Krauss, Clifford. 2007. As ethanol takes its first steps, Congress proposes a giant leap. *New
    York Times*, Washington section. Dec. 18..

19 Goodell, Jeff. 2007. Rolling Stone: The Ethanol Scam: One of America's Biggest Political
    Boondoggles, Issue 1032. Aug 9, 2007.

20 Doombosch, R., and Ronald Steeblik. 2007. Biofuels: Is the Curse Worse than the
    Disease? Round table on Sustainable Development, Office of the General Secretariat,
    OECD, Rome

21 ibid.

22 Renewable Fuels Association. http://www.ethanolrfa.org/industry/statistics/#F

23 U.S. Senate. 2007. Energy Independence and Security Act of 2007. As agreed to by Senate.
    http://thomas.loc.gov/cgibin/ query/F?c110:25:./temp/~c110wMU9UK:e97001.

24 Brasher, Philip. 2007. Biofuels on candidates' radars on campaign trails. Des Moines
    Register. Dec. 16.

25 Holt-Giménez, Eric. 2007. Biofuels: Myths of the Agrofuels Transition, Food First.
    http://www.foodfirst.org/node/1711

26 CNBC Stock Market News . 2007. Venture capital investments in biofuels, including
    ethanol and biodiesel, grew to $740 million in 2006 from $110.5 million in 2005." Green
    Technology Revs Up Venture Capitalists ,20 Apr 2007, http://today.msnbc.msn.com/
    id/18204222

27   Altieri, Miguel A. and Eric Holt-Giménez, "UC's Biotech Benefactors: The Power of Big Finance and Bad Ideas", The Berkeley Daily Planet, 02-06-07, www.berkeleydailyplanet. com

28   Corporate Europe Observatory. 2007 The EU's agrofuel folly: policy capture by corporate interests. http://www.corporateeurope.org/agrofuelfolly.html

29   Philpott, Tom. 2007. Corn ethanol to the max. Dec. 12. http://gristmill.grist.org

30   Archer Daniels Midland Company. 2007. ADM Statement Regarding Expanded Renewable Fuel Standard. Dec. 19.

31   Scully, Vaughan. 2007. Effects of the Biofuel Boom: Market Views. Business Week. August 27.

32   Archer Daniels Midland Company. 2007.

33   International Institute for Sustainable Development. 2006. Global Subsidies Initiative. Biofuels: At What Cost? Government Support for Ethanol and Biodiesel in the United States. October.

34   Briggs, Don, 2007. Energy Bill is filled with surprising details. *Daily Advertiser*. Dec. 16.

35   Goodell, Jeff. 2007.

36   Barrion Nuevo, Alexi. 2007. Rise in Ethanol Raises Concerns About Corn as a Food. New York Times. http://query.nytimes.com/gst/fullpage.html?res=9A06E7DC1430F936A3 5752C0A9619C8B63&sec=&spon=

37   Hasan, Hamza. 2007. The US Ethanol Industry. Food First. http://www.foodfirst.org/ taxonomy/term/250

38   ETC Group. 2007. Peak Oil + Peak Soil = Peak Spoils. ETC Group Communique. N. 96, November/December, 2007.

39   Voss, Stephen and Dan Weeks. 2007. BP, Associated Foods Plan $400 Million Biofuels Plant. *Bloomberg*. June 26.

40   Stern Review. 2006. The Economics of Climate Change. October 30. p.171.

41   Rosenthall, Elizabeth. 2008. Biofuels Deemed a Greenhouse Threat. New Your Times. http://www.nytimes.com/2008/02/08/science/earth/08wbiofuels.html?_ r=3&pagewanted=1&ref=world

42   Harris, Edward. 2008. Rainforests fall at 'alarming' rates. Associated Press. http://www. commondreams.org/archive/2008/02/03/6818

43   Tilman, David and Jason Hill. 2007. Corn Can't Solve Our Problem. *Washington Post*. March 25. B01. http://www.washingtonpost.com/wp-dyn/content/ article/2007/03/23/AR2007032301625_2.html

44   Stern Review. 2006. The Economics of Climate Change. October 30. p.171.

45   Crutzen, P.J., A.R. Mosier, K.A. Smith, and W.Winisarter. "Nitrous oxide release from agro-biofuel production negates global warming reduction by replacing fossil fuels' Atmospheric Chemistry and Physics. Discujss., 7 11191-11205, 2007

46   Roach, John. 2005. National Geographic News. May 25. http://news.nationalgeographic. com/news/2005/05/0525_050525_deadzone.html

47   Kinney, Dennis. 2007. More ethanol, more corn, more nitrogen and bigger dead zone in

the Gulf. Institute for Agricultural Trade Policy. August 14.

48   Ring, ed. 2007. Is biofuel water positive? June 4. http://www.ecoworld.com/blog/2007/06/04/corn-ethanol-water/

49   Holt-Giménez & Altieri. 2007. UC's Biotech Benefactors: the Power of Big Finance and Bad Ideas. *Berkeley Daily Planet*. February 6.

50   Corporate Europe Observatory. 2007. The EU's agrofuel folly: The comeback of the biotech industry, 13 June.

51   ibid.

52   Baker, Mindy L., Dermot J. Hayes, and Bruce A. Babcock, Working Paper 08-WP 460, February 2008, Center for Agricultural and Rural Development. pp. 22-23. Iowa State University, Ames, Iowa 50011-1070, www.card.iastate.edu

53   Adam, David and Alok Jha. 2008. EU Reviews Biofuel Target as Doubts Grow. http://www.guardian.co.uk/environment/2008/jan/15/biofuels.carbonemissions.

Text Box References:

Box #2: Increase in Grain Prices:

1   Elobeid, Amani and Chad Hart. 2007 Ethanol Expansion in the Food versus Fuel Debate: How Will Developing Countries Fare? Journal of Agricultural & Food Industrialization, Special Issue: Explorations in Biofuels Economics, Policy and History. Vol. 5. Article 6

2   Brown, Lester R. 2008. Ethanol Production Will Drive World Food Prices Even Higher in 2008. Earth Policy Institute. January 24

Box #3: The North-South Connection:

1   Rosen, Stacy, USDA, personal Communication. February 7, 2008

2   Romoser, Annalise. "Biofuel means bust for Colombian campesinos" 18 October 2007 http://news.nacla.org

Box #4, Biotech's Monopoly Profits:

1   De Falco, Neil, 2008, Monsanto: Seed of Profit in a World of Drought. Investopedia. Community http://research.investopedia.com/news/1A/2008/Monsanto Seed Of Profit in a World of Drought_MON.aspx?partner=aol. Jan 31.

2   Forbes http://forbes.com/markets/2008/01/03/monsanto-agricultural-food-markets-equity-cx_er_0103markets12.html

3   Syngenta full year results 2007, Feb 7, 2008 4 Forbes, ibid.

Box# 5, Seed Monopolies:

1   GRAIN 2007, Corporation Power: Agrofuels and the expansion of agribusiness. *Seedling*.

2   Monsanto 2007 Annual Report

3   ETC Group. 2006. The World's Top Ten Seed Companies. http://www.etcgroup.org/en/materials/publications.html?pub_id=656

Box #6, Certified Sustainable Agrofuels:

1   Jeff Goodell, Rolling Stone: The Ethanol Scam: One of America's Biggest Political Boondoggles, Issue 1032

CHAPTER II

THE FREE MARKET IN AGROFUELS:
REGULATION AND TRADE IN THE AMERICAS

BY GRETCHEN GORDON AND JESSICA AGUIRRE

LOS ANGELES HARBOR

Across the Americas, governments and private investors are rolling out a bold strategy for economic development through the cultivation of a new cash crop: energy. Over the last few years a global trade in agrofuels[I] (ethanol and biodiesel) has taken hold. While both Brazil and the U.S. have had biomass energy programs since the 1970s, it wasn't until the recent spike in petroleum prices and growing surplus of commodities in the early 2000s that the model of producing biofuels for domestic consumption was recast as a global free market in industrial agrofuels. Though the current drop in oil prices and the economic downturn have brought a temporary slow in agrofuels investments, legislated demand is growing, setting the stage for a future rebound of the agrofuels expansion. As agrofuels take on an increasingly global Industrial scale, their social and environmental impacts become more acute, and the question of *how* and if those impacts can be controlled becomes a critical one.

Global trade and investment in agrofuels took off over the last five years with the passage of gasoline blending mandates in the U.S. and EU, which assured investors of new markets and increasing demand[II] With U.S. cropland at near

---

I. **"Biofuels"** is the general term for liquid fuels made from biomass. Their most common forms are ethanol and biodiesel which are utilized in a pure form, or more commonly blended with petroleum gasoline or diesel fuels. Ethanol is currently produced from starch alcohols, including corn, sugar cane, and sugar beet. Biodiesel is predominantly made from oil seeds, including oil palm, soy, rapeseed, canola, jatropha, and castor.

"Agrofuels" is a term that has been adopted by many social movements and organizations in the Americas and Europe to refer to biofuels made from fuel crops grown on a large agro-industrial scale. The term allows a distinction from the traditional model of small-scale, non-industrial biofuels frequently made in owner-operated facilities for local consumption. This report concerns itself with industrial agrofuels, not small-scale biofuels.

II. Most recently, the U.S. Energy Independence and Security Act of 2007 mandated the use of 9 billion gallons of renewable fuel in 2008, rising to 36 billion gallons by 2022, 21 billion gallons of which is to come from cellulosic ethanol

capacity and the EU unable to meet production demands, these graduated renewable fuels standards establish a guaranteed future market for agrofuels imports, the vast majority of which will come from Latin America, Asia, and Africa. Agribusiness, genetic engineering and energy companies, together with venture capitalists and international financial institutions, have driven a flood of investment into agrofuels production.

Export production of agrofuels is currently being marketed as a model for economic development throughout the Americas. Mounting evidence has shown, however, that the agrofuels push in large part is doing more harm than good. Scientific studies have demonstrated that the expansion of industrial corn ethanol in the U.S. can actually lead to greater net greenhouse gas emissions due to intensive production methods and resultant indirect land use changes in other countries, including deforestation.[1] Agrofuels grown on land that was cleared

AGRICULTURAL DEFORESTATION NOVO PROGRESSO, PARA, BRAZIL

from rainforests or savannas have been shown to have "greater greenhouse gas impacts than the fossil fuels they displace."[2] Sugarcane ethanol and oil palm development in countries such as Brazil and Colombia has been linked to deplorable labor conditions, human rights abuses, and forced displacement

or advanced biofuels. The European Union Renewable Energy Directive of 2008 established a 10% requirement for alternative fuel content in the transportation sector by 2020.

of communities.[3, 4] Agrofuels have come under further attack for contributing to the current global food crisis marked by unprecedented commodity price volatility.[5]

In light of these serious consequences, the blind embrace of agrofuels is being reconsidered. European Union states have been engaged in negotiations to craft sustainability criteria for agrofuels procurement in a revision of their renewable fuel mandates. A number of politicians in the U.S. have called for the elimination of agrofuels consumption targets and subsidies.[6, 7] But while the halo of agrofuels may have dimmed, the faith that we can grow and trade our way out of mounting energy needs and tightening environmental constraints remains remarkably resilient among companies and policymakers alike.

Public and industry researchers are busy investigating ways to employ technology to provide a "green" image for the agrofuels trade through the development of second generation or cellulosic fuels, which utilize agricultural waste materials or non-food plants such as switchgrass. EU policymakers in December 2008 scrapped plans to distinguish between "good" and "bad" agrofuels, watering down sustainability requirements while renewing their consumption mandates. At the same time, other nations (including India and New Zealand) are entering the field with their own agrofuels targets while the UN and heads of state call for greater liberalization of agrofuels trade. Multinational agribusiness companies are redoubling efforts to combat the recent agrofuels public relations fallout while capitalizing on the new Obama administration's support for agrofuels. Despite the debate over which fuel stocks to grow and how to trade them, the basic framework for a global free market in agrofuels remains unquestioned and the drive to establish a global commodities market in agrofuels is proceeding apace.

In order to be effective, any revision of agrofuels policy needs to consider the global market context in which the agrofuels expansion is playing out. In our current deregulated markets, the horizontal and vertical concentration of both energy and agriculture industries will continue to promote a large-scale, resource-intensive monoculture model with inherent negative environmental and social impacts.

Efforts to mitigate these impacts through narrow regulation of agrofuels alone, without regulating agriculture and financial markets will be ineffective. At the same time, the pressure of agrofuels industries and the confines of international trade rules are already limiting the range of options under consideration for regulating agrofuels. At best, the push for a free market in industrial agrofuels threatens to distract from real solutions to the energy crisis and equitable development needs. At worst, it threatens to greatly exacerbate current climate, food, and development crises.

SOYBEAN FIELD AND AGRICULTURAL DEFORESTATION.

The Project for a Free Market in Agrofuels

The project for a free market in agrofuels occurs on several fronts. It is advanced within global trade negotiations, such as those at the World Trade Organization (WTO), and through other international agreements including bilateral credit, investment, and cooperation agreements. But it also moves forward at the behest of global capital, independent of national governments. Global investment in agrofuels rose from $5 billion in 1995 to $38 billion in 2005.[8] The majority of this new investment is directed towards a specific export-driven agribusiness model already well established in the global soy and agricultural feeds trade. The project includes a general push to increase the advancement of industrial agriculture, the volume of trade and investment in agrofuels, and investment in export-oriented infrastructure including ports and roads. At the same time, proponents are looking toward international trade negotiations to eliminate barriers to free trade in agrofuels, most visibly import tariffs and subsidies which favor domestic producers or otherwise 'distort' the free market.

Another less visible aspect of trade liberalization, often with more significant impacts, is the elimination of what are referred to as non-tariff barriers to trade and investment. These 'barriers' include an almost endless range of government regulations which impact the freedom of global investment–from environmental and public health regulations, to agricultural and tax laws to land zoning rules. A key goal of agrofuels trade liberalization is also to increase intellectual property protections for technology and biotechnology, including eliminating government restrictions on the use of genetically modified (GM) organisms or requirements for technology transfer. So, for instance, while biotech has been shut out of the EU market because of restrictions on GM crops for food, the industry has secured access for the cultivation of the same GM crops for agrofuels.

The final component of the free market in agrofuels is the creation of a global agrofuels commodities market which would open up greater outlets for capital, and more lucrative opportunities for investment return. The agrofuels market provides an outlet for surplus grains and other commodities—like corn, sugar, and soy—which have in the past suffered from overproduction and plummeting prices. Turning grains and oilseeds into fuels imbues them with added value, increasing profit potential. Additionally, the creation of a full-scale commodities market in agrofuels allows for agrofuels traders to win big in a high-risk market, earning profit not just from sales, but from gambles on futures and other financial risk mechanisms. [III] Unfortunately, while the development of markets and production capacity is receiving great attention and investment, the question of how to regulate a new commodities market in agrofuels remains conspicuously unaddressed. If the financial crisis has demonstrated anything, it is the damage that can be wrought by unregulated markets and speculative capital, a threat that is even more acute when played out in our agriculture and food systems.

Consequences for Sustainable Development

The model of agrofuels expansion is one of industrial export agriculture: large-scale, intensive, monoculture production. In many regards, it is not that different from the old cash crop plantation model ubiquitous in Latin America, except for

---

III. While there are commodity futures contracts on ethanol, the market is only in its nascent stages due to limited volume, number of buyers and sellers, and low liquidity.

the high degree of mechanization now involved. While biofuels can be produced in a small-scale sustainable manner that meets local consumption needs, that is not the model which is currently being pushed by governments, investors, and financial institutions. While some agrofuels importing governments may be exploring the possibilities for establishing agrofuels sustainability criteria, it is the expansion of a resource-intensive, deregulated, export-driven structure, not biofuels *per se*, which poses the greatest threat to both climate preservation and equitable development.

The machine of free trade in industrial agriculture is not tooled for environmental or social sustainability. In fact, its track record shows just the opposite. Conspicuously absent from the discussion of trade in agrofuels as a solution to the world's climate crisis is the responsibility that both trade and industrial agriculture bear in creating that crisis. Global trade accounts for approximately one-fifth of global carbon dioxide emissions, while industrial agriculture and related deforestation has been estimated to make up one-third of global emissions and approximately two-thirds global water use.[9, 10, 11] Thus, a climate solution based on global trade in industrial agriculture would seem like an oxymoron. But that is the basic blueprint of the free market in agrofuels.

The singular focus on lowering vehicular greenhouse gas emissions in the developed world has obscured the absurdity of pursuing agrofuels development as a climate mitigation strategy. In the case of biofuel powerhouse Brazil, three quarters of the nation's greenhouse gas emissions come not from cars, but from deforestation, which is increasing with the agrofuels boom.[12] Similarly, the clearing of native forests for agrofuels plantations in Colombia and throughout Asia is causing microclimate change and bringing on new environmental crises through loss of biodiversity and critical habitats.[13] Large-scale monoculture production requires heavy application of chemical inputs, bringing with it soil nutrient depletion, habitat destruction, and air and water contamination, as well as increased greenhouse gas emissions. Industrial agriculture and related deforestation has been estimated to make up one-third of global carbon dioxide emissions, while global trade accounts for approximately one-fifth of global emissions.[14]

From a development perspective, it is important to keep in mind who benefits from a free market in agrofuels, and who bears the costs. Hong Kong-based brokerage CLSA predicts the global agrofuels market will be worth nearly 150 billion dollars a year by 2020.[15] That market, however, is following in the mold of an agricultural trade system that is rigged to the benefit of multinational agribusiness. Starting in the 1970s, the industrialization of agriculture, the subsidization of agribusiness, and the proliferation of free trade and deregulation have gradually replaced local market access for the majority of small producers with global market access for a few mega producers. The agrofuels boom even more effectively propels this concentration of market power by inextricably linking food and energy markets. While some small farmers have been able to benefit from local agrofuels markets, as the agrofuels trade becomes more lucrative there is increasing consolidation of industries, markets and land.[16,17] Without effective policies that address concentration and the power of agricultural oligopolies, the vast majority of small producers cannot access or benefit from a global market. Consequently, the greatest benefits of a free market in agrofuels are only accessible to those corporations with sufficient infrastructure, capital and market share to harness the cheapest labor and resources, gain access to foreign consumers, and shoulder the risk of volatile markets.

Just as the benefits of the free market in agrofuels are not evenly distributed, nor are the costs evenly shared, falling disproportionately on those most vulnerable; small farmers, poor consumers, and rural and indigenous communities which are squeezed out of access to land, food, and natural resources. The agrofuels boom has the potential to direct great amounts of foreign investment to developing nations. But, as with any extractive industry, strong policies are needed to make sure that investment works for development, and does not just generate profits for investors. Agrofuels liberalization as a development strategy, however, rests on the flawed logic of liberalized markets, assuming that favorable conditions for foreign investors will trickle down to generate local development – an assumption that time and again has proven false.

Can the Problems with Agrofuels be Fixed with Regulation?

In response to concerns over the negative impacts of agrofuels, policymakers are scrambling to find quick regulatory fixes while continuing to promote agrofuels development. Several governments with mandatory targets for fuel blending are in the process of establishing environmental certification and labeling protocols. These regimes would specify minimum standards for imported or domestically produced agrofuels, including feedstock type or origin, production methods, greenhouse gas emissions, or labor conditions in order for fuels to qualify for government incentives. But regulating agrofuels production chains that cross multiple borders and have diverse spillover impacts is no easy task. First, there is no international consensus on what sustainable agrofuels production would look like and there is legitimate concern that standards setting processes often lack adequate input from the communities most affected by those standards. Second, even if standards are agreed to, the question remains how they are to be enforced. This is not to say that government standards should not be established. Enforceable regulation of agrofuels production is sorely needed. However, its effectiveness will be severely compromised if it is done in isolation, or in piecemeal fashion. Setting downstream agrofuels sustainability standards is an inadequate redress for the promotion of a production model that is in many ways inherently environmentally and socially unsustainable.

Effective regulation of agrofuels faces another set of legal obstacles in addition to these logistical and political obstacles. The existing trade regime—embodied in the WTO, its underlying General Agreement on Tariffs and Trade (GATT) and myriad bilateral and multilateral agreements—greatly restricts the ability of national governments to regulate agrofuels production or to implement sustainability criteria. Many of the policy proposals at the forefront of the debate on how to address the climate and food system impacts of agrofuels production run head-on into international trade rules that aim to eliminate tariff and "non-tariff" barriers to trade. There are three main facets of trade law that can work to significantly limit the potential for effective agrofuels regulation. First is the principle that countries may not discriminate between different trading partners.[IV] Second, under the principle of *national treatment*, foreign imports or investors must be afforded treatment "no less favorable" than that afforded to their domestic counterparts.[V] In other words, government actions and regulations cannot discriminate explicitly, or in their effects, between "like" domestic and foreign goods or investors. Lastly, trade rules that govern regulations, such as certification labeling protocols, prohibit those which create "unnecessary obstacles" to trade, or which are "more trade-restrictive than necessary."[VI]

So what does the trade regime mean for agrofuels regulation? It means that it is very difficult for governments to promote local small-scale biofuels produc-

IV. GATT Article I
V. GATT Article III
VI. Agreement on Technical Barriers to Trade (TBT) Article 2.2

ers or to devise environmental and social sustainability certification programs through mandatory regulations without making themselves vulnerable to challenges under international trade rules. While governments are generally free to

regulate the production of agrofuels within their borders, regulations that tie tax breaks, incentives, subsidies, or tariff levels to the way in which agrofuels are produced are open to challenge by trade partners if they are deemed contrary to trade rules. While many agrofuels importing nations

INDUSTRIAL SOYBEAN PLANTATION, BRAZIL

have established blending mandates and other government incentives for agrofuels, conditioning those incentives to the use of domestic feedstocks, the meeting of minimum labor standards, or regulations to control for indirect impacts, including indirect land use or life cycle greenhouse gas emissions, could be met with trade sanctions.

Agrofuels policies requiring domestic content or the use of "homegrown" fuels are an obvious target for a trade challenge under the *national treatment* principle. This includes U.S. states' gasoline blending credits which are contingent on the use of in-state grown feedstocks.[18] There are also several bills currently under consideration in the U.S. Congress which require a percentage of agrofuels from domestic facilities.[19] Another example of potentially conflictive policies is the use of *border adjustments*. Border adjustments include carbon taxes on imports, or requirements that importers not certified to meet a base level of domestic climate protection purchase green-house gas emissions credits in the importing country's carbon market. These two options have been under consideration for agrofuels as well as in the broader context of climate policy, the idea being that until comparable global climate policies are in place, countries implementing stricter emissions regulations could put their domestic industries at a disadvantage compared to foreign imports from countries with weaker regulations. GATT rules, however, conflict with most border adjustment proposals, and the threat of a WTO challenge has already led the European Union to scrap plans for border adjustment legislation.[20]

Agrofuels certification schemes which identify minimum standards for labor conditions or indirect environmental impacts also present another likely conflict with trade rules. A considerable gray area in WTO rules is how to treat regulations dealing with how a good was produced. According to several GATT and WTO tribunal rulings, goods can be treated differently based on their final physical characteristics, but not on factors relating to *how* they were produced (referred to as Process and Production Methods, or PPMs).[VII] So, for instance, a country can have different policies (be those tariff rates, tax policies, or regulatory standards) for long-sleeve shirts and short-sleeve shirts (be those tariff rates, tax policies, or regulatory standards) for long-sleeve shirts and short-sleeve shirts and still be in compliance with WTO rules. However, under several GATT rulings, a country couldn't have different policies for shirts based on whether or not they were made with child labor. To apply this to agrofuels, that means that ethanol is ethanol—regardless of whether it was made from corn or cane, produced by a sustainable cooperative on rehabilitated land, or produced on rainforest land cleared by exploited workers—yet to control for the environmental and social impacts of agrofuels, regulations need to take into account how fuels are produced, from what feedstock, and under what conditions.

The GATT text itself does not outright ban the consideration of PPMs. GATT and WTO trade tribunals have ruled against PPMs on several occasions, but they have also upheld the legitimacy of PPM-based regulations in limited cases, leaving an opening for those that are distinguishable by a clear consumer preference or based on international standards adopted through consultative multilateral negotiation, or a good faith effort thereof. In the area of agrofuels and many climate solutions more broadly, however, neither clear consumer preference nor international agreement on universal standards is a near-term reality. Additionally, even if international standards could be reached, those standards could serve as a ceiling, leaving national governments attempting to adopt higher standards vulnerable to challenge. While countries could potentially use multilateral environmental agreements to justify certain aspects

---

VII. See Panel Report, *Mexico – Tax Measures on Soft Drinks and Other Beverages*, ¶ 8.36, WT/DS308/R (October 7, 2005) in which the WTO ruled that cane sugar and beet sugar sweeteners are "like products" to be treated equally, and Panel Report, *Spain – Tariff Treatment of Unroasted Coffee*, L/5135 - 28S/102 (adopted June 11, 1981) which ruled against regulations distinguishing between coffee beans based on different production and cultivation methods.

of agrofuels regulations, this is a flexibility that still needs to be carved out in WTO judicial practice.

While it is possible that certification schemes that involve some of the direct land use impacts of agrofuels production could potentially withstand WTO challenge, regulation of Indirect Land Use (ILU) impacts would be much more difficult to justify. A direct impact is, for instance, the clearing of peatland for the planting of oil palm. Much of agrofuels' most pervasive impacts, however, are indirect, such as when soy or sugarcane production for agrofuels displaces cattle ranching, which then leads to the clearing of rainforest. Additionally, many current agrofuels regulatory proposals attempt to address indirect impacts by utilizing life cycle analysis (LCA), which examines the impacts of a product from production to disposal. California's renewable fuels mandate, for instance, uses LCA of net greenhouse gas emissions to determine qualifying fuels. Because LCA calculations and ILU impacts are even further removed from a product's final physical characteristics than PPMs, it is highly likely that if a challenge were brought, a WTO tribunal would consider LCA or ILU-based regulations as "unnecessary" or "more burdensome than necessary" under the WTO agreement on Technical Barriers to Trade (TBT).

According to the WTO, since 2000, twenty WTO member nations have notified the WTO of thirty-seven agrofuels measures, that is to say measures which are not based on established international standards.[21] While the TBT recognizes protection of human, animal or plant health or the environment as legitimate objectives for technical regulations, those regulations still must be deemed to be "no more trade restrictive than necessary," and cannot be aimed at promoting domestic competitiveness. The vagueness of this requirement leaves government regulations vulnerable to the determination of trade tribunals as to whether alternative regulatory options could have been employed. While the GATT does include exceptions for regulatory measures necessary for the protection of health or the conservation of natural resources (GATT, Article XX), this defense has rarely prevailed in trade disputes. WTO tribunals have to a very limited extent more recently ruled to allow a possibility of PPMs based on environmental impacts, following several high profile rulings against environmental policies.[VIII] However, agrofuels standards based on social impacts

---

VIII. See U.S.-Shrimp (United States–Import Prohibition of Certain Shrimp and Shrimp Products, Appellate Body Report adopted on 12 October 1998, WT/DS58/AB/R) case in which the WTO Appellate Body Report left the possibility of PPM regulations falling under GATT article XX (General Exceptions).

such as labor conditions or effects on food systems would not fall within this exception.[22]

While most agrofuels standards may never be brought before a trade tribunal, trade rules are nonetheless already impacting regulatory efforts. The threat or potential for a costly challenge alone has been a powerful limiting factor on the range of options under consideration by national governments. Brazil has made clear its opposition to mandatory sustainability criteria for agrofuels and has the commercial power to back up that position in WTO negotiations.[23] In recent EU discussions of agrofuels policy, legally binding labor standards have been shelved in deference to WTO rules, while final negotiations took place under the threat of a WTO challenge by eight agrofuels producing nations. In the end, the EU's "sustainability" criteria were stripped of any legally-binding reference to indirect land-

SUGAR CANE BURN

use in calculating greenhouse gas emissions.[24] The evisceration of EU agrofuels standards reflects the political interests of certain EU member states in promoting agrofuels industries and also provides evidence that the power of the WTO is not necessarily its rulings, but how it can be utilized politically to influence regulatory efforts.[25, 26]

Putting the Breaks on the Agrofuels Expansion

The project of trade liberalization depends on complex political negotiation between the most powerful countries and financial players. In some cases the end result is textbook style market liberalization. And in some cases it is massive subsidies and government intervention. How the free market in agrofuels will play out at a policy level remains to be seen. However, on a fundamental level, the liberalization of agrofuels trade means *more* agrofuels trade. It means the expansion of a production model that has been shown to have serious negative social and environmental impacts. And it means that local communities and national governments will have less power to control those impacts.

Acknowledging the conflicts between effective agrofuels regulation and our current trade system is not a call for policymakers to refrain from regulating, but rather to be aware of the incompatibility between environmental and social goals and a deregulated, free market regime. Proposals such as sustainability certification schemes cannot be assumed to be "easy fixes" to the complex environmental and social impacts of agrofuels trade, especially its indirect impacts on the environment and our food systems. Social movements have long called for the exclusion of agriculture from trade rules based on the belief that the fate of our food systems is too important a question to leave up to the market, private investors, or the WTO. This is even more evident in the context of agrofuels and the current food crisis.

Rather than deferring to trade rules, regulators must demand their reform. They can do this in trade negotiations, or by passing domestic legislation that pushes the envelope on regulatory space, forcing flexibility into WTO rulings. However, as currently devised, our trade regime functions to promote the growth of multinational capital, not to promote environmental and social sustainability. The EU experience with agrofuels sustainability criteria demonstrates the chimera of achieving effective standards amid foreign and domestic industry pressure. In this context, the potential for a trade challenge is a powerful means of deflating regulatory efforts or justifying regulations that benefit multinational capital. Whether it is domestic agrofuels industries or foreign exporters who are shaping the direction of agrofuels regulatory policies, those most affected by agrofuels expansion—small farmers, poor consumers, and indigenous and rural communities—don't have a seat at the table.

Just as the agrofuels expansion is proceeding on multiple fronts, a strategy to change directions will require multiple approaches, including regulating trade and production and reforming trade rules to allow that to happen. However, the first, and critical, priority must be to stop the drive for expansion created by agrofuels consumption mandates and investment projects. The damage being wrought by the agrofuels trade is now undeniable. It is also in many cases irreparable. The communities that are being destroyed by agrofuels expansion cannot be restored. The forests and other carbon sinks that are being uprooted for agrofuels monocultures cannot be replaced. The local food systems that are dismantled by agrofuels production cannot be recreated. If the agrofuels expansion is allowed to develop into an unregulated global commodity market in agrofuels, we could very quickly see the concentrated speculative booms and busts that brought the recent financial meltdown turn to our food systems and rural communities. With these stakes, it's unacceptable to press ahead with a destructive model in the hopes that safeguards can be figured out along the way. When a vehicle is out of control, you first take your foot off the accelerator.

The promises of the free market in agrofuels—to solve our energy and climate problems and to bring economic development—have proven empty. The agrofuels expansion is instead exacerbating climate change and poverty through the promotion of a resource-intensive industrial agriculture model that destroys natural habitats and squeezes out local producers. Real solutions to the food and climate crises will be found through strategies of energy and food sovereignty —in conservation and equitable resource distribution – not in the next new wonder fuel. It is possible to re-craft our agriculture and energy systems to use fewer resources while at the same time supporting equitable and sustainable development. But it is not possible to do so if we keep using the same free market model that got us here in the first place.

Photo and Image Credits:

1. Los Angeles Harbor: Photo by Rick Jonasse Food First/Birdseye Studio

2. Agricultural Burn, Novo Progresso: Leonardo L. Freitas, Creative Commons License (details: http://creativecommons.org/licenses/by-nc-sa/2.0/deed.en) Photo URL: http://www.flickr.com/photos/leoffreitas/1469376131

3. Agricultural Deforestation, Central Brazil: Gretchen Gordon, Food First.

4. Industrial soy production, Brazil: Leonardo F. Freitas Creative Commons License (info:

http://creativecommons.org/licenses/by-nc-nd/2.0/) Photo URL: http://www.flickr.com/photos/leoffreitas/789119835/

5.   Sugar Cane Fire: Photo by Steve Gibson, Creative Commons License (info: http://creativecommons.org/licenses/by/2.0/deed.en) Photo URL: http://www.flickr.com/photos/photohome_uk/1489690006/

6.   "Gasohol": Photo by Todd Ehlers Creative Commons License (info: http://creativecommons.org/licenses/by-nc-nd/2.0/deed.en) Photo URL: http://www.flickr.com/photos/eklektikos/22948054/

References:

1   Searchinger, Timothy,. 2008. Use of U.S. Croplands for Agrofuels Increases Greenhouse Gases Through Emissions from Land Use Change. Science Vol 319 no 5867, February 2, 2008, pp. 1238 - 1240

2   Fargione, J., Jason Hill, David Tilman, Stephen Polasky, Peter Hawthorne. 2008. Land Clearing and the Biofuel Carbon Debt Science 29 February 2008:
    Vol. 319. no. 5867, pp. 1235 - 1238

3   Amnesty International. 2008. "The State of the World's Human Rights," London:76; accessed July 14, 2008http://www.bbc.co.uk/portuguese/reporterbbc/story/2008/03/080327_timebiocombustiveisbg.shtml.

4   Constanza, Vieira. 2008. "Colombia: Oil Palms, Rights Abuses Hand in Hand in Northwest," InterPress Services. http://www.ipsnews.net/news.asp?idnews=43813

5   Reuters. 2008. Biofuels Blamed for Food Price Crisis – Report. http://uk.reuters.com/article/businessNews/idUKL0340750020080704

6   Reuters. 2008. UPDATE 1-Key EU Lawmaker Proposes New 2015 Biofuel Target http://uk.reuters.com/article/oilRpt/idUKL0434441520080704, accessed 14 July, 2008;

7   Perrone, Mathew, Associated Press. 2008. GOP Senators Seek Hold on Ethanol Mandate May 6, 2008.

8   Grunwald, Michael. 2008. The Clean Energy Scam. Time Magazine, March 27 2008.

9   Peters, Glen P.; and Edgar G. Hertwich 2007. CO2 Embodied in International Trade with Implications for Global Climate Policy', Industrial Ecology Programme. Norwegian University of Science and Technology (NTNU), NO-7491 Trondheim, Norway, 18 December, 2007.

10 Stern, Sir Nicholas. 2006. British Government 'Stern Review: The economics of climate change' 2006: 4; Annex 7.f

11 Santa Barbara, Jack. 2007. The False Promise of Biofuels. International Forum on Globalization and Institute for Policy Studies San Francisco, September 2007. p. 9

12 Rohter, L. 2007. Brazil, Alarmed, Reconsiders Policy on Climate Change. New York Times, 31 July 2007

13 Biofuel Watch, Carbon Trade Watch, TNI. 2008. Agrofuels: Towards a reality check in nine key areas. TNI: http://www.tni.org/reports/ctw/agrofuels.pdf? p. 17, 18.

14   Stern, Sir Nicholas. 2006. Stern Review: The economics of climate change. British
     Government. Annex 7f.

15   Wilson, E. 2008. The Biofuels Debate: Find another planet and plant it with soybeans.
     The Spectator. http://www.spectator.co.uk/the-magazine/business/223871/find-
     another-planet-and-plant-it-with-soybeans.thtml

16   Grain. 2007. Corporate Power: Agrofuels and the expansion of agribusiness' Seedling,
     July 2007. Accessed 07/33/08 http://www.foodfirst.org/node/1723.

17   Mackenzie, D. 2008. Rich Countries Carry out "21st Century Land Grab" New
     Scientists, December 4, 2008 http://www.newscientist.com/article/mg20026854.200-
     rich-countries-carry-out-21st-century-land-grab.html?full=true

18   Doornbosch, R. and Ronald Steenblik. 2007. Biofuels: Is the Cure Worse than the
     Disease? Round Table on Sustainable Development, Paris September 11, 2007 p. 26

19   Syunkova, A. 2007. WTO-Compatibility of Four Categories of U.S. Climate Change
     Policy. National Foreign Trade Council, December 2007 p. 7.

20   Inside US Trade. 2008. Under U.S. Pressure, EU Backs Off Carbon Import Taxes For
     Now. 02/25/2008.

21   World Trade Organization. 2006. The Multilateral Trading System and Climate Change.
     p 6. http://www.wto.org/english/tratop_e/envir_e/climate_change_e.pdf

22   United Nations Conference on Trade and Development. 2008. Making Certification
     Work for Sustainable Development: The Case of Biofuels. . New York: United Nations,
     2008, p. 39. http://www.unctad.org/en/docs/ditcted20081_en.pdf

23   Folha de São Paulo. 2008. Brasil Tenta Derrubar na UE 'Taxa Verde' ao Alcool. http://
     www1.folha.uol.com.br/folha/dinheiro/ult91u415927.shtml

24   Renewenergy. 2008. EU Agrees 10% 'Green Fuel' Target in Renewables Deal http://
     www.euractiv.com/en/transport/eu-agrees-10-green-fuel-target-renewables-deal/
     article-177812

25   Harrison, P. 2008 Human Rights, Rare Species on EU Biofuels Agenda. Reuters. http://
     www.planetark.com/dailynewsstory.cfm/newsid/49092/story.htm

26   Harrison, P. Eight Nations Warn EU over Biofuel Barriers. Reuters, Nov 6, 2008 http://
     in.reuters.com/article/businessNews/idINIndia-36366820081106

CHAPTER III

AGRIBUSINESS' FIELD OF DREAMS: IFIs AND THE LATIN AMERICAN AGROFUELS EXPANSION

BY RICHARD JONASSE

SUGAR CANE HARVEST, MATO GROSSO DU SUL, BRAZIL

For over twenty years, the World Bank, the Inter-American Development Bank (IDB), and the IMF have been building an infrastructural and regulatory haven for industrial agriculture in Latin America. These International Finance Institutions (IFIs) have fostered global agribusinesses through a set of deregulatory Structural Adjustment Programs (SAPs) that have made Latin America conducive to the inflows of capital and the outflows of goods. Their policies lowered barriers to foreign investments and the global commodities trade, eliminated government supports for local smallholder farmers, and fostered market-based land distribution systems.[1] Brazil embraced many of these prescriptions in the 1990s under the Cardozo government.[2] Coming on top of Brazil's thirty years of state support for their ethanol industry, these policy shifts primed the country for what has become an ethanol and biodiesel boom.

The result of the SAPs has been an influx of global capital into Latin American food systems, leading to monopolization and concentration, along with the externalization of the environmental and social costs of industrial agriculture. It has also lead to increased land concentration exemplified in Brazil, which already had one of the highest rates of uneven distribution in the world.[3] The pressure of agrofuels production on the availability of land has caused destruction in the Amazon rainforest and the savannahs of the Cerrado region, and further threatens food security in a country where nearly 40% of the people do not have enough to eat.[4] The consequences have been especially dire for the legions of landless workers who must either migrate to sprawling cities or follow the farm labor routes to difficult, low paying jobs, and sometimes slavery, where they are exposed to brutal working conditions, agro-toxins, and other hazards.[5]

Large-scale export agriculture is not new to Brazil—it has been the predominant model since the region was a Portuguese colony[6]—but by providing loans for Latin American agrofuels, the IDB and the World Bank are subsidizing the expansion of a destructive social model in Brazil and throughout Latin America in the name of "rural development."

Some environmental and social institutions are trying to rein in the negative consequences of these dramatic changes. In the first half of 2008 the Brazilian environmental ministry, IBAMA, embargoed the farms of Soybean King (and biodiesel magnate) Blairo Maggi over rainforest destruction and destructive farming practices.[7] The state of Sao Paolo placed a 120-day moratorium on ethanol plant construction to study the environmental impact of ethanol production there.[8] Brazil's environmental minister, Marina Silva, resigned rather than acquiesce to President Luiz Inácio Lula da Silva's plan to issue permits for plantation development in the Amazon. Her successor, Carlos Minc, has banned purchases of soy from the Amazon until July 2009.[9] When President Bush visited Brazil to sign a biofuels agreement with Brazilian President Lula da Silva in 2007, Via Campesina and the Brazilian Landless Workers Movement (MST) held massive protests and occupied agribusiness corporations throughout the country because the accord invited multinational corporations to take control of land and Brazil's agricultural system.[10] These efforts to stem the tide do not have the power to change IMF and WTO policies however, and foreign investment dollars continue to flow into Latin America and the Caribbean—with corrosive effects on human rights, environmental integrity, and food sovereignty.

Many among the landed elite welcome the influx of capital.[11] Foreign investors have purchased more than 20 million hectares of Brazilian agricultural land in the past two years, and foreign corporations monopolize many non-agricultural aspects of the export value chain. The entire production of raw materials for fertilizers is controlled by Bunge, Mosaic, and Yara. Monsanto and Nortox produce all of the nation's herbicide glyphosate. AGCO, Fiat, and New Holland control the agricultural machinery sector. Syngenta sells transgenic crops and, alongside Monsanto and Bayer, pressured the government into legalizing their GM corn.[12] ADM and Cargill are dominant agroprocessors, and many of Cargill's plants accept only Monsanto strains.[13] In one sense, agrofuels are just another investment opportunity within this larger amalgamation. The difference between food and agrofuels lies in the fact that demand for food is relatively inelastic while there are few limits to the global economy's thirst for agrofuels.

The IDB, the IFC, and Agrofuels

Citing inflationary pressures on food prices, the World Bank's International Bank for Reconstruction and Development has shied away from loans for agrofuel production. The Bank's private arm, the International Finance Corporation (IFC), however, is keeping a hand in Latin American agrofuels as part of its general promotion of industrial agriculture as a development strategy.[14] For mostly financial reasons the IFC is moving cautiously,[15] but where it steps in there are dire implications for labor, the environment, and food security. The IDB on the other hand is making agrofuels a cornerstone of its regional development policy. In 2005, the IDB raised the ceiling on direct lending to private companies to $200 million ($400 million in extraordinary circumstances), up from $75 million,[16] and has since used this increase to place some big bets in the agrofuel sector.

Free market fundamentalism aside, why would the development banks support agrofuels—which compete with food for agricultural resources—while billions of people around the world are starving or undernourished? Part of the answer is that agrofuels require practices that put agricultural modernization on autopilot. Due to the scale of agrofuel production; its processing requirements; the standardization of the inputs needed; and the price pressures of global

SUGAR CANE FIELDS, GUYANA

competition, agrofuels inevitably require the vertical integration and monocrop agribusiness efficiencies that the IFIs have been striving to instill.[17] Agriculturally speaking, agrofuels start out looking and acting very much like food, but after processing they become fungible, global, export commodities that are synonymous with the petrochemicals that fuel global economic growth. This draws developing countries deeper into the global economy which, according to supply-side economics, means the benefits will trickle down to everyone. The 'benefit' of the relative handful of dangerous, low paying jobs in the cane, palm, and soy industries appears to be the IFIs' concept of 'rural development.'

Another important reason why IFI support agrofuels is their own need to remain relevant. Given their success in opening world markets to finance capital, the development banks are having a difficult time finding projects that will accept their loans—except in places where finance capital dare not tread. While private corporations can bribe local governments and ignore environmental and social externalities with impunity, the World Bank and regional development banks must make a *prima facie* effort to help local populations—even though their structural role is to channel capital investments.[18] It turns out that even the weakened social and environmental scrutiny given to IFI loans make them less competitive, because as publicly funded institutions they are more open to criticism than corporations. This has led, ironically, to a liquidity crisis within the development banks themselves, and they have responded by joining the 'race to the bottom' in order to remain competitive with the private capital they have fostered.

The IDB and Hemispheric Integration

The IDB is the largest multilateral lender in Latin America.[19] It was already known for its anemic environmental safeguards, lack of transparency, and weak accountability mechanisms when current President Alberto Moreno stepped in and made things worse.[20] Before joining the IDB, Moreno oversaw privatization and trade liberalization of Colombia, as the country's Economic Development Minister. He also served as Colombia's Ambassador to the U.S. for seven years, procuring $4 billion in US military and economic assistance programs and helping negotiate the fraught Colombia-US Free Trade Agreement.[21] This made him a favored choice for the IDB within the Bush administration.[22] Moreno has continued his pro-business policies at the IDB. As one insider put it, "the Bank could not have less in place to deal with civil society."[23] He has since joined Jeb Bush (along with former Brazilian Agriculture Minister Roberto Rodrigues) in the transnational public/private lobbying group, the Inter-American Ethanol Commission.

The IDB's promotion of agrofuels is part of a coordinated regional expansion project, alongside the (US$19 billion[24]) infrastructure "gigaproject"[25] called the Initiative for Integration of Regional Infrastructure in South America

(IIRSA), and the Sustainable Energy and Climate Change Initiative (SECCI). The intellectual and (de)regulatory framework for these programs was etched in the *Initiative for the Americas* in 1989, under George H.W. Bush.[26] This agreement led to a *Hemispheric Energy Initiative* hammered out by regional energy ministers in Washington, DC in October, 1995. The latter called for lowering barriers to foreign investors and transnational corporations in *every aspect* of the Latin American energy sector, from production to pump, and the promotion

> Thirteen companies involved in [Brazil's agro-fuels] sector...have linkages with 44 European financial institutions from ten European countries (Austria, Belgium, France, Germany, Italy, Netherlands, Portugal, Spain, Switzerland and the United Kingdom). ...Bunge has links with 31 European financial institutions, Agrenco with 19, and Tereos with 13.
>
> Van Gelder, Jan Willem and Hassel Kroes. 2008. European financing of agrofuel production in Latin America. Banktrack.org.

renewable energy—primarily agrofuels.[27] The IFIs' have lent their institutional backing to the plan: the IMF through its structural adjustments, the World Bank through infrastructure and energy projects,[28, 29] and the IDB through direct agrofuel loans and its IIRSA and SECCI programs.

IIRSA and SECCI
The Initiative for the Integration of Regional Infrastructure in South America (IIRSA) is strongly linked to the Free Trade Areas of the Americas agreements and the needs of Southern elites.[30] While the IDB only directly funds 7% (64% of the funding comes from the 16-country *Andean Development Corporation* and 21% from private sources[31]), the IDB offers institutional support and helps provide loan guarantees for private capital investments. IIRSA's goal is to link ten "hubs" in the South American countries to the global economy by way of an integrated transportation, energy, and telecommunications infrastructure.[32]

IIRSA's project list includes roads and highways, rails, airports, canals, river dredging, port expansion, petro-energy projects, pipelines, telecommunications expansion, and border centers.[33] Beyond regional integration, one of the reasons given for the creation of IIRSA was the need to provide an outlet for investment capital.[34] This project gives capital plenty of profitable work to do— privatizing South America's commons while carving out routes between its natural resources and the global economy; and leaving behind a trail of dams, deforestation, social dislocation, and billions of dollars in debt.

The Sustainable Energy and Climate Change Initiative (SECCI) supports agro and passive energy research and development, and energy-related projects throughout Latin America. Currently, SECCI is primarily throwing its weight behind increasing agrofuels expansion and decreasing the risks of private Latin American investments, but it has a hand in ethanol export infrastructure projects as well. While there were only six SECCI loans for the entire year in 2007, sixteen were

IIRSA PROJECT: SANTOS PORT EXPANSION IN BRAZIL

approved for 2008[35] and the IDB has continued expanding bioenergy projects in 2009.[36] These projects tend to be studies that look at agrofuel potential, and recommend tailored government reforms that hold the door for global capital. The program is also promoting the export of Brazilian technology, expertise, and capital throughout Latin America.

The Agrofuels "Blueprint"

In support of these two programs, the IDB released a plan for regional economic growth in 2007 entitled *A Blueprint for Green Energy in the Americas: Strategic Analysis of Opportunities for Brazil and the Hemisphere*.[37] It is an exhaustive country-by-country look at bioenergy potential in Latin America. The report looks well beyond the Americas to global markets, climate agreements, and the cheap land in Africa. It is a battle plan for the transformation of the entire region into a global leader in bioenergy and an economic juggernaut:

> Much of the world is in the midst of a major reexamination of—and investment in—clean energy. Soaring oil prices and increasingly acute concerns about climate change have turned what used to be a cottage industry into a booming business. By 2010, it is estimated that US$100 billion will be invested in clean energy, compared to US$38 billion in 2005, and just over US$5 billion a decade before.[38]

The IDB wants to capture that investment capital for Latin America. The report looks to India's Bangalore, Boston's Route 128, and China's Shenzen as aspirational models. It is appropriate that these are all high-tech industrial zones because the IDB's plan is to promote industrial agrofuels production for the global economy. IIRSA and SECCI play a prominent role in the Biofuels Report, which recommends lucrative lines of finance for their infrastructure and energy projects. The IDB has pledged US$3 billion in loans and guarantees for Latin American agrofuels, including US$570 million in Brazil alone, under its Rural Development Program.[39]

The IDB is positioning Brazil—its biggest contributor after the U.S.—to spearhead the agrofuels boom in Latin America. Brazil is embracing this role, using its standing as an agrofuels and energy giant to promote itself as a major global power, and exporting its expertise and technology.

The IDB and the Consolidation of Brazil's Ethanol Industry

In an increasingly competitive investment field, the IDB must find a way into the agrofuels capital markets alongside a bevy of private corporations.[40] It earns its keep by certifying the labor and environmental sustainability of agrofuel projects, and ferrying projects through loan application processes. Its flagship endeavor consists of three loans for ethanol refineries/farmland to subsidiaries of Companhia Nacional de Açúcar e Álcool (CNAA). CNAA is a joint venture between the Dutch corporation Global Foods Holdings, N.V. and Brazilian Companhia Energética Santa Elisa S.A.—which recently merged with Companhia Açucareira Vale do Rosário to form Santelisa Vale Bioenergia S.A.[41] In reality, this is a merger between two powerful Brazilian families: the Junqueira family (Vale do Rosario) and the Biagi family (Santa Elisa, Vale do Rosario), who have created the second largest sugar conglomerate in Brazil.[42] The Biagi family was Cargill's doorway into the Brazilian sugar industry, via the sugar giant Crystalsev, which also has connections with global investors Carlysle Group/Riverstone (coal, oil, LPG, ethanol) and the global equity firm Golden Holdings.[43]

Santelisa has recently consolidated and restructured in order to attract US$210 million from Goldman Sachs/Discovery Capital[44] and US$85 million from the Brazilian Economic and Social Development Bank (BNDESPAR),[45] which allows Santelisa to be publicly traded on the Novo Mercado (Brazilian New Market).[46] Santelisa also partnered with the Maeda Group to create Tropical

BioEnergia S.A., and then sold a 50% stake to British Petroleum for a mere US$59 million—which used the toehold to invest US$1 billion in two ethanol plants/farmland: a 115 million gallon per year ethanol refinery in Edeia, Goias, plus another yet to be named, which will raise total capacity to almost 264 million gallons of ethanol by the middle of 2010.[47]

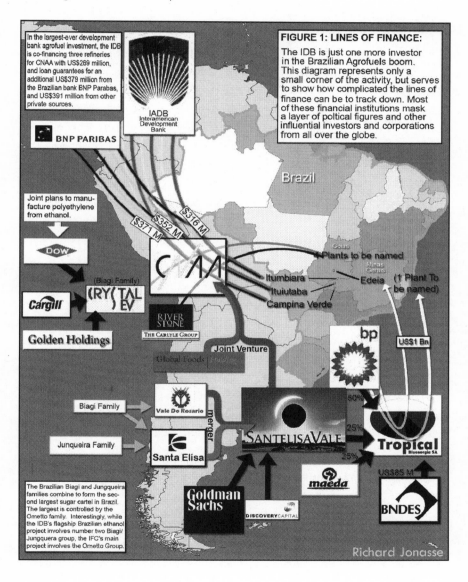

In the largest-ever development bank agrofuel investment, the IDB is co-financing three refineries with US$269 million of its own, and loan guarantees for an additional US$379 million from the Brazilian bank BNP Parabas.[48] Each will produce 55 million gallons of ethanol per year for the CNAA subsidiaries for a total of 165 million gallons: one in Ituiutaba, Minas Gerais (total cost US$352 million); another in Itumbiara, Goiás (total cost US $316 million); and a third in Campina Verde, Minas Gerais (total cost US $371 million). At the Brazilian average of 7500 gallons per hectare these refineries will require 22,000 hectares of land.

The IDB environmental assessment for the project states that the current use of sugarcane for ethanol consumes 2% of the total area available for food production in Brazil. By their own calculations 22 million more hectares of cane plantations will be added by 2025, bringing the total to 8% of the available farmland—not counting soy plantations and other fuel crops. By 2025, the current plantations will be less fertile and looking to move to fresher pastures. The human and environmental costs of the expansion will be immense. The IDB claims that the increased land use for agrofuels will not hurt food prices however, and backs this with an IMF report that offers a familiar refrain by calling for increased global trade to make up the balance.[49]

The International Finance Corporation: "Reducing Poverty, Saving Lives"

As with the IDB, the IFC's weak labor and environmental standards lend *prima facie* credibility to global investors and transnational corporations. The Dutch Rabobank, which invested a total of US$ 330 million in the IFC's Amaggi Soy debacle in the Amazon,[I] specifically cited IFC labor and environmental certifications as the reason it felt safe to invest: "Rabobank's reasoning was that if IFC approves this project and they classify it only as a class B, low-risk project, we can safely invest [an additional] $230 million ... in this corporation."[50] The IFC loan for this "low-risk" project resulted in a World Bank internal investigation, and the aforementioned embargo of Blairo Maggi's farms.

The IFC lends its imprimatur to private investments by relying on "corporate responsibility"—a euphemistic term for self-certification of labor conditions and environmental stewardship. Furthermore, since the Bank's environmental and social requirements tend to rely on weak local criteria, the preconditions for

I. The IFC's loan to Blairo Maggi of Ammagi Soy is a well known cautionary tale. It wound up in an investigation by the Bank's ombudsman at the request of then Bank President James Wolfensohn. For more information go to: http://www.corpwatch.org/article.php?id=11756 or http://www.brettonwoodsproject.org/art-107739

loans are disturbingly similar to the criteria employed by unencumbered private investors, whose sole motivation is profit, not development.

From 2005 to 2007, the area covered by sugar cane plantations in São Paolo alone grew from 3 million to 4.5 million hectares.[51] One US$50 million IFC loan is going to a project to help Cosan S.A. Industria e Comercio[II] expand its ethanol production. U.S.-based Cargill owns a majority stake in Cosan. Cosan is the largest sugar and ethanol company in the world, and part of billionaire Rubens Ometto Silveira Mello's Ometto Group, which owns several of Brazil's second-tier sugar companies as well.[III, 52] Its 2006 IPO raised US $ 405 million,[53] and it is attracting investments from Tate & Lyle, Mitsubishi, Hong Kong's Kuok Group (palm growers), and twin French sugar companies, Sucden and Tereos. Ometto also holds stakes in sugar breeding and biotech companies. To help access foreign markets, Cosan announced a merger of its sugar operations with Nova America at Santos Port in São Paulo State in April, 2008.[54] It is currently investing US $1 billion in a 618 km ethanol pipeline to the port.

Life on a Cosan Plantation:

"Silva, who is 45 and started cutting cane this year, says he's reluctant to stop working. His pay and his job hinge on how much cane he can cut in a day. The cane Silva slashes feeds an ethanol plant owned by Cosan SA Indústria & Comércio, Brazil's biggest exporter of a fuel that politicians around the world trumpet as a clean, renewable alternative to gasoline. Halfway through Silva's 10-hour shift, the slender, 5-foot-2-inch-tall ... worker collapses. He takes shelter under a bus, where he trembles with fever. That's where São Paulo state labor prosecutor Mario Antônio Gomes finds him as he inspects the plantation. Gomes orders Elton Rodrigo Franco, a driver for the planta-tion, to take Silva to a hospital in Capivari, about 50 miles (80 kilometers) away.... A doctor at the hospital diagnoses Silva with lung fibrosis, a scarring of the lungs that often afflicts cane cutters, according to the labor inspector's report. He may die if he keeps cutting cane, the report says. 'I don't know if I can keep going much longer, but I want to try,' says Silva sprawled across a gurney in the small hospital. 'I can't return home without any money.'"

Smith, Michael & Carlos Caminada. November, 2007. Ethanol's Deadly Brew. Bloomberg Press. http://www.bloomberg.com/news/marketsmag/mm_1107_sto-ry3.html

---

II.   Cosan tried at one point to take over Biagi and Junqueira's *Vale do Rosario*, but was fended off.

III. An interesting note here is that while the IFC is exclusively involved with Brazil's largest sugar producer, the Olmetto conglomerate, the IDB handles the number two Biagi/Junqueira cartel. It's highly likely that IFC and the IDB negotiated this division of aid at some point.

As with the Amaggi loan, the IFC proved its value to Cosan by granting the project a "B" classification for moderate environmental impacts and labor conditions. The IFC set the guidelines, and then allowed Cosan to perform self-audits on labor and environmental standards. The IFC monitored compliance by reviewing copies of corporate memoranda and "management-certified completion of top priority corrective measures."[55] This is lot of faith in the corporate responsibility of a private company that manages 240,000 ha of land and crushes 26 million tons of cane each year. The IFC belayed any concerns by "reviewing [Cosan's] annual monitoring reports" to ensure that it "meet(s) the applicable World Bank/IFC environment and social policies and the environmental, health and safety guidelines."[56] The loan was granted, largely on Cosan's word.

A recent study by the Center for International Environmental Law, Bank Information Center, BankTrack, Oxfam Australia, and the World Resources Institute found a high incidence of abuses of international human rights standards in IFC-financed projects. Out of 335 recognized categories the IFC was in full compliance on only two, partial compliance with four, and failed to comply on 329.[57] It appears that the IFC has wholly abandoned the credo "Reducing Poverty, Saving Lives"; creating profits for investors while leaving the socially and economically vulnerable to live in continual, cyclical poverty.

Conclusion: The costs of development

The IFIs' promotion of agrofuels has little to do with either poverty reduction or climate change. There is a direct and overt contradiction between the negative impacts of industrial agrofuel production and what is officially touted as lifting people out of cyclical rural poverty. The nitrogen oxides released by industrial agriculture, the petro-inputs required, the destruction of the soil, and the global trade model itself do more to contribute to climate change than to mitigate it. Susan George points out that "those who argue for expanding exports as the road to growth put their faith in comparable advantage, and while they focus on what exports may earn they rarely tell us what they cost."[58]

The loans described above reward keeping labor in the most precarious position possible. They reward the maximum extraction of every available resource. They also reward corporate externalization of social and environmental costs, and leaving behind polluted and degraded landscapes. But perhaps even more damaging is the IFIs' promotion of the indiscriminant commoditization of everything, including agricultural products and resources—a free market model that the recent and ongoing global food crises have revealed as spectacularly bankrupt.

These development institutions need to begin to pay back their social and environmental debts they are accumulating in the Latin American countryside and throughout the Global South. This can be accomplished by promoting a more humane development model that supports communities and sustainability over the long term. It requires a re-envisioning of the way that markets should function and develop— from the bottom-up rather than from the top down. It also requires creating incentives for maintaining agricultural resources over the long term and keeping communities together.

CHILDREN OF LANDLESS WORKERS, PERNAMBUCO, BRAZIL

This is far more humane and more difficult than the path of "creative destruction" that the IFI's appear to be following. It takes more time to develop, but focusing on sustainable relationships between people and the land provides far more resilience than the boom and bust cycles of the IFIs' failed extractive model.

Photo and Image Credits:

1. Cane Stubble, Sao Paolo, Brazil: John McQuaid Creative Commons License (http://creativecommons.org/licenses/by-nc/2.0/deed.en) Photo URL: http://www.flickr.com/photos/mcquaid/3014893212/in/set-72157608776245780/

2. Cane_fields_guyana Photo by Kefoe Creative Commons License = (details: http://creativecommons.org/licenses/by-nc-nd/2.0/deed.en) Photo URL: http://www.flickr.com/photos/bigheadedbrownie/699085100/

3. IDB/IIRSA Project: Santos Port expansion in Brazil: flamingbear / Mattie Creative Commons License (http://creativecommons.org/licenses/by-nc-sa/2.0/deed.en) Photo URL: http://www.flickr.com/photos/savoie/2045666486/

4. Lines of Finance: Rick Jonasse. Food First.

5. Children of landless workers in Pernambuco, Brazil. Maria Hsu Creative Commons License (http://creativecommons.org/licenses/by/2.0/) Photo URL: http://www.flickr.com/photos/14323530@N05/2156119259/

References:

1 Sauer, Sérgio, 2006. The World Bank's Market-Based Land Reform in Brazil. in Rosset, Peter, Raj Patel, & Michael Courville. Promised Land: Competing visions of agrarian reform. Oakland: Food First Books.

2 ibid.

3 Lee, Rennie. 2007. Allied with Brazilian Agribusiness, Syngenta Resists Governor's Decree to Expropriate Site. Center for International Policy. Accessed 10/29/08: http://americas.irc-online.org/am/4239

4 ibid.

5 Brazilian Landless Workers Movement (MST). 2006. The perverse nature of agribusiness for Brazilian society. MST. Accessed 10/29/08: http://www.mstbrazil.org/?q=mstinforma109

6 Brazilian Landless Workers Movement (MST). 2006.

7 Amazonia. 2008. Trade with IFC-funded farm in the Amazon is embargoed as a result of illegal activities. Amazonia.org. Accessed 06/14/08: http://www.amazonia.org.br/english/noticias/noticia.cfm?id=265777

8 Thomson Financial News. 2008. Brazil's Sao Paulo state suspends new ethanol plants pending environmental study. Available at: http://www.forbes.com/markets/feeds/afx/2008/05/16/afx5019776.html. Accessed 05/21/08.

9 Reuters. 2008. Brazil throws weight behind Amazon soy ban. Accessed 07/07/08: http://www.reuters.com/article/environmentNews/idUSN1734831620080617

10 Kenfield Isabella, R. Burbach. 2007. Militant Brazilian Opposition to Bush-Lula Ethanol Accords. ZNet. Accessed 02/17/2008: http://www.zmag.org/znet/viewArticle/1738

11 Lee, Rennie. 2007.

12 Stedile, João Pedro. 2008. International Capital Dominates Brazilian Agriculture. Monthly Review. Accessed 12/15/08: http://www.monthlyreview.org/mrzine/stedile120808.html

13 Baker, Marcia Merry & Dennis Small. 2005. Brazil's Agricultural 'Success' In the Cerrado Is a Disaster. Economics. Accessed 11/02/08.

14 International Finance Corporation. 2008. Global Agribusiness. Accessed 11/02/08: http://www.ifc.org/agribusiness

15 Bank Information Center. 2008. Unaccountable and Unsustainable, IDB champions corporate interests at expense of citizens. Accessed 10/08/08: http://www.bicusa.org/en/Article.3715.aspx

16 Bank Information Center. 2008a. Inter-American Development Bank/Lending. Accessed 12/15/08: http://bicusa.org/en/Institution.Lending.4.aspx

17 International Finance Corporation. 2008. Global Agribusiness: Creating Opportunity in Emerging Markets. Accessed 11/08/08: http://www.ifc.org/ifcext/agribusiness.nsf/AttachmentsByTitle/CreatingOpportunity_Agribusiness/$FILE/Vertical+Creating+Opportunity_Ag_Final.pdf

18 Qureshi, Zia. 1995. Globalization: New Opportunities, Tough Challenges. Washington DC: World Bank. Accessed 03/20/09: http://www.worldbank.org/fandd/english/0396/articles/050396.htm

19 Bank Information Center. 2008c. Inter-American Development Bank/Overview. The Bank Information Center. Accessed 04/11/08: http://www.bicusa.org/en/Institution.4.aspx.

20 Bank Information Center. 2008d. Accountability at the IDB. Accessed 11/11/08: http://www.bicusa.org/en/Issue.20.aspx

21 IDBWatch. April 4, 2008. A botched realignment? Moreno leadership at the IDB in question. Accessed 10/22/08: http://www.amazonwatch.org/documents/IDBWatch_Issue1_finallorez.pdf

22 Bank Information Center. 2008e. Inter-American Development Bank/Structure. Accessed 11/08/2008: http://bicusa.org/en/Institution.Structure.4.aspx

23 IDBWatch. April 4, 2008. P. 2.

24 IFIs.Choike.Org. 2008a. Evaluation of IDB Action in the Initiative for Integration of Regional Infrastructure in South America (IIRSA). Choike.org. accessed 11/14/08: http://ifis.choike.org/informes/876.html

25 Holt-Giménez, Eric, and Lyra Spang. 2005. IIRSA Update #1: A Report on the South American Integration Initiative. The Bank Information Center. Accessed 03/17/08: http://www.bicusa.org/en/Article.1946.aspx.

26 Ruiz Caro, Ariela. 2008. Energy Integration and Security in Latin America and the Caribbean. The Americas Program. Accessed 04/15/08: http://americas.irc-online.org/am/5109

27 Summits of the Americas Secretariat. 2008. First Summit of the Americas: ENERGY. Washington: Summits of the Americas. Accessed 11/09/08: http://www.summit-americas.org/Miami%20Summit/Energy%20(revised)%20Eng.htm

28 The World Bank. 2008. Energy in Latin America and the Carribbean. Accessed 12/08/2008: http://web.worldbank.org/WBSITE/EXTERNAL/COUNTRIES/LACEXT/EXTLACREGTOPENERGY/0,,menuPK:841447~pagePK:34004175~piPK:34004435~theSitePK:841431,00.html

29 The World Bank Group. 2008. Private Participation in Infrastructure Update Note 11. Accessed 11/11/08: http://ppi.worldbank.org/features/Oct2008/2007EnergyDataLaunch.pdf

30 Zibechi, Raul. 2006. IIRSA: Integration Custom-Made for International Markets. Americas IRC. Accesssed 06/05/08: http://americas.irc-online.org/pdf/reports/0606iirsa.pdf

31 IFIs Latin American Monitor. 2008. Evaluation of IDB Action in the Initiative for Integration of Regional Infrastructure in South America (IIRSA). Accessed 11/11/08: http://ifis.choike.org/informes/876.html

32 Holt-Giménez, Eric, and Lyra Spang. 2005. IIRSA Update #1: A Report on the South American Integration Initiative. The Bank Information Center. Available at: http://www.bicusa.org/en/Article.1946.aspx.

33 IIRSA. 2006. Project Information Sheets: Priority Investment Portfolio in South America. Washington: Inter-American Development Bank. 04/15/2008. http://idbdocs.iadb.org/ wsdocs/getdocument.aspx?docnum=834687

34 Holt-Giménez, Eric, and Lyra Spang. 2005.

35 Interamerican Development Bank. Projects Database. Washington: IDB: http://www. iadb.org/projects/

36 McElhinny, Vince. 2009. Global Crisis is Good News for IFIs in Latin America. Bank Information Center: Accessed 01/13/09: http://www.bicusa.org/admin/ Document.100712.aspx

37 Rothkopf, Garten 2007. A Blueprint for Green Energy in the Americas: Strategic Analysis of Opportunities for Brazil and the Hemisphere. Inter-American Development Bank. http://www.iadb.org/biofuels/. Accessed 03/12/2008.

38 ibid, p.1

39 Ortiz, Lucia 2008. Multilateral Banks: feeding the exportation of biofuels and the disputes over land use in Brazil. Friends of the Earth. http://ifis.choike.org/informes/790.html. Accessed 03/17/2008.

40 Bank Information Center. 2008e. Unaccountable and Unsustainable, IDB champions corporate interests at expense of citizens. Accessed 10/08/08: http://www.bicusa.org/en/ Article.3715.aspx

41 Riveras, Inae. February, 22, 2008. Rosario sees Santa Elisa merger within weeks. Reuters. Accessed 04/22/08: http://www.reuters.com/article/mergersNews/ idUSN2247915520070222

42 Voice of America. August, 14, 2008. Brazil Increases Consumption, Export of Sugar-Based Ethanol. Accessed 09/04/08: http://www.voanews.com/english/2008-08-14-voa52.cfm

43 Grain. 2007. The Sugar-Cane-Ethanol Nexus. Grain.org: Available at: http://www.grain. org/seedling/?id=488 accessed 11/2008.

44 Reuters. July 27, 2007. Goldman to invest $210 mln in Brazil Santelisa Vale. Accessed 09/15/08: http://www.reuters.com/article/fundsFundsNews/ idUSN2722042620070727

45 Reuters. January 07, 2008. Brazil's BNDES buys sugar miller Santelisa stake. Accessed 09/15/08: http://www.reuters.com/article/companyNews/idUSN0732074220080107

46 Brazilian National Development Bank. January/07/2008. BNDESPAR will acquire R$ 150 million in shares of Santelisa Vale . BNDES. Accessed 09/08/2008: http://www. bndes.gov.br/english/news/not003_08.asp

47 Renewable Energy. may 20, 2008. BP Steps Into Brazilian Ethanol. Accessed 09/13/08: http://renewenergy.wordpress.com/2008/05/20/bp-steps-into-brazilian-ethanol/

48 Interamerican Development Bank. July, 23, 2008. IDB lends $269 million for three Brazilian ethanol plants. IDB. Accessed 09/08/2008: http://www.iadb.org/news/ articledetail.cfm?language=English&ARTID=4696

49 InterAmerican Development Bank. 2008. ITUMBIARA BIOENERGY PROJECT (BR-L1170). P. 18. IDB: Documents Available Through: http://www.iadb.org/projects/ Project.cfm?project=BR-L1170&Language=English. Accessed 05/06/2008.

50 Lilly, Shasha. 2004. Paving the Amazon with Soy: World Bank Bows to Audit of Maggi Loan. CorpWatch. available at: http://www.corpwatch.org/article.php?id=11756. accessed 04/10/2008.

51 Thompson Financial News. 2008. Brazil's Sao Paulo state suspends new ethanol plants pending environmental study. Available at : http://www.forbes.com/markets/feeds/afx/2008/05/16/afx5019776.html Accessed 0519/08.

52 Grain. 2007. The Sugar-cane–Ethanol Nexus. Available at: http://www.grain.org/seedling/?id=488. Accessed: 03/14/2008.

53 JornalCana. 2006. Grupo Cosan divulga balanço da safra 2005/06; empresa aumenta moagem em 30%. Available at: http://www.jornalcana.com.br/conteudo/noticia.asp?area=Producao&secao=Exclusivas&ID_Materia=23008 Accessed 05/10/08

54 Reuters, 2008. Cosan, Nova America to Merge Santos Port Sugar Ops. available at: http://www.reuters.com/article/companyNews/idUSN1146577620080411 accessed 05/10/08.

55 International Finance Corporation. 2005. Cosan Corrective Action Plan (CAP). IFC. Available at: http://www.ifc.org/ifcext/spiwebsite1.nsf/2bc34f011b50ff6e85256a55007 3ff1c/99378c64cc153f0085256fb90076555d/$FILE/CAP%20Cosan%20260105%20 FINAL.pdf. Accessed 04/05/2008.

56 ibid.

57 Herz, Steven, Kristen Genovese, Kirk Herbertson, & Anne Perrault. August, 2008. The International Finance Corporation's Performance Standards and the Equator Principles: Respecting Human Rights and Remedying Violations? The Center for International Environmental Law, Bank Information Center, BankTrack, Oxfam Australia, and the World Resources Institute. Accessed 09/15/08: http://www.ciel.org/Publications/IFC_Aug08/Ruggie_Submission.pdf

58 George, Susan. 1988. A Fate Worse Than Debt: A radical new analysis of the Third World debt crisis (Or, the world financial crisis and the poor). p. 143. Food First Books, Grove Press, New York.

CHAPTER IV

WILL SUSTAINABILITY STANDARDS WORK? A LOOK AT THE ROUNDTABLE ON SUSTAINABLE BIOFUELS

BY ANNIE SHATTUCK

Luciana Soldi Bullara

CANE FIELD AFTER HARVEST

Three years into the agrofuels boom, few can deny the industry's negative consequences. Agrofuels have recently been blamed for volatile food prices, deforestation, poor energy balance, land grabs, increased greenhouse gas emissions, land concentration, disruption of rural communities, poor working conditions, and a number of other social and environmental damages.

Calls for regulation of "sustainable" agrofuels have emanated from the European Union, mainstream environmental organizations in the U.S., and the State of California. Some organizations are calling for a moratorium on agrofuels, a removal of the mandates, and elimination of subsides. Other NGO's and industry groups are calling for continued support for "smart" agrofuels. The largest efforts to regulate for "sustainable" or "smart" agrofuels include the European Commission's sustainability standards, the state of California's nascent Low Carbon Fuel Standard, and the Roundtable on Sustainable Biofuels, a voluntary set of standards drafted by a group of major industry players and corporate-dominated nonprofits.

The Roundtable on Sustainable Biofuels (RSB) is the only global initiative attempting to regulate the agrofuels sector. The Roundtable is a partnership between the World Wildlife Fund, British Petroleum, Shell Oil, the Brazilian Sugarcane Industry, the Federation of Swiss Oil Companies, Petrobras (the Brazilian state-owned oil and ethanol company), and Bunge (one of the largest grain traders in the world), among others. Over the past year, the RSB has been touring the globe, seeking consultation on "Version Zero" of its sustainable biofuels standard. The global, multi-stakeholder group has spoken with civil society and industry groups on nearly every continent. The standards attempt to address issues as diverse as land rights, food security, conservation areas, labor, and ecosystem services.

The Roundtable hopes to create a voluntary third party certification system, analogous to Fair Trade for coffee or the Forest Stewardship Council's certification for lumber. Any agrofuels sold with the RSB seal would theoretically guarantee that consumers are purchasing truly sustainable (and fair) fuel. Big non-governmental organizations, including the International Union for the Conservation of Nature, the Natural Resources Defense Council and the World Wildlife Fund (WWF) have been intimately involved with the Roundtable.

The Roundtable has counted on the good intentions and input of scores of experts truly concerned with the destructive impacts of agrofuels. On the surface the RSB's draft standards appear comprehensive and far-reaching, but are their criteria likely to succeed? It remains unclear how key elements of the standard will be defined and how the product will be delivered. The progress thus far and experiences with other certification schemes may give a picture of the RSB's future performance. Initiatives like the RSB have the potential to curb some of the worst abuses of the industry, but if sustainability initiatives merely provide enough cover to convince the public that agrofuels are an efficient and socially-valuable energy source, they will do so at the expense of real solutions to both the food and energy crises.

Past Experiences:
"Responsible" Soy, "Sustainable" Palm Oil, Certified Lumber

"In Argentina, forests are burning because cattle farmers have been forced to find new pastures to make way for GM soy. As the Round Table [on Responsible Soy] meets in Buenos Aires to redefine the meaning of 'responsible,' the intensive farming methods it relies on are depleting the soil, polluting the ground water and damaging wildlife." Stella Semino, Grupo de Reflexion Rural[1]

"The soy production boom in Paraguay is having devastating effects. Small landowners are being forced to sell their farms to the big producers because they cannot compete in this aggressive industrial market place. Rural communities that once grew their own food have been driven from the land into the cities where they struggle to find work and live in poverty." *Javiera Rulli from the social research center BASEIS, Paraguay[2]*

The Roundtable on Sustainable Biofuels is not a new endeavor. The World Wildlife Fund has been sponsoring industry roundtables since 2004. The Roundtable for Sustainable Palm Oil and the Roundtable for Responsible Soy, launched in 2004 and 2006 respectively, followed much the same pattern of industry/stakeholder consultation, meetings, standards development, etc. "Version Zero" standards are also based on the popular (though controversial) sustainable lumber certification by the Forest Stewardship Council.

The Forest Stewardship Council, established in 1994, certifies forest products based on a set of social and environmental criteria. The criteria, developed through three years of consultations with industry, civil society, consumer, and producer groups, guarantee the end user that the lumber in question was produced sustainably. Since the founding of the FSC, demand for sustainably produced lumber has increased dramatically. The market success of the FSC has led to a spin off of a host of industry "self-certification" schemes. The FSC however, remains the only certification program with widespread recognition from the public and mainstream environmental organizations. The FSC has grown so rapidly that there are few lumber products that cannot be sourced from a "sustainable" forest or plantation.

The FSC has not been without its critics however. The group has come under fire for certifying monoculture plantations, allowing limited clearcuts, and for poor social performance of some of its standards. Cases of negligence on the part of certifying agencies have led to outcry from civil society groups in Brazil and South Africa.[3, 4] In one case, the agency granted certification to a company that planted 96,000 hectares of Eucalyptus illegally. The Brazilian government eventually required the company to remove the trees, replant the land to native forest, and pay a fine of over US$12 million.[5] This and other cases of abuse led to calls for reform at the FSC plenary meeting in 2008. Some groups have pulled their support for the FSC completely, while others remain staunchly behind the certification, citing past success and continued demand for sustainable lumber.

The WWF's industry roundtables have been far more controversial than the FSC. Both of the previous roundtables—the Roundtable on Sustainable Palm Oil and the Roundtable on Responsible Soy—drew resistance from social movements, farmers organizations, and civil society. Few local producer organizations participated in either roundtable, with the Roundtable on Responsible Soy dominated by corporate interests and large landowners like

Brazil's infamous soybean magnate, Blairo Maggi, whose World Bank loan was accused of egregious labor abuses, including slavery, and rainforest destruction.[6] Though these roundtables first began seven years ago, palm oil development continues to be a significant source of greenhouse gas emissions, catapulting Indonesia into third place among climate polluters—and the march of soy into the Amazon goes unchecked.

Forest Stewardship Council Principles:

1. Compliance with all applicable laws and international treaties.
2. Demonstrated and uncontested, clearly defined, long–term land tenure and use rights.
3. Recognition and respect of indigenous peoples' rights.
4. Maintenance or enhancement of long-term social and economic well-being of forest workers and local communities and respect of worker's rights in compliance with International Labour Organisation (ILO) conventions.
5. Equitable use and sharing of benefits derived from the forest.
6. Reduction of environmental impact of logging activities and maintenance of the ecological functions and integrity of the forest.
7. Appropriate and continuously updated management plan.
8. Appropriate monitoring and assessment activities to assess the condition of the forest, management activities and their social and environmental impacts.
9. Maintenance of High Conservation Value Forests (HCVFs) defined as environmental and social values that are considered to be of outstanding significance or critical importance.
10. In addition to compliance with all of the above, plantations must contribute to reduce the pressures on and promote the restoration and conservation of natural forests.

From Forest Stewardship Council: http://www.fsc.org/pc.html

The Roundtable on Sustainable Palm Oil, the WWF's first industry roundtable, has been in operation since 2002. Some of the largest players in the palm industry have been involved from the beginning. Groups like Cadbury Schweppes, Rabobank, and Wilmar International, a partially owned subsidiary of Unilever, (whose Director of Sustainable Agriculture is president of the RSPO), have committed to the groups standards—which include respect for land rights, fair labor conditions, and an end to deforestation. The RSPO includes an NGO-led "smallholder taskforce" to help smallholders participate in the certified market, and two locally based NGO's that help bring the voices of small farmers and indigenous people to the table.

GUATEMALA: CLEARED FOREST AND DIVERTED WATERCOURSE FOR A PALM PLANTATION

Thus far, the Roundtable has not been able to significantly curb land conflicts or deforestation. According to a 2008 report by Friends of the Earth International, some 400,000 hectares of "Permanent Forest Estates" were allocated for conversion to plantation in the Malaysian state of Sarawak.[7] In 2006 alone, there were over 350 agrarian conflicts over palm oil development in Indonesia.[8] While some civil society groups are calling on companies in the RSPO to live up to their promises of sustainability, others are calling the group's efforts "greenwashing" and claim the "RSPO is designed to legitimate the continuous expansion of the palm oil industry".[9]

In August of 2008, United Plantations was the first company to be certified under RSPO standards. According to the standards, a company plantation can be certified only if all their holdings meet certain minimum requirements;

including no land conflicts, unmediated labor disputes, or replacement of primary forest, and a plan to achieve certification for all plantations. According to Greenpeace, while the company's Malaysian plantation was certified, United Plantations holdings in Indonesia failed to comply with the RSPO's minimum standards for partial certification. Four community members were jailed for protesting oil palm development on their land in the Indonesian village of Rutu. One of the arrestees was still in prison when United Plantations converted the man's farm to oil palm.[10] Furthermore the Indonesian plantations were planted in "High Conservation Value Areas," on drained peatlands and recently cleared forests, prompting Greenpeace to call the RSPO's first test-case a "failure."[11] The RSPO responded, saying "we will do everything we can to improve things that are not up to standard yet ... as with any scheme that's in its infancy, the RSPO will evolve and strengthen over time."[12]

The Roundtable on Responsible Soy (RRS)was conceived in 2004 in a similar fashion to the RSPO. The group was originally called the Roundtable for Sustainable Soy, though the group had to re-brand itself due to embarrassing media coverage on the absurdity of certifying vast monocultures of genetically modified soy as "sustainable." The Roundtable on Responsible Soy has drawn even more criticism than the RSPO.

In April of 2008, a delegation of Campesino leaders from Paraguay traveled over 20 hours by bus to address the Roundtable on Responsible Soy in Buenos Aires. Participants in the meeting paid US$400 to be included, an amount of money that a member of the Campesino delegation declared he had never before seen in his life.

FINAL REMNANTS OF FOREST ARE BURNED ON A SOY PLANTATION IN MATO GROSSO, BRAZIL

The Campesino leaders were escorted from the "open, multi-stakeholder discussion" by police and the meeting was barricaded, but not before the delegates from Paraguay read a declaration signed by over 200 NGO's and farmer's organizations.[13] The declaration leaves no room for doubt on the position of social movements:

Agribusiness is responsible for the devastation of our soils, deforestation, contamination of rivers and aquifers, biodiversity loss, and the plunder of the natural and cultural heritage which once supported our communities. The expansion of soybean monoculture threatens the territorial, cultural and food sovereignty of countries as well as the rights of the Indigenous and rural communities. Soy agribusiness excludes, impoverishes and weakens the population. This industrial agricultural model violates economic, social, cultural and environmental rights and, as it expands, its destructive methods of operation wipe out everything in its path, resulting in rural migration, marginalization of rural populations, and ultimately the criminalization of the poor and social movements....

...Agribusiness expands more and more, and many European Governments respond to criticisms and complaints about the current situation in our countries by blindly and naively trusting WWF´s [World Wildlife Fund] Round Tables for Sustainable Business. We are dismayed that they are following it as being successful examples, specifically towards the creation of new legal criteria for the sustainable production of biofuels. By doing this the EU Governments will fall into the trap of corporate greenwashing.

Social movements from the North and the South reject outright all attempts by corporations and NGOs to mobilize public opinion in support of their notion of sustainable or responsible GM soy monoculture. We disapprove of the projects of corporate social responsibility (CSR) that, through roundtable dialogue and voluntary measures, attempt to cover up the crimes committed by the corporations. Through CSR, corporations try to usurp the State and create private social policy making.

We resist the agribusiness model of neocolonial domination and the way in which corporations systematically misrepresent [and] distort many of our own social movement discourses and statements. We denounce the corporate greenwashing of the niche market of certification...." From ... (from *For a Third Time We Reject the Fallacy of Responsible Soy* 2008)[14]

Delivery Systems

It is still too soon to tell what kind of system the RSB will use to verify and deliver certified sustainable biofuels to market. It will be difficult to guarantee that companies have lived up to their claims on a product like fuel. Unlike other common certified products, like Fair Trade Coffee, Organic produce, or even certified 2x4s; fuel is delivered through a centralized network. Separate pumps for "sustainable" agrofuels (and another for "unsustain-

TORTUGUERO PALM PLANTATION, COSTA RICA

able" agrofuel, along with regular diesel and 3 octane scales of unleaded) are unlikely to appear at gas stations any time soon. Certified and conventional agrofuels will be blended.

Internal discussions around verification in the RSB have highlighted the need for transparency along the whole supply chain, from plantation to pump; though the RSB does plan to accept complimentary certifications, like the FSC and the RSPO.[15] While both the Forest Stewardship Council and the Roundtable on Sustainable Palm Oil include complete chain of custody certification, their delivery and verification process is much more complex.

The Roundtable on Sustainable Palm Oil allows a tiered claims system. Buyers of palm oil that has been segregated from its non-certified counterparts along the entire supply chain (at all stages of production, processing, refining and manufacturing) are allowed to make the claim "Contains only RSPO Certified Sustainable Palm Oil." This oil may be from a single certified plantation (and in theory traceable to the original plantation) or from multiple RSPO certified sources.

The RSPO also employs "Mass Balance" and "Book and Claim" systems. The Mass Balance system allows the end buyer to purchase a known quantity of certified palm oil mixed in with oil from other sources. The "Book and Claim" system adds one more step between the consumer and a certified plantation. Under this system, manufacturers buy a credit —assumed to be the difference between market prices for a volume of certified and conventional palm oil— and continue to buy palm oil from the global market. Certified plantations can then sell their oil into conventional supply chains. Under the "Book and Claim" system, the end product, even if it bears the RSB seal, will not actually have come from a certified plantation. Both systems allow the end user to make the claim "Supports the production of RSPO certified palm oil." In order to gain certification, a plantation must meet all the standards, and the company involved must meet minimum standards at all their other plantations.

The Forest Stewardship Council has a similar standard called "Controlled Wood." Under this standard, conventional lumber can be mixed with certified lumber if the company can prove that the non-certified wood meets a set of basic criteria. The wood cannot have come from illegally harvested sources, high conservation value areas, natural forest that has been converted to plantations, forest areas where traditional or civil rights violations are occurring, or areas where genetically modified trees are grown.

The standard, much like the RSPO's partial certification standard, has been highly controversial. A 2008 Greenpeace report documented 40 cases of controversial logging operations with links to Finnish companies producing or seeking to produce FSC controlled wood.[16] Controlled wood was among the major issues prompting calls for reform at the 2008 General Assembly meeting. One thing is clear: transparency is lost as the certification schemes become more and more complex.

An Eye on the Roundtable: The RSB Standards

The actual RSB standards were largely based on the Roundtable for Sustainable Palm Oil and the Forest Stewardship Council certification, among others.[17] While the original steering board was dominated by industry, the RSB is in the process of adopting a new governance structure. Eleven chambers will represent different stakeholder groups that send two representatives each, one from the Global North and one from the Global South, to the new standards board which is supposed to make decisions by consensus. Some of the RSB Standards, like 7) avoiding areas of High Conservation Value and 1) "production shall follow all applicable local laws" are easily understood, relatively easy to audit, and of obvious value. Other principles, while laudable at face value, will in practice be more complicated to audit and implement.

Despite the fact that the RSB is based on FSC certification, the social provisions in the RSB certification appear weaker than those in the FSC's. For example, in article 3.1 of the FSC certification states that "Indigenous peoples shall *control* forest management on their lands and territories unless they delegate control with free and informed consent to other agencies." The RSB version of that clause (article 2) States that "Stakeholder consultation shall demonstrate *best efforts* to reach consensus through free prior and informed consent." The key guidance on that article, however, provides that "consensus" can be achieved with a

C. Muniz

CHILDREN AT MARIO LAGO LANDLESS WORKERS
MOVEMENT CAMP, RIBERAIO PRETO, BRAZIL

hand-selected group of stakeholders. The FSC certification provides that indigenous people will be compensated for traditional knowledge (3.4). No such provision for local agricultural knowledge exists in the RSB. The FSC recognizes "customary [land] tenure" (2.2), and will automatically disqualify a project from certification in case of a land tenure dispute (2.3). While the RSB standard includes a provision for land rights including customary rights, it does not automatically disqualify a project in case of a dispute, couching the qualification on an undefined "legitimate contest."

Insofar as environmental variables are comparable across sectors, the FSC comes out stronger as well. The FSC standards include a provision for control and monitoring of exotic species use. The RSB does not touch on the subject, even though many of the second generation fuel crops, like Eucalyptus and Miscanthus are invasive.[18] On *paper*, the FSC also provides for genetic diversity in its forests, where no such provision exists in the RSB standard. The RSB standard also explicitly allows for GMOs, which means that the RSB could conceivable certify as "sustainable" vast monoculture plantations of genetically modified crops.

Some of the standards in the RSB Version Zero seem difficult to achieve if not out-and-out unattainable. Principle 9b, for example, "Biofuel production shall

---

Roundtable on Sustainable Biofuels Principles:

1. Biofuel production shall follow all applicable laws of the country in which they occur, and shall endeavor to follow all international treaties relevant to biofuels' production to which the relevant country is a party.
2. Biofuels projects shall be designed and operated under appropriate, comprehensive, transparent, consultative, and participatory processes that involve all relevant stakeholders.
3. Biofuels shall contribute to climate change mitigation by significantly reducing GHG emissions as compared to fossil fuels.
4. Biofuel production shall not violate human rights or labor rights, and shall ensure decent work and the well-being of workers   .
5. Biofuel production shall contribute to the social and economic development of local, rural and indigenous peoples and communities.
6. Biofuel production shall not impair food security.
7. Biofuel production shall avoid negative impacts on biodiversity, ecosystems, and areas of High Conservation Value.
8. Biofuel production shall promote practices that seek to improve soil health and minimize degradation.
9. Biofuel production shall optimize surface and groundwater resource use, including minimizing contamination or depletion of these resources, and shall not violate existing formal and customary water rights.
10. Air pollution from biofuel production and processing shall be minimized along the supply chain.
11. Biofuels shall be produced in the most cost-effective way. The use of technology must improve production efficiency and social and environmental performance in all stages of the biofuel value chain.
12. Biofuel production shall not violate land rights.

From Forest Stewardship Council: http://www.fsc.org/pc.html

not deplete surface or groundwater resources," disregards the fact that significant quantities of water are needed to refine and grow agrofuels. For corn ethanol, the figure amounts to some 780 gallons of water per gallon of fuel.[19] Regions where agrofuels are produced, like the Midwestern U.S. have already been drawing on aquifers faster than the rate of recharge for decades (Ibid.). Other standards are still vague and difficult to measure, like "biofuels shall maintain optimal soil health" without defining how the RSB will measure healthy soil (be it carbon content, amount of topsoil, soil biota, chemical residues, rotation practices, erosion levels, etc.).

The "Elephant in the Room"

In terms of standards, the RSB certainly has some kinks to work out, but the "elephant in the room" is how their standard (or any sustainability regulation) will address the market-mitigated, or indirect, effects of the industry. Arguably, the most destructive impacts of the biofuels industry come through their pressures on the market: land conversion and subsequent greenhouse gas emissions, food price inflation and volatility, land concentration, rural employment and food sovereignty.

In February of 2008 a study in Science by Timothy Searchinger of Princeton University found that counting the indirect greenhouse gas emissions from land use change, ethanol is actually worse for the environment than gasoline.[20] Around the same time, a leaked World Bank report claimed that 75% of food price inflation was primarily due to surging demand from agrofuels.[21] Other reports assigned less blame to the industry for food prices, while still other analysts pointed out that by linking food and energy markets, a new level of volatility and speculative activity was introduced into previously stable markets.[22]

These effects are extremely difficult for a single producer or importer to deal with, but some market mitigated effects can be dealt with in an overall standard. Because agrofuels increase the demand for agricultural acreage, the carbon footprint of a given fuel will be vastly different dependent on where it is grown, and what crops or vegetation it displaces. If a farmer switches from corn/soy rotations in the Midwestern U.S. to strictly corn, which in turn causes more land in Brazil to be planted to soy, (which displaces cattle ranchers into the Amazon), the climate effects may be worse than fossil fuels.

Asking the original producer of that corn to account for those indirect emissions is impossible, but for policy considerations it may be possible to calculate an average value for indirect land use change emissions.

The State of California is in the process of writing the rules for their new Low Carbon Fuel Standard. The standard counts greenhouse gas emissions from field to tank, including refining energy and production methods. After months of controversy, the California Air Resources Board decided to include indirect land use change emissions in its life-cycle assessment of alternative fuels. The board is in the process of coming up with default emissions values to be used in the net calculation. The original 2007 Energy and Security Act (the 2007 Energy Bill which includes Renewable Fuels Mandates) called for a National Academies study of indirect land use impact of agrofuels to be completed within 18 months. That study has not been funded.

But some environmental groups are asking California to take a precautionary approach in regards to indirect land use change. The groups cite new evidence from Cornell University that indirect land use change makes agrofuels more carbon intensive than fossil fuels.[23]

The RSB is not including calculations for indirect land use change, which ensures their carbon accounting will vastly underestimate the climate impact of agrofuels, but this is not due to any fault on the part of the Roundtable. The controversy around the State of California's calculations illustrates how poorly equipped standards in general are for dealing with macro-level, market-mitigated effects. At this point any standard is highly unlikely to include an accurate accounting of greenhouse gas emissions from agrofuels.

Indirect Social Effects: "La soja mata!"
The food vs. fuel debate that made headlines in 2008, (and pitted livestock companies against the grain traders and ethanol producers), is an overly simple way of looking at the industry's effect on food security. Holistic effects of the industry, not just on the price of food, but price volatility, land concentration, rural employment, industrialization, corporate consolidation, and income distribution, all affect the price of food and food security.

The RSB does not attempt to deal with this complexity, but instead deals with food security issues by raising yields, prioritizing "marginal lands," and utilizing "waste" products. But as Nobel prize-winning economist Amartya Sen noted, hunger is a function of poverty not scarcity. Raising yields of basic commodities alone will do little to prevent hunger without addressing the structural inequalities that leave nearly a billion people too poor to buy the ample food that is already produced. As author Wendell Berry notes, there is no waste in agriculture.[24] Waste products like corn stover are essential to maintaining soil health and preventing massive erosion. Likewise, the myth of "marginal lands" also rhetorically sidesteps structural issues. In a recent report, Jonathan Davies of the World Initiative for Sustainable Pastoralism puts it succinctly, "These marginal lands do not exist on the scale people think. In Africa, most of the lands in question are actively managed by pastoralists, hunter-gatherers and sometimes dryland farmers."[25]

The RSB cannot be asked to fix the food system, but it could help avoid some of the structural inequalities that cause hunger that are exacerbated by the agrofuels industry: land concentration, monopoly control of genetic resources, monoculture, and rural employment. In order to address food security and rural development in a meaningful way, it matters who owns the means of production, not just whether or not workers have a right to organize. It matters whether or not the feedstock is a monoculture of proprietary GM crops. It matters if industrial agrofuel plantations pave over family farms, and whether exporting agrofuels concentrates land in fewer and fewer hands.

The RSB does not deal with the issue of ownership – in fact it acknowledges that many of their standards will be difficult for smallholders to follow. As far as income distribution, it only asserts that local minimum wage laws be followed (no mention of living wage, access to health services etc.). While agrofuels supposedly will bring about rural development: we are seeing quite the opposite. If agrofuel plantations displace family farms, as they are doing in much of the world (i.e. Hurtado and Mendonça, this volume), jobs will be lost from the rural economy, and the jobs that are left, are hardly to be desired. Cane cutting, for example, is one of the most backbreaking, dangerous, and abuse-ridden labor markets in Brazil (see Mendonça this issue). For landless sugarcane workers, industrial agrofuels is hardly a pathway out of poverty.

The RSB cannot engage the structural issues around food security because locally-owned, democratically-controlled, decentralized food and energy systems would cut into the bottom line of the corporations with monopoly market power over our food and fuel systems – many of which are participants in the Roundtable. Global trade in industrial, corporate-owned, agrofuels will never be "sustainable" for the small producer.

A Model for the Future...

While the RSB has the real potential to curb some of the worst practices of the industry, the standard cannot reform the model as a whole. Industrial agrofuels production preferences the model of global commodities trade, land concentration, and monoculture plantations that creates environmental damage and injustice. In essence, industrial agrofuels can never be sustainable. By focusing on the effects that industry can and will agree to in a standard, the RSB runs the risk of legitimizing a destructive model.

Certifications are controversial. Neither the FSC nor the WWF Roundtables have been without their critics. For all the good intentions and efforts to reach smallholders, few small farmers' organizations are participating in the RSB. At the 2008 International Conference on Biofuels a declaration from farmers' movements had this to say about certification schemes: "The proposals for social and environmental certification of agrofuels, looking at different experiences [like FSC, RSPO, RSB] do not reduce but rather hide the impacts, serving largely as an instrument to legitimize the international trade in agrofuels."[26]

Cleaning up the worst abuses of a historically destructive industry is a noble goal. But the global trade in agrofuels has no historical precedent. The industry is being artificially created as a matter of public policy. And this is where initiatives like the RSB and calls for sustainable regulation in general, run into dangerous territory. These initiatives are trying to clean up an industry that probably would not exist without public funding. The need for sustainability regulation alone means that the public subsidies that are meant to jump-start renewable energy, reduce greenhouse gas emissions, stimulate the rural economy and help reduce dependence on foreign energy sources are failing.

In the United States as in the European Union, the market for agrofuels is artificially constructed. In the U.S., the market for industrial agrofuels was created in the form of a 10% gasoline blending mandate (soon to be 12-13%), supposedly to reduce dependence on foreign energy sources, revitalize the farm economy, and reduce greenhouse gas emissions. The 10% blending mandate is supported by subsides to ethanol to the tune of $13 billion a year, amounting to about $1.38 per gallon of ethanol.[27]

Seventy-five percent of renewable energy funding in the U.S. goes to agrofuels, leaving just 25% of the monies for solar, micro-hydro, geothermal, wind, green retrofitting, and improved efficiency.[28] A study by Marc Jacobsen of Stanford

University compared the environmental performance of different technologies for powering a personal vehicle and found that ethanol (including cellulosic ethanol) rated worst, while electric hybrids run on solar or wind rated among the best.[29] Studies like Jacobsen's beg the question, "Why ethanol at all?" Instead of attempting to make dirty vehicle fuels marginally more green, why don't we put those public dollars towards truly sustainable energy and food systems?

Instead of supporting an industry that may or may not meet any social or environmental policy goals, those subsidies could be used to create food and energy sovereignty – a matrix of locally controlled, regionally appropriate food and energy systems. There is no reason to jeopardize the food security of hundreds of millions of people to power cars in the American Southwest that could be much more efficiently run on solar and plug-in technology. Instead of supporting agrofuels from Brazil, those same subsidy dollars could support wind farms in Texas, wave energy in  Oregon, utility-scale solar in California, and green retrofitting throughout the developed world. Rather than promoting an international trade in agrofuels, why not support farmer co-ops and small-scale biofuel – with caps on support above a certain volume of production. This would help farmers in the Midwestern U.S. produce energy for local consumption and buffer against price volatility. Siting energy sources near the point of consumption, investing in small businesses and decentralized energy solutions, and guaranteeing support like grain reserves, extension, and credit to family-scale agriculture will genuinely spur the rural economy and help reduce dependence on foreign sources.

Looking at existing models such as the FSC, RSPO, and RRS, suggests that sustainability initiatives for biofuels are highly unlikely to stop the destruction being wrought by the agrofuels industry. If the RSPO is any indication, it could take another six or seven years for the first "sustainable" plantations to come on line. By that time, most of the damage may already have been done. In the best case scenario, the RSB will create islands of sustainability in the midst of a largely destructive sea, demand will increase for sustainable fuel, consumers will pay a premium for it, and the standards can be used as a lever for access to a lucrative, boutique market. In the worst case scenario – marginal participation in the Roundtable will be enough to staunch the negative PR that has plagued the agrofuels industry from day one—without delivering any real results.

Regardless, the RSB will provide a veneer of sustainability to an industry that desperately needs it. And here is where, even if the RSB succeeds in building a boutique market for certified agrofuels, sustainability certifications may do more harm than good. If the time and money invested into participation in the RSB helps companies market agrofuels as a long-term renewable energy solution, the investment will pay off 1000 times in tax breaks, subsidies, and mandates. Despite best intentions, the RSB runs a serious risk of becoming cheap marketing for a dirty industry.

Photo and Image Credits:

1.   Sugar Cane, Minas Gerais, Brazil. Photo by Luciana Soldi Bullara. Creative Commons License (details: http://creativecommons.org/licenses/by-nc/2.0/deed.en).). Photo URL: http://www.flickr.com/photos/lusoldi/149401652/
2.   Land Cleared for Palm Plantation, Guatemala: Photo by Laura Hurtado. Food First.
3.   Soy Fields/Amazon Mato Grosso: Leonardo F. Freitas creative commons License (details: http://creativecommons.org/licenses/by-nc-sa/2.0/) Photo URL: http://www.flickr.com/photos/leoffreitas/789180675/in/photostream
4.   Tortuguero Palm Plantation, Costa Rica. Gary Colet Creative Commons License = (http://creativecommons.org/licenses/by-nc-nd/2.0/deed.en) Photo URL: http://www.flickr.com/photos/garycolet/495136239/
5.   Mario Logo Landless Workers Movement Camp: Photo by C. Muniz Creative Commons License (details: http://creativecommons.org/licenses/by-nc-nd/2.0/deed.en). Photo URL: http://www.flickr.com/photos/7607113@N03/1948356953
6.   Traffic: Photo by Kathy McEldowney, Creative Commons License (details: http://creativecommons.org/licenses/by-nc-nd/2.0/deed.en) Photo URL: http://www.flickr.com/photos/k2d2vaca/703476356/

References:

1.   ASEED Europe. 2008. "Round Table set to certify damaging soy" New report published by groups from Europe, the U.S. and South America. ASEED Europe, 22 April 2008 [cited March 8 2009]. Available from http://www.aseed.net/index.php?option=com_content&task=view&id=555&Itemid=211.
2.   Ibid

3. Timberwatch. 2008. Life as Commerce – Certification in South Africa. Global Forest Coalition [cited March 10 2009]. Available from http://www.globalforestcoalition.org/paginas/view/33.

4. WRM. 2008. Brazil: Historic federal court decision sentences Veracel Celulose (Stora Enso-Aracruz) for environmental violations, July 2008 2008 [cited March 10 2009]. Available from http://www.wrm.org.uy/bulletin/132/Brazil_2.html.

5. ibid.

6. Bretton Woods Project. 2009. IFC funds Amazon deforestation, undermines safeguard policies. Bretton Woods Project, January 26 2005 2005 [cited March 26 2009]. Available from http://www.brettonwoodsproject.org/art-107739

7. FOEI. 2008. Malaysian palm oil - green gold or green wash? Friends of the Earth International, October 2008[cited March 9 2009]. Available from http://www.foei.org/en/publications/pdfs/malaysian-palm-oil-exec-sum.

8. Serikat Petani Indonesia. 2007. It's cars versus humans. Serikat Petani Indonesia, 26 July 2007 [cited March 8 2009]. Available from http://www.spi.or.id/en/?p=10.

9. WRM. 2008. International Declaration Against the 'Greenwashing' of Palm Oil by the Roundtable on Sustainable Palm Oil (RSPO). World Rainforest Movement, 16 October 2008 2008 [cited March 8 2009]. Available from www.wrm.org.uy/subjects/agrofuels/International_Declaration_RTSPO.pdf.

10. Greenpeace Netherlands. 20098 United Plantations certified despite gross violations of RSPO standards, November 2008 [cited March 8 2009]. Available from http://www.greenpeace.org.uk/files/pdfs/forests/UnitedPlantationsReport.pdf.

11. Ibid.

12. Unilever. 2008. November 2008: Unilever buys first batch of certified sustainable palm oil. Unilever. [cited March 8 2009]. Available at: http://www.unilever.com/sustainability/news/november2008unileverbuysfirstbatchofcertifiedsustainablepalmoil.aspx.

13. Samulan, Andrea. 2008. "Multi-Stakeholder" Process Misses the Mark (Police and barricades installed to prevent access). Rainforest Action Network, 24 April 2008 [cited March 8 2009]. Available from http://understory.ran.org/2008/04/24/multi-stakeholder-process-misses-the-mark-police-and-barricades-installed-to-prevent-access/.

14. For a Third Time We Reject the Fallacy of Responsible Soy 2009. March 2008 [cited March 8 2009]. Available from http://www.lasojamata.org/node/110/.

15. Hammel, Debbie. 2009. Personal Communication. Oakland, California, March 4, 2009.

16. Harkki, Sini 2008. Out of Control: High Conservation Value Forest Logging Under FSC Controlled Wood in Finland. Greenpeace, October 2008 [cited March 8 2009]. Available from www.greenpeace.org/raw/content/finland/fi/dokumentit/out-of-control-high-conservat.pdf.

17. RSB. 2008. Roundtable on Sustainable Biofuels Global Prinicples and Criteria for Sustainable Biofuels Production Version Zero. Energy Center, Ecole Polytechnique Federale de Lausanne [cited March 8 2009]. Available from http://cgse.epfl.ch/page70341.html.

18. Rosenthal, Elizabeth. 2008. New biofuel sources may not be food, but they could prove

invasive. International Herald Tribune. May 20, 2008.

19. National Research Council. 2008. Water Implications for Biofuels Production in the United States: The National Academies Press.

20. Searchinger, Timothy, and Ralph Heimlich,2 R. A. Houghton,3 Fengxia Dong,4 Amani Elobeid,4 Jacinto Fabiosa,4 Simla Tokgoz,4 Dermot Hayes,4 Tun-Hsiang Yu. 2008. Use of U.S. Croplands for Biofuels Increases Greenhouse Gases Through Emissions from Land-Use Change. Science 319 (5867):1238 – 1240

21. World Bank. Rising Food Prices: Policy Options and World Bank Response. World Bank. 2008 [cited September 25, 2008. Available at: http://siteresources.worldbank.org/NEWS/Resources/risingfoodprices_backgroundnote_apr08.pdf.

22. Holt-Gimenez, Eric and Raj Patel. 2009. Food Rebellions! Crisis and the hunger for justice. Oakland, California: Food First Books

23. Howarth, R. W., S. Bringezu, M. Bekunda, C. de Fraiture, L. Maene, L.A. Martinelli, O.E. Sala. 2009. Rapid assessment on biofuels and the environment: overview and key findings. Executive Summary. In R.W. Howarth and S. Bringezu, editors. 2009 Biofuels: Environmental Consequences and Interactions with Changing Land Use Proceedings of the Scientific Committee on Problems of the Environment (SCOPE) International Biofuels Project Rapid Assessment, 22-25 September 2008, Gummersbach, Germany.

24. Berry, Wendell. 2007. Introduction. In The Soil and Health. A Study of Organic Agriculture, edited by A. Howard: The University Press of Kentucky.

25. Gaia Foundation. 2008. Agrofuels and the Myth of Marginal Lands. A briefing by The Gaia Foundation, Biofuelwatch, the African Biodiversity Network, Salva La Selva, Watch Indonesia and EcoNexus, September 2008 [cited March 10 2009]. Available from www.gaiafoundation.org/documents/Agrofuels&MarginalMyth.pdf.

26. Holland, Nina. 2008. Brazil's Agrofuel Push in Sao Paulo. Corporate Europe Observatory, 21 November 2008. [cited March 10 2009]. Available from http://www.corporateeurope.org/brazilconference.html.

27. Steenblik, Ronald. 2007. Biofuels – At what cost? Government support for ethanol and biodiesel in selected OECD countries. Global Subsidies Initiative; International Institute for Sustainable Development [cited March 8 2009]. Available from http://www.globalsubsidies.org/files/assets/oecdbiofuels.pdf.

28. Environmental Working Group. 2009. Ethanol's Federal Subsidy Grab Leaves Little For Solar, Wind And Geothermal Energy Environmental Working Group [cited March 8 2009]. Available from http://www.ewg.org/node/27498.

29. Jacobson, Mark Z. 2009. Review of solutions to global warming, air pollution, and energy security. Energy and Environmental Science 2:148-173.

PART TWO

The Social and Environmental Consequences of Agrofuels

CHAPTER V

THE ENVIRONMENTAL AND SOCIAL CONSEQUENCES OF "GREEN CAPITALISM" IN BRAZIL

BY MARIA LUICA MENDONÇA

AMAZON SOY PLANTATION

The Brazilian government has assumed a prominent role in defending the expansion of monoculture agrofuel production. Brazil's foreign policy priority is gaining access to agrofuel markets, especially in the European Union, Japan, and the United States. It is also encouraging other countries in the Southern cone to adopt this model, by transferring the required technology.

George W. Bush's visit to Brazil on March 9, 2007 consolidated Brazil's alliance with the U.S. in a memorandum that encourages ethanol production in several countries. At the time Brazilian President, Luiz Inácio Lula da Silva said: "We should create projects for poor nations so that they don't only see rich countries as exploiters. We want to see biomass generate sustainable development in South America, Central America, the Caribbean and Africa. We all feel the obligation of taking care of the environment."[1]

According to Nicholas Burns, the U.S. Undersecretary of State for Political Affairs under President George W. Bush, this alliance could bring about a "global revolution" because the U.S. and Brazil are responsible for over 70% of ethanol production in the world. For the U.S. government, the purpose of this visit was to improve Bush's image in Latin America and to guarantee a monopoly over energy sources (traditional and alternative) for a few corporations. The biotech industry, the petroleum industry and the automobile industry are all taking advantage of the widespread and legitimate concern about global warming as an opportunity for profit.

The consequences of this "green capitalism" could be just as devastating as conventional wars. Brazil is the fourth largest emitter of carbon dioxide in the world. This is largely due to the destruction of the Amazon rainforest, which represents 80% of carbon dioxide emissions in the country.[2] The expansion of monoculture agrofuel for the production aggravates this problem by pushing the agricultural frontier into the Amazon region and the Cerrado—the biologically diverse savannah that covers approximately one fifth of Brazil's land area.

Studies show that the expansion of industrial agriculture presents a greater threat of global warming than carbon dioxide emissions from fossil fuels,[3] yet the Brazilian government attempts to convince the international community that Brazilian ethanol is sustainable.

The Expansion of Sugarcane Plantations in the Cerrado

The Cerrado is known as the "father of the waters" because it supplies Brazil's main hydrographic basins: the Amazon, Paraguay, and São Francisco. This biome covers around two million square kilometers between the Amazon rainforest, the Atlantic forest, the Pantanal and the Caatinga, including the states of Minas Gerais, Mato Grosso, Mato Grosso do Sul, Goiás, the Federal District, Tocantins, southern Maranhão, western Bahia, and part of Sao Paulo.

BIODIVERSE CERRADO, MINAS GERAIS, BRAZIL

The Cerrado is as important as the Amazon rainforest because it is rich in biodiversity; it is home to over 10,000 species of plants, 935 bird species and nearly 300 mammals;[4] many of which are under the threat of extinction. Despite its importance, the destruction of the Cerrado has not been as visible as that of the rainforest. Studies indicate that every year around 2 million hectares of the Cerrado are deforested.[5] It is estimated that more than half of the region has already been destroyed. At this pace, it will be completely gone by 2030.[6]

In the last few years, the Brazilian government chose the Cerrado as the main area for the expansion of sugarcane plantations because it has a favorable topography, with high quality flat lands and abundant water. Data from the Brazilian Institute of Geography and Statistics (IBGE) indicate that in 2007 sugarcane plantations occupied 5.8 million hectares in the Cerrado.[7]

An investigation done by the Center for the Study of Applied Economics of the University of Sao Paolo estimates that in the next five years, about US$14.6 billion will be spent on the construction of 73 new sugar mills in the South Central region.[8] In August 2008, an agreement between the Environment Ministry and the Agriculture Ministry resulted in a series of modifications to the Environmental Crimes Law. One was a decree by President Lula that allows sugarcane mills in the Pantanal. According to data from the National Institute for Space Research (INPE), from IBGE, and from the Environment Ministry (MMA); new mills are being installed within ecological reserves and over natural water sources.[9] A report by the Society, Population and Nature Institute (ISPN) confirms this:

> Deforestation for the creation of sugarcane plantations directly harms rural populations that subsist on the biodiversity in the Cerrado. Another consequence is that small-scale food producers leave their plantations because they are attracted to the temporary cane-cutting jobs. This process could reduce the amount of food produced in the region and could aggravate migration to urban peripheries.[10]

As demand for biofuels grows, Brazil is increasingly seen as the "granary" for sugarcane and soy. In an interview published by the Washington Post, Carlo Lovatelli, the commercial director of the multinational Bunge corporation— which controls 93% of Brazilian soy for export—said that, "If the U.S. races after ethanol, soybean prices tend to climb and demand will be supplied by Brazil." He added: "The Cerrado is perfect for agriculture and it will be used, there is no doubt about that."[11]

According to geography professor Antônio Thomaz Júnior of the State University of Sao Paulo (UNESP), "The expansion of sugar cane in Brazil for ethanol production could extend to areas where food is currently cultivated, in addition to threatening the integrity of important biomes, such as the Amazon region and the Pantanal."[12] Researcher Sérgio De Zen cautions that, "even if it seems that ethanol is an economically viable alternative that will substitute [for] fossil fuels, it has turned into an environmental threat."[13]

Another worry stems from the amount of water needed for biofuel production. Jan Lundqvist, the director of the Scientific Committee of the International Water Institute of Stockholm, warns:

> The amount of water currently used in the whole world for food production is around 7 million cubic meters. In 2050, it is estimated that the amount will rise to 11 million cubic meters, almost double than what is used today. Projections indicate that the amount of water required for biofuel production will increase in the same proportion as the demand for water for food production. That would mean that between 20 and 30 million cubic meters of water would be needed by 2050. This is more water than is available.[14]

In addition to supply problems, water quality impacts pose a concern. A study published by the U.S. National Academies on the impact of ethanol production on U.S. water sources, concludes that:

> The quality of groundwater, water from rivers, coastal water and spring water could be affected by the increased use of fertilizers and pesticides for biofuels. High nitrogen levels are the main cause for the decrease in oxygen in regions known as "dead zones" that are lethal to many aquatic creatures.[15]

The Destruction of the Brazilian Amazon Region

A 2008 study conducted by Matthew Hensen of the University of South Dakota found that deforestation in Brazil represented 47.8% of worldwide tropical forest destruction for the period between 2000 and 2005.[16] INPE calculates that over the last 20 years, one hectare of forest has disappeared every ten seconds in Brazil. Out of a total of 4 million square kilometers of original forest, around 700 thousand are already deforested. The Institute of Amazon Environmental

Research says another 670 thousand square kilometers may be destroyed by 2030 if the current predatory model is maintained,[17] and the ISPN predicts

that deforestation could completely destroy the Brazilian Amazon region in 40 years.[18]

According to the INPE, 11,200 square kilometers were deforested between August 2006 and July 2007. The System for Real-time Detection of Deforestation (DETER) reg-

DEFORESTATION FOR SOY PLANTATIONS
IN THE AMAZON REGION

istered 4,732 square kilometers deforested between August 2007 and March 2008.[19] In April 2008, over 1,100 square kilometers of forests were lost.[20] The highest rate of deforestation occurred in the state of Mato Grosso, accounting for 54% of the total, followed by Pará (18%) and Rondônia (16%).[21] In June 2008, the Amazon Institute of People and the Environment (Imazon) registered more than 600 square kilometers lost in these regions. This was a 23% increase from June 2007. According to Paulo Barreta, a representative for Imazon, this is a direct consequence of the expansion of agriculture in the region.[22]

The American environmentalist Lester Brown, one of the pioneers in this issue, was quoted in the newspaper Folha de Sao Paulo, warning that "biofuels are the most serious threat to the world's biodiversity." He said "Brazil should start to develop alternative sources of energy, including solar energy and wind power, which have huge potential," adding, "What we need to do is to think about a new economic model based on renewable sources of energy, that has a diversified transportation system and that reuses and recycles everything. ... If we do not restructure the world economy, economic progress will not be sustainable."[23] Yet, the Brazilian government still insists on defending large-scale monoculture biofuel expansion, and has introduced a series of administrative and economic measures to facilitate this.

"Grilagem:" Land Thievery

The term *"grilagem"* refers to the fraudulent appropriation of public and leaseholder lands, especially in regions along the agricultural frontier. The main mechanisms used in grilagem are illegal land registrations, with the tacit collusion of judges. This practice has been used by large land owners to gain control over vast areas of land, and with it political and economic power. Transnational corporations have gradually acquired control over formerly public lands to produce export commodities on a large scale.

In July 2008, Brazil's Senate approved a provision that increased the amount of public land that can be sold in the Amazon without competitive bidding from 500 to 1,500 hectares. According to Senator and ex-minister for the environment Marina Silva (who voted against the measure) "that is going to increase land thievery, and consequently will increase deforestation in the Amazon region. It will also promote the privatization of public forests."[24] On August 6, 2008, President Lula signed the measure into law but vetoed a provision that limited this measure to the ecological-economic zone of the Amazon region.

This represents a very serious problem in the Amazon because it allows for predatory activities such as illegal logging, industrial agriculture, and cattle farming. In July 2008, a study done by Imazon estimated that about 42 million hectares of land in the Amazon are possessed illegally. According to forest engineer Paulo Barreta, one of the coordinators of this study, "In practice grilagem is about the free privatization of the forest."[25] Barreta estimates that in addition to fraudulent possession, there are around 40 million hectares for which there are duplicate land titles. He believes that actual illegal land possession in the Amazon may be as high as 80 million hectares.

Most land possession irregularities were found in the states of Pará and Mato Grosso, with 16 and 9.6 million hectares respectively. Even Brazil's National Institute for Colonization and Agrarian Reform (INCRA), responsible for public lands in the Amazon, recognizes that over 710.2 thousand square kilometers of land in the Amazon region are outside of its control. This area represents 14% of the region and 65% of lands under INCRA's purview. Most of this, about 288.6 thousand square kilometers, is in the state of Pará.[26] According to professor Ariovaldo Umbelino, of the University of Sao Paulo (USP):

> More than 212 million hectares of public lands are not registered by INCRA, by state Land Institutes, or by the real estate registry. In other words, even though these lands are fenced, they do not

legally exist for the State. Another 84 million hectares appear in the INCRA registry as possessions, and within those, only 21 million hectares could be made legal by the existing legislation. The 1988 Constitution allows for the regularization of possessions of up to 50 hectares and 100 hectares in exceptional cases. This means that larger areas cannot be legalized.[27]

The Expansion of Sugarcane Cultivation in the Amazon Region

On July 29, 2007, the Brazilian Agriculture Minister Reinhold Stephanes, declared to the newspaper O Globo that "Cane does not exist in the Amazon region. We have no knowledge of sugarcane in the region." President Lula has constantly repeated this denial to evade criticism, especially from countries that import Brazilian ethanol. In June 2008, in his speech at the FAO conference, President Lula stated that "only 0.3% of all of Brazil's sugar cane plantations" are in the Amazon region. "Our sugar cane plantations, in other words, are about as far away from the Amazon as the Vatican is from the Kremlin."[28]

Nonetheless, in 2006, Brazil's National Commodities Supply Corp. (CONAB)—linked to the Ministry of Agriculture—declared that the northern region of Brazil had the highest indexes of increased sugarcane production in the country. Between 2007 and 2008 CONAB registered an increase in sugarcane production in the Amazon from 17.6 million to 19.3 million tons.[29] The increase was 68.9% in Tocantins, 55.1% in Amazonas and 34.3% in Pará. Production in the three states was 1.6 million tons, a 46.8% increase from the previous harvest.[30] In Tocantins, there was a 13% expansion (from 4.5 thousand to 5.1 thousand hectares), followed by Mato Grosso with an increase of 10%, and Amazonas with an 8% increase (from 4.8 thousand to 5.2 thousand hectares). In Pará the area covered with sugarcane is probably around 10.5 thousand hectares. According to a study done by USP, Pará is one of the main areas in which ethanol production has increased.[31]

These facts have produced immense concern, both in Brazil and abroad. According to researcher Écio Rodrigues from the Federal University of Acre (UFAC), "carbon dioxide released from the destruction of forests cannot be compensated by cane production. This is why everybody is worried about Brazil's transformation into a biofuel superpower."[32]

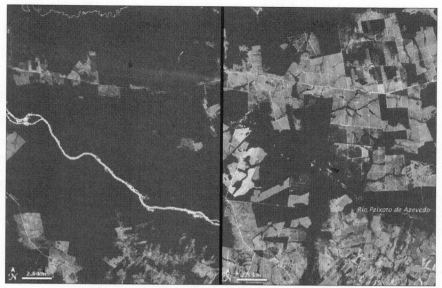

CLEARED FORESTS IN MATO GROSSO IN 1992 (LEFT) AND 2006

The False Concept of "Degraded" Lands

A census done in 2006 confirmed that there had been a 275.5% agricultural expansion in the northern Amazon region. Between 1990 and 2006 there was an 18% yearly increase in soy plantations and an 11% increase in the amount of livestock raised in the Amazon.[33] Between 2006 and 2007, the soy harvest in the northern region increased by 20%.[34] These strong pressures on the agricultural frontier generate doubts about the government's capacity to monitor sugarcane production and implement enforcement mechanisms when the law is broken. Sérgio Leitão, the public policy coordinator for Greenpeace in Brazil, says that fines have been successfully levied in only 2% of illegal deforestation cases.[35]

A law proposed by parliament member Rosa de Freitas (number 2323/07) hopes to stop fiscal and financial incentives for ethanol production in the Amazon region, including the states of Acre, Amapá, Amazonas, Pará, Rondônia, Roraima and part of Mato Grosso, Tocantins and Maranhão. Rosa de Freitas maintains that "sugarcane is extremely harmful in terms of deforestation, and monoculture production has grave environmental consequences." She suggests that the zoning proposed by the government "will not only allow for but will also serve as an incentive for sugarcane cultivation."[36]

Health Risks for Workers and Local Populations

A May 6, 2008 document published by the Public Ministry of Labor of Mato Grosso do Sul concluded that sugarcane burning ...

> leads to the formation of potentially toxic substances, such as carbon monoxide, ammonia, and methane, among others. Particles are less than or equal to 10 micrometers (PM10, inhalable particles) represent the highest health risk and have received the most attention. Ninety four percent of it is constituted of fine and ultra fine particles; that is, particles that reach the deepest parts of the respiratory system, cross the epithelial barrier, reach the pulmonary gap and are responsible for triggering serious illnesses.[37]

The document cites several scientific studies, such as that of Dr. Marco Abdo Arbex, which "reveals that atmospheric pollution generated by the burning of sugarcane has led to a considerable increase in the amount of people getting medical treatment for asthma." Also cited were other cardiac, arterial and cerebrovascular illnesses, along with "acute effects [more people in the hospital and more deaths from arrhythmia] and chronic effects due to long-term exposure [an increase in the death rate for cerebrovascular and cardiac illnesses]."[38]

The document goes on to describe the "lack of labor legislation compliance and worker intoxication from chemical products; worker deaths because of the inhalation of carcinogenic gases; the incidence of respiratory problems due to carbonic, ozone, nitrogen and sulfur gases released when sugarcane is burned [also responsible for acid rain] which also releases the undesired soot of burnt straw [which contains carcinogenic substances]." The study concluded that the "data provide evidence that cane-cutting workers' exposure to the materials released during the cane burning process represents important risks that have to be considered as possible causes of death of some of these workers." It adds, "Working conditions expose cane cutters to pollutants that place them at risk to various illnesses, especially to respiratory problems and lung cancer."[39]

Worker Rights Violations

In many parts of Brazil, the rise in ethanol production has led to the displacement of peasants from their lands and has created a type of dependency referred to as "cane economy," where only insecure employment exists. The land monopoly impedes the development of other agricultural sectors, leading to unemployment and stimulating migration, as well as the submission of workers to degrading labor conditions.

The biofuel industry looks "efficient" because it is based on the exploitation of cheap labor, and sometimes slave labor. Workers are paid according to the amount of cane they cut and not per hour. In the state of Sao Paulo, a worker's goal is to cut between 10 and 15 tons of cane per day. For that, 30 strokes per minute for eight hours per day are necessary. According to information from the Rural Workers Union of Cosmópilis (SP), the current minimum wage is R$ 475 (about US$ 200) a month. Workers receive R$ 2.92 (US$ 1.26) per ton of cut and piled cane.

There is new invented transgenic sugarcane which is lighter, and produces a higher concentration of sucrose. While this is more profitable for mill owners; it means even greater exploitation of workers, who are still paid by the ton and must therefore work harder to get their quotas. According to an investigation by Fundacentro, an organ of the Ministry of Labor and Employment (MTE), "100 square meters of cane used to add up to 10 tons. Today you need 300 square meters for 10 tons."[40]

The exploitation of cañeros (cane workers) has led to serious health problems and has even killed many workers. Between 2005 and 2006, the Pastoral Service for Migrants registered 17 deaths of migrant workers in Sao Paulo. In 2007, five deaths were registered for excessive work in that same state.

- 52 year old José Pereira Martins, died of a heart attack after cutting cane in the city of Guariba. He had migrated from the municipality of Araçuaí in Minas Gerais.

- 20-year-old Lourenço Paulino

CANE WORKER IN SÃO PAOLO, BRAZIL

de Souza from Tocantis, was found dead in Sao José, in Barretos.

- 34 year old Adailton Jesus dos Santos died. He had migrated from Piauí to the sugarcane plantations in Sao Paulo.

- 33 year old José Dionísio de Souza died after having migrated from Minas Gerais.

- 28-year-old Edílson Jesus de Andrade died in the municipality of Guariba. He had migrated from Bahia and was buried in Sao Paulo.

There are similar cases in Sao Paulo's sugarcane sector. In 2005, the Regional Labor Delegation registered 416 deaths, due mostly to work accidents or because of illnesses such as heart attacks, cancer, and burning to death.

On April 15, 2007, an employee in Santa Luiza in the Motuca municipality, died from suffocation and another was gravely injured while they were burning sugarcane. Adriano de Amaral (31 years old) died because there was no water in the hose he was using to control the fire. He was the father of a seven year old and had a baby 20 days old. Another 44-year-old worker, Ivanildo Gomes, was burned over 44% of his body.

In the state of Sao Paulo it is estimated that half of the labor force is made up of migrant workers, especially from the northeast and Minas Gerais. Workers spend up to $250 Reals (approximately US$106) a month out of an average R$413 (US$175) to survive, and have very little left over to send to their families, who also depend on the income. By the end of the harvest, many migrants do not have enough money to return home. In 2007, there were over 40 cases tried by the Regional Labor Agency of the 15th region against sugar mills, suppliers and labor contractors in Sao Paulo for breaking labor laws.

Slave labor is common in the sugar sector. These workers tend to be migrants from the northeast or from the Vale do Jequitinhonha in Minas Gerais, attracted by middlemen that recruit workers for sugar mills. In 2006, the Attorney General's Office of the Public Ministry inspected 74 sugar mills in Sao Paulo state and they were all fined. In March 2007, public prosecutors of the MTE rescued 288 workers from slavery in six sugar mills in Sao Paulo. In another operation in March, the oversight group of the Regional Labor Delegation in Mato Grosso do Sul rescued 409 workers from the alcohol factory Centro Oeste Iguatemi. Among them were 150 indigenous men. In July 2007, public prosecutors from the Labor Ministry freed 1,108 cañeros from the Pagrisa plantation.[41] The

International Labor Organization (ILO) reported that:

> ... there were workers who received less than R$ 10 per month because illegal deductions made by the company took up almost their whole wage. The food provided to workers was often rotten, and several were suffering from nausea and diarrhea. According to testimonies given by some workers, the water they drank was the same water used for irrigation, and it was so dirty that it looked like bean soup. Housing, according to Humberto, was excessively crowded and the sewer was visible. Most workers came from Maranhao and Piaui, and there was no transportation available to take them to the estate in Ulianopolis, some 40 kilometers away.[42]

On November 13, 2007 the Debrasa factory was closed by the Special Inspection Group. Debrasa belongs to the Brazilian Sugar and Alcohol Company/Agrisul in Brasilandia, a municipality located 400 kilometers from Campo Grande in Mato Grosso do Sul. Around 800 indigenous workers were found in degrading conditions. A report states that the workers were found in "precarious housing and without hygiene, with visible sewage systems, without the necessary sanitary conditions and constantly lacking water. Transportation depended on uninsured vehicles that lacked authorization to transport workers." It also mentioned that workers were not paid on time and that the Unemployment Guarantee Fund Termination Report was not respected.[43]

Every year, hundreds of workers are found in substandard conditions in sugarcane plantations: they often lack work permits, they are not provided with necessary protection equipment, they live without clean water or an adequate diet, they do not have access to showers, and they live in precarious housing. Many times workers even have to pay for things they need to work, such as boots. In cases of workplace accidents, they do not receive adequate treatment.

Conclusion

The expansion of the agrofuel industry has had a devastating affect on smallholder farmers and laborers in Brazil. From grilagem and land evictions to the exploitation of landless laborers, the harmful consequences of this industry far outweigh the benefits. The environmental destruction of the Cerrado and the Amazon is taking away things that can never be returned, and all that Brazilians get in return are lives of difficult migrant labor, an increased concentration of land, and more wealth in the hands of those who are powerful enough to take what they want.

A change in consumer patterns is essential, because no current sustainable energy source can supply the world's demand for energy. But this option has been mostly excluded from the debates around reducing greenhouse gasses. The first step should be to invest heavily in public transportation, in addition to working towards a better handling of waste, greater energy efficiency, and the development of alternative energy sources that are truly renewable.

A change in energy production that looks to preserve life on this planet would also require a change in our idea of "development" and the way our societies are organized. Development of new sustainable sources of energy requires, first, reflection on who is going to be served by the new model, who it will benefit, and what its purpose will be.

The agricultural model should be based in agroecology and in the diversification of production. It is important that we rediscover and promote the practices of peasant agriculture, diversified ecosystems, and strengthen rural social organizations in order to construct a new model that works toward food sovereignty.

Photo and Image Credits:

1. Amazon Soy Field. Leonardo F. Freitas creative commons (share alike, license info: http://creativecommons.org/licenses/by-nc-sa/2.0/deed.en) Photo URL: http://www.flickr.com/photos/leoffreitas/789151757/in/set-72157600605933144/
2. Cerrado, Minas Geras, Brazil: JAIRO BD Creative Commons License (details: http://creativecommons.org/licenses/by/2.0/deed.en) Photo URL: http://www.flickr.com/photos/jairo_abud/2227576199/
3. Amazon Deforestation for Soy. Leonardo F. Freitas Creative Commons License (info: http://creativecommons.org/licenses/by-nc-sa/2.0/) Photo URL: http://www.flickr.com/photos/leoffreitas/789136737/in/set-72157600605933144/
4. Deforestation in Mato Grosso, Brazil. NASA Earth Observatory. Deforestation in Mato Grosso, Brazil. http://earthobservatory.nasa.gov/IOTD/view.php?id=35891
5. Cane Cutter, Brazil. John McQuaid Creative Commons License (info: http://creativecommons.org/licenses/by-nc/2.0/) Photo URL: http://www.flickr.com/photos/mcquaid/3014055075

References:

1 Folha Online. 2007. Veja a íntegra da declaração conjunta dos presidentes Bush e Lula. http://www1.folha.uol.com.br/folha/mundo/ult94u106039.shtml.
2 Grain.org. 2007. Soya nexus in South America. Seedling (July 2007). http://www.grain.org/seedling_files/seed-07-07-en.pdf

3   La Via Campesina. 2007. Small scale sustainable farmers are cooling down the earth. Back ground paper. November 9, 2007: http://www.viacampesina.org/mail_en/index.php?option=com_content&task=view&id=457&Itemid-37..

4   The Nature Conservancy. 2009. The Cerrado. http://www.nature.org/wherewework/southamerica/brazil/work/art5082.html.

5   Machado, Ricardo B.; Ramos Neto, Mário B.; Silva, José Maria C. 2005. Cerrado deforestation and effects on biodiversity conservation. In-Abstracts Universidade de Brasília, Brazil, July 2005. ternational, SAUS quadra 3 lote C Ed. Business Point sala 722. 70070-934 - Brasília-DF – Brazil. http://news.mongabay.com/2005/0721-cbc_cerrado.html.

6   Brannstrom, Christian, Wendy Jepson, Anthony M. Filippi, Daniel Redoa, Zengwang Xu and Srinivasan Ganesh. 2008. Land change in the Brazilian Savanna (Cerrado) 1986–2002: Comparative analysis and implications for land-use policy. *Land Use Policy*, 25(4): 579-595. http://www.sciencedirect.com/science?_ob=ArticleURL&_udi=B6VB0-4RPVJ6S-1&_user=10&_rdoc=1&_fmt=&_orig=search&_sort=d&view=c&_acct=C000050221&_version=1&_urlVersion=0&_userid=10&md5=dda465546515739915b42a574b8cb61f.

7   Fernandez, Sarah. 2008 Cana pressiona área de proteção no Cerrado. Prima Pagina: http://www.pnud.org.br/meio_ambiente/reportagens/index.php?id01=2902&lay=mam

8   Macedo, Isaias C. 2007. The current situation and prospects for ethanol. SciELO Brasil: http://www.scielo.br/scielo.php?script=sci_arttext&pid=S0103-40142007000100012&tlng=en&lng=en&nrm=iso.

9   Fernandez, Sarah. 2008. Plantio ocupou, em 2007, 162 mil hectares do bioma que hoje o governo indica como áreas de conservação. Prima Pagina: http://www.pnud.org.br/meio_ambiente/reportagens/index.php?id01=2902&lay=mam

10 Conexão Tocanitins. 2007. O Estado de São Paulo, Cana coloca em risco o cerrado brasileiro. Conexão Tocanitins: http://conexaotocantins.com.br/noticia/cana-coloca-em-risco-o-cerrado-brasileiro/926

11 Valle, Sabrina. 2007. Losing forests to fuel cars: ethanol sugarcane threatens brazil's wooded savanna. Washington Post, July 31. http://www.washingtonpost.com/wp-dyn/content/article/2007/07/30/AR2007073001484.html.

12 Juliano Barros, Carlos . 2007. Cana pode prejudicar meio ambiente e produção de alimentos. Reporter Brasil: http://www.reporterbrasil.com.br/exibe.php?id=984.

13 Brito, Agnaldo. 15/04/07. O Estado de S. Paulo, Cana invade os pastos e expulsa os rebanhos. LEAD.org: http://www.lead.org.br/article/view/3477/1/285

14 Varejão Wallin, Claudia. 13/08/07. Biocombustível causaria falta de água. BBC Brasil: http://noticias.terra.com.br/ciencia/interna/0,,OI1825830-EI299,00.html.

15 National Research Council of the National Academies. 2008. Water Implications of Biofuels Production in the United States. Washington D.C. The National Academies Press. Accessed 01/18/09: Press. Washington D.C. http://www.nap.edu/catalog.php?record_id=12039.

16 Hansen, Matthew C., Stephen V. Stehman, Peter V. Potapov, Thomas R. Loveland, John R.

G. Townshend, Ruth S. DeFries, Kyle W. Pittman, Belinda Arunarwati, Fred Stolle, Marc K. Steininger, Mark Carroll, and Charlene DiMiceli. 2008. Humid tropical forest clearing from 2000 to 2005 quantified by using multitemporal and multiresolution remotely sensed data. PNAS :105 (27) 9439-9444.

17 Betto, Frei. 15/02/08. Amazônia devastada. Correio da Cidadania: http://www. correiocidadania.com.br/content/view/1429/.

18 Aparecido Dias, Jefferson. 16/06/2008. O Ministério Público e a expansão da atividade sucroalcooleira. Última Instância: http://ultimainstancia.uol.com.br/ensaios/ler_noticia. php?idNoticia=52197.

19 Folhade São Paulo. 15/5/2008. Inpe prevê desmatamento maior em 2008. http://www. cptpe.org.br/modules.php?name=News&file=article&sid=1288.

20 Barbieri, Gisele. 03/06/08. Amazônia sofre com crescimento acelerado do desmatamento. Radioagência Notícias do Planalto: http://www.radioagencianp. com.br/index.php?option=com_content&task=view&id=4757&Itemid=43.

21 Wordpress.com. 28/1/2008. A Rebrip e o desmatamento da Amazônia. http://ecourbana.wordpress.com/2008/02/08/a-rebrip- e-   o-desmatamento- da-amazonia

22 Radioagência Notícias do Planalto. 29/07/08. Desmatamento na Amazônia registra alta no mês de junho. http://www.radioagencianp.com.br/index.php?option=com_content&t ask=view&id=5118&Itemid=43.

23 São Paulo. 2/7/2007. Entrevist, Lester Brown, Biocombustíveis são maior ameaça à diversidade na Terra. http://www1.folha.uol.com.br/fsp/brasil/fc0207200721.htm

24 Diário de Pernambuco,.10/07/2008. Mais área pública na Amazônia. http://www. pernambuco.com/diario/2008/07/10/brasil10_0.asp.

25 Agência Brasiliera de Inteligência. 6/6/2008. Amazônia: 8,5% das terras têm posse ilegal. O Estado de São Paulo: http://www.abin.gov.br/modules/articles/article.php?id=2672

26 Folha Online. 27/06/2008. País ignora o que ocorre em 14% da Amazônia, diz Incra. http://www1.folha.uol.com.br/folha/brasil/ult96u416673.shtml.

27 Umbelino, Ariovaldo. 08/08/2008. Brasil de Fato, Lula é o presidente companheiro dos grileiros da Amazônia. Brasil de Fato: http://www.brasildefato.com.br/v01/agencia/ analise/lula-e-o-presidente-companheiro-dos-grileiros-da-amazonia.

28 Lula da Silva, Luiz Inácio. 2008. Statement at the FAO High-Level Conference on World Food Security: the Challenges of Climate Change and Bioenergy Food and Agriculture Organization of the United Nations, 3-5 June, in Rome, Italy. http://www.fao.org/ fileadmin/user_upload/foodclimate/statements/brazil_lula.pdf

29 Betto, Frei .2008. Amazônia, Ecocídio Anunciado. Adital: http://www.adital.com.br/site noticia.asp?lang=PT&cod=3159

30 Jornal Valor Econômico, 01/06/2006. Amazônia aumenta sua produção de cana, só não no Pará. Pará Negócios: http://www.paranegocios.com.br/anterior_cont.asp?id=1670.

31 Jose Pinto, Raimundo (ed.). 2007. Amazônia aumenta sua produção de cana, só não no Pará. (July 30). http://www.paranegocios.com.br/anterior_cont.asp?id=1670.

32 Calixto, Bruno. 16/06/2008. Cana-de-açúcar avança na Amazônia com recursos públicos. Amazonia.org.br: http://www.reporterbrasil.org.br/agrocombustiveis/clipping.php?id=25.

33 Betto, Frei. 11/02/08. Amazônia, Ecocídio Anunciado. Adital: http://www.adital.com.br/site/noticia.asp?lang=PT&cod=31596.

34 Organizadores Comissão Pastoral da Terra Rede Social de Justiça e Direitos Humanos. 2008. Os impactos da produção de cana no Cerrado e Amazônia. http://www.cptnac.com.br/pub/publicacoes/f0557ab0e850048922e143f615076ebb.pdf.

35 Soalheiro, Marco Antônio. 2007. Cana e Rebanho Bovino Impulsionam Desmatamento na Amazonia. Agência Brasil: http://www.malima.com.br/amazonia/blog_commento.asp?blog_id=55.

36 Araújo, Chico. 29/7/2008. , Projeto proíbe incentivo à cana-de-açúcar na Amazônia. Tribuna do Juruá: http://www.tribunadojurua.com/index.php?option=com_content&task=view&id=561&Itemid=40.

37 Hess, Sônia Corina & Heiler Ivens de Souza Natali. 2008. PARECER TÉCNICO, REF.: OF/PRT24ª/GAB-HISN/Nº 134/2008. Ministério Público do Trabalho de Mato Grosso do Sul.

38 ibid.

39 ibid.

40 UOL Economia. 2007. Febre do etanol ignora milhares de trabalhadores explorados em canaviais. Accessed 03/09/09: http://noticias.uol.com.br/economia/ultnot/efe/2007/03/07/ult1767u88021.jhtm

41 Organizadores Comissão Pastoral da Terra Rede Social de Justiça e Direitos Humanos. 2008. Os impactos da produção de cana no Cerrado e Amazônia. http://www.cptnac.com.br/pub/publicacoes/f0557ab0e850048922e143f615076ebb.pdf.

42 ibid.

43 ibid.

CHAPTER VI

AGROFUELS AND THE LOSS OF LAND FOR FOOD IN GUATEMALA

BY LAURA HURTADO

PLANTING PALMS IN FRAY BARTOLOMÉ LAS CASAS, GUATEMALA

Introduction

The present food crisis has placed the issue of food security, and therefore, of the fundamental right to life, at the center of global discussions and concerns. Analysts have rightfully argued that the food crisis is the result of multiple factors, including: the rise in petroleum prices and the resulting increases in energy, fertilizer and agricultural input costs; the diversion of grains and land into agrofuel[I] production;[II] and a rise in global demand for grains and food—triggered by a rise in consumption by the so-called "emerging" economies: Brazil, India and China.[1] Moreover, food has become the object of speculation in the commodities markets, and is now of interest to national and international financial capital. Food price volatility has also increased in the context of climate change and more frequent "natural" disasters. This study, originally conducted for ActionAid in Guatemala, focuses on the loss of land previously used for food production due to the expansion of agrofuel (primarily African palm and sugarcane) plantations. Already weakened by neoliberal policies via the IMF and free trade agreements, the expansion of agrofuels in Guatemala has resulted in a considerable reduction in the production of basic grains and foods.[III] In the last decade, Guatemala went from being self-sufficient in food, to being dependent on imports of yellow maize, rice, wheat, and soy

I. The term "agrofuels" is used in this report in the sense adopted by the 2007 World Social Forum on Food Sovereignty in Mali, as a rejection of the association that the term "biofuel" attempts to make with life ("bio") and the "sustainability" of the practices associated with it. In Guatemala, the spread of monoculture plantations for agrofuel production, rather than contributing to the sustainability of Guatemalan lives and natural resources, has become a threat to the livelihoods of thousands of families and peasant communities, as well as a threat to their food and nutritional security.
II. The United States currently uses 10% of world maize production for ethanol production.
III. According to FAOSTAT, between 1990-2005 Guatemalan national production of wheat fell 80.4%, bean production fell 25.9%, rice 22.7%, and maize 22.2% (http://faostat.fao.org/).

from the U.S.[2] It has thus become increasingly vulnerable to international price volatility, and dependent on the world market.

In the transformation to agrofuel production, small-scale family farmers have lost their lands, and forests and natural resources are being lost. Forests contribute significantly to peasants' livelihoods; they provide basic necessities through integrated productive systems. The loss of agricultural lands for food production goes hand in hand with extensive land use changes in areas that, until recently, were forests and wetlands that provided local populations with incomes, medicines, and basic necessities such as game and firewood.

For the past five years, agribusinesses have been appropriating the lands of large, medium and small landowners for African palm and sugarcane cultivation. Cane ethanol production has been going on, at a slower pace, since 1983—but it is now increasing at a rapid pace. African palm growers and processors are getting ready to produce biodiesel on a large-scale in the coming years. Governments and International Financial Institutions (IFIs) have facilitated this process through their policies, without taking into account the implications for agrarian social structures, the population's right to food, and the possibilities for continued human development in the country.

The analysis of this issue in Guatemala is made difficult by a lack of national statistics, maps, images and up-to-date data. This study is based on the information that was available, plus data from municipal governments, recent studies, interviews and other primary data collected in the field. With this information we can make some comparisons and claims, even if they are only indicative in nature. National and multilateral institutions should generate specific, current information to be analyzed and considered when creating public policy to confront the food crisis. As suggested by Renato Maluf, the president of the National Council of Food and Nutrition Security of Brazil (CONSEA), "There are numerous possible responses to the present crisis, except to ignore its seriousness and depth."

The Expansion of Agrofuel Plantations

The unprecedented expansion of agrofuel production, primarily palm and sugarcane, is rapidly transforming Guatemalan agriculture. Neither the fourth Agricultural Census (2003)[3] nor the latest Agricultural Survey (2007)[4] reveal the land use changes that have occurred since 2003 in the lowlands in northern Guatemala, particularly in the municipalities of Ixcán (Quiché department),

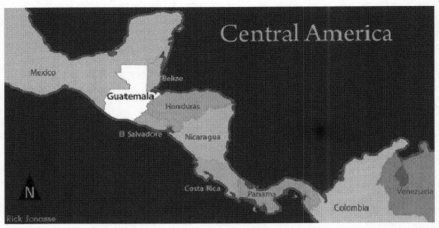

Sayaxché and San Luis (Petén), Chisec, Fray Bartolomé Las Casas, Chahal and Panzós (Alta Verapaz), and El Estor (Izabal).[IV] Agrofuel crops had been introduced earlier on the southern coast of the country, but it was not until 2003—encouraged by the growing global market for agrofuels—that they expanded rapidly both in the south and north.

According to the Guatemalan National Institute of Statistics (INE), there were forty-nine African palm plantations in 2003, covering 31,185 hectares[5] and producing 7,040,225 quintals[V] of palm oil, for essences and for the food and soap industries. The 2007 Agricultural Survey revealed that the number of palm plantations rose to 1,049 that year, and the total area reached 65,340 hectares—doubling in only four years, while output went up 250%. Calculations suggest that 83,385 hectares had been planted by 2008, and estimates published in mid-July of that year predict that by 2010 the number could reach 100,000 hectares.[6]

Sugarcane production, traditionally concentrated in the southern coast, is also expanding rapidly, both because of a higher sugar export quota to the U.S.[VI] and because of the growing demand for ethanol internationally. In 2003,

---

IV. The IV Agricultural Census (INE, 2003) stated that the departments of Escuintla, Izabal, Quetzaltenango, San Marcos, Suchitepéquez and Retalhuleu dedicate the most land to palm plantations, and the departments of Escuintla, Suchitepéquez, Santa Rosa, and Retalhuleu dedicate the largest area to sugarcane cultivation. The 2007 Agricultural Survey did not document the phenomenon, nor did it forecast its development, even though it was already happening

V. 704,022,500 kg.

VI. 704,022,500 kg.

sugarcane covered an area of 188,775 hectares. By 2007, the Agricultural Survey estimated that it had increased to 260,896 in four years. Ethanol production from sugarcane was 49 million liters in 2006, ranking Guatemala 19th in global ethanol production.[7]

In February 2007, after the owners of the sugar refinery Chabil Utaj, S.A. expanded throughout the Polochic Valley in the department of Alta Verapaz, the sugar sector appeared to be reaching its limit. At the time, the manager of the Guatemalan Sugarcane Farmers Association, Armando Boesche, told the press that there were no more lands available for sugar production. But, the sugar sector has continued to expand in Sayaxché and Ixcán. There is talk about the expansion of sugarcane plantations into the municipality of Fray Bartolomé Las Casas.

Table 1 summarizes the information available,[8] along with estimates from June 2008, regarding the expansion of African palm and sugarcane between 2003 and 2008.

Table 1. Estimates of Area Cultivated with African Palm and Sugarcane, 2003-2008[9]

	Total cultivated area per product (in ha)	
	African palm	Sugarcane
Agricultural Census 2003	31,051	188,775
Agricultural Survey 2007	65,340	260,896
Additional area in the Polochic Valley 2007[1]	995	5,376
Additional area in Izabal	n.a.	n.a.
Additional area in Fray Bartolomé[2]	2,488	n.a.
Additional area in Ixcán[3]	3,982	n.a.
Additional area in Sayaxché[4]	10,483	3,500
2008 Estimated Total	83,288	269,772

Data Source Information for Table 1:

1 Data from INDESA and Office IUSI Panzós.

2 Data from PADESA and Office IUSI Fray Bartolomé Las Casas.

3 Data from Palmas del Ixcán, Voegele, E. 2008, July, 01. Fondos estadounidenses realizan inversión en el agro guatemalteco. El Periodico Guatemala. Accessed 03/09/09: http://www.elperiodico.com.gt/es/20080701/economia/59513

4 Data estimated from personal field interviews.

In 2007, palm corporations were projecting rapid growth and considering expanding into both small and large privately owned lands in the lowlands of

Northern Guatemala. At the time, Eduardo Castillo, the oils director for the Food Manufacturers Union, told the press, "We have not yet encountered a limit to the amount of land used to cultivate African palm; however, we could reach such a limit in about ten years."[10]

Jatropha

Press sources have publicized the investments of corporations, the Guatemalan government and the U.S. government to establish plantations for *Jatropha curcas* for biodiesel. One investor has already created a nursery of 700 hectares, with an investment of Q 75 million (US$ 9.27 million), with intentions of creating a 50,000 hectare plantation by 2009. This investor already produces 3,000 gallons of biodiesel daily, but production could grow to 200,000 hectares—through an association of small-scale "cluster" producers—for export to Mexico and the United States. The U.S. Agency for International Development (USAID) is helping finance a project to establish a jatropha biodiesel processing plant to help "fight rural poverty."[11] Jatropha is also expanding into the department of Petén.

Concentration Within Agrofuel Production

The production and processing of palm and sugarcane is primarily concentrated in the hands of six large companies that own plantations and processing plants. Until recently, African palm production had only been used for oil essences and oils for the food and soap industries, both nationally and for export to El Salvador and the United States. It was not until the agrofuels boom occurred within the context of the climate and energy crises that these companies expanded their plantations and processing plants.

Sugarcane production is concentrated in fifteen sugar refineries, some of which have joined with corporations that operate in Central and South America. The main sugar refinery in Guatemala is Pantaleón, which has grown by acquiring its competitors. In 1984 it assumed control of the Concepción refinery. In 1998 it acquired the Monte Rosa refinery, the second most important in Nicaragua, positioning itself as one of the main refiners in Central America. In 2000, these three companies (Monte Rosa/Concepción/Pantaleón) acquired the El Baúl refinery and the Tierra Buena refinery, and all were integrated as subsidiaries of the corporation Pantaleón Sugar Holdings. In 2005, Pantaleón made an alliance with Colombia's Grupo Manuelita and Brazil's UNIALCO to construct a sugar producing and ethanol processing plan in Vale do Pará, Brasil.[12]

Table 2. Principal Producers of African Palm Oil in Guatemala:

Company	Region(s) in Guatemala	National, Regional, and Transnational Alliances
HAME/ REPSA Group Hugo Armando Molina Espinoza	Escuintla Coatepeque (Quetzaltenango), Ocós (San Marcos), Sayaxché (Petén)	
INDESA/ PADESA Juan Maegli	El Estor (Izabal), Panzós, Chisec, Fray Bartolomé Las Casas y Chahal (Alta Verapaz)	Unilever, El Salvador Ignacio González, Costa Rica
AGROCARIBE/ Extractora del Atlántico Grupo Torrebiarte y Arriola Fuxet	Finca Berlín, Morales (Izabal) Acapetahua, Acacoyagua, Mazatán, Mapastepec y Villa Comaltitlán,in the region of Soconusco y Chiapas (México)	Propalma, México Green Earth Fuel/Palmas del Ixcán
Palmas del Ixcán (subsidiary of U.S. Green Earth Fuels)	Ixcán (Quiché), Rubelsanto y Playitas, Chisec; y Lachúa, Cobán (Alta Verapaz)	Green Earth Fuels Carlyle Group, Riverstone Holdings & Goldman Sachs AGROCARIBE Reservas Naturales Privadas del Ixcán
Grupo Kong	Sayaxché (Petén)	Colombian Producer

Table 3: Principal Sugar Producers in Guatemala:

Company	Region(s) in Guatemala	Owners or Corporation
Pantaleón (ethanol) Concepción El Baúl	Santa Lucía Cotzumalguapa, Escintla Escuintla	Pantaleón Sugar Holdings
Magdalena (ethanol exporter)	Escuintla	Leal
Santa Ana	Santa Lucía Cotzumalguapa, Escuintla	Botrán
Palo Gordo (ethanol exporter)	San Antonio, Suchitepéquez	De la Hoz, Bonifasi, Abascal
Los Tarros La Unión	Santa Lucía Cotzumalguapa, Escuintla	Aparicio Hnos.
Madre Tierra	Mazatenango, Suchitepéquez	Campollo Codina
San Diego Trinidad	Escuintla	Fraterno Vila
Guadalupe Chabil Utzaj	Escuintla Panzós y La Tinta, Alta Verapaz El Estor, Izabal	Widmann (also associated with Madre Tierra and Concepción).
El Pilar	Retalhuleu	Campollo Weissemberg
Santa Teresa	Villa Canales, Guatemala	Escamilla
La Sonrisa	Cuilapa, Santa Rosa	Pivaral

The Concentration of Agrarian Property

The expansion of agrofuel production is leading to the concentration of landholdings, which runs counter to the *Agreement on Socioeconomic Aspects and the Agrarian Situation*, created within the framework of the 1996 Guatemalan Peace Accords.[13] This agreement addressed the democratization of land possession, and the improvement of peasants' access to land and natural resources. Information from the Ministry of Agriculture, Animal Industry, and Nutrition (MAGA) shows that the only way to expand palm cultivation is to use land that has been recently "regularized"[VII] ("registered") by the State in favor of peasant families and communities, most of which are indigenous. This is especially true in the north, in the department of Petén, and the Northern Transverse Strip region.[VIII,14]

Industry expansion is leading to the concentration and reconcentration of agrarian property, which is eroding peasants' ability to own or rent land.[15] The *concentration* of agrarian property refers to processes whereby peasant land plots and/or medium and large-scale farmers and stock breeders are aggregated into larger properties for agrofuel plantations. This is happening in the municipalities of Ixcán, Chisec, Fray Bartolomé de Las Casas, and Sayaxché. In these places palm companies are purchasing land from individual owners and communities whose members are co-owners in *pro indiviso*.[IX] Most of these small-scale owners are peasant families that acquired land through Guatemala's Colonization Programs in the 1960s and 70s, or land belonging to groups of families that were forced to move there because of repression and violence during the internal armed conflict. All of these land owners had been allowed to obtain property deeds after the signing of the 1996 Peace Accords.

The *reconcentration* of agrarian property refers to the aggregation of old *large* estates into even larger estates, which are being acquired by national and

---

VII. There is no precise translation of this term into English. It is a process of simultaneously mapping land plots on a cadastre, sorting out overlapping ownership issues, and giving legal claim to land. The closest functional term might be "registration," but that is not always accurate.

VIII. The original study superimposes both areas (the land registered by FONTIERRAS and the potential area for the expansion of African palm) over the private farms in the country's southern coastal areas.

IX. The possession or occupation of lands or tenements belonging to two or more persons.

transnational agribusinesses for the expansion of their plantations. This is happening in the Polochic River Valley, in the municipalities of La Tinta and Panzós (Alta Verapaz) and El Estor (Izabal), where Chabil Utzaj S.A. has bought almost all the old farms measuring between 90 and 1,350 hectares for sugarcane plantations[16] This corporation sought to purchase 5,400 hectares of land in just this one region. Similarly, African palm companies are gathering large stock-breeding estates and unproductive private lands in the municipalities of Chisec, Fray Bartolomé de Las Casas, and Chahal in the Northern Transverse Strip Generally speaking, agribusinesses first seek to purchase private property to ensure optimum conditions for their investments. If land owners refuse to sell their land, they try to establish rent contracts. Through these contracts, they can assure their control over the land for the duration of plantations' useful lives. In the municipality of Fray Bartolomé Las Casas, for example, African palm rent contracts have been established for the next 25 years. The costs of breaking the contracts are so onerous that they would result in the loss of land for the small landholders.

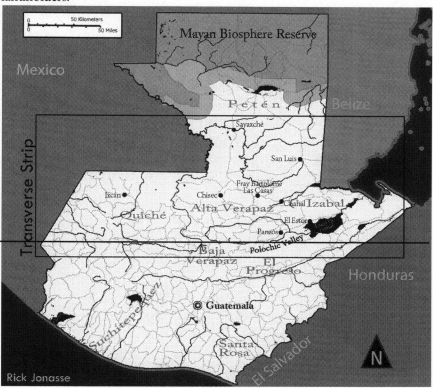

WOMAN DESOLATE OVER BEING FORCED TO LEAVE HER HOME IN YALCOBÉ, GUATEMALA

Methods Used by Agribusinesses to Gain Land

The methods used to acquire and concentrate land ownership vary from one region to the next. Those who buy land in the department of Petén have tended to use more aggressive and violent methods to force owners to sell to them. They begin with offers above local land prices and descend into threats, coercion, and violence. They also gain land through the gradual purchase of plots of land that enable them to deny peasants secure access to water and transportation networks.

South of Petén, in Fray Bartolomé Las Casas, palm companies first try to persuade small-scale land owners to sell their land. If landowners refuse, they offer a variety of leasing options. In either case the price paid by the company is large in comparison with local peasant economies, *in the short term.* The long-term consequences—in terms of absolute job and income dependency—are not evident at the time, nor is currency deflation, the rise in prices of basic goods, or property devaluation due to land degradation. Peasants do not always figure in the total annual income they derive from their property—from agricultural production, livestock, handicrafts and commercial activities.

Representatives of African palm corporations discuss increasing demand for land and the varying prices in the different regions among themselves. In addition, palm companies sometimes collude in informal land distribution arrangements. For example, the Santa Isabel River might be the border between the HAME and PADESA-controlled lands.[X] PADESA would then advance (in alliance with individual producers) toward lands in Chahal and Chisec, while the Green Earth Fuel does the same,[17] starting from Cobán and moving towards Ixcán.

The State and International Financial Institutions' Support for Plantations
Studies have shown that the registration of land ownership undertaken by FONTIERRAS[XI] (*Fondo de Tierras*, or the Land Fund) in the lowlands of the north of Guatemala has accelerated the buying and selling of recently-registered land plots.[18] The Land Fund Law—following the World Bank's directive to 'create and/or dynamize land markets'—has reduced the ability of the State to provide land to families and peasants over the past ten years. Agricultural businessmen were present at the original transfer of deeds, and thus knew who the new owners were and tried to convince them to sell their land plots. In cases where collectively owned properties are bought, the transfer of ownership generally does not follow legal proceedings.

Given the rising demand for land, some businessmen have hired personnel to deal with the difficult process of registering land ownership before the Land Fund. The state institutions have responded much more readily to companies' demands than their responses had been to peasant demands over the past thirty years. Most land titles now being registered could or would not have been accepted under the former system.

The State's agrarian institution is aware of the dynamics of land registration, but has not adopted policies to benefit peasants. On the contrary, state institutions have made it easier for agribusinesses to quickly buy and sell land. In addition, the agribusinesses have been exonerated from the Land Capacity and Use Study

---

X. Guatemalan Financial Corporations.
XI. FONTIERRAS is the government agency authorized to purchase farmland for redistribution to poor farmers. Under the tutelage/pressure of the World Bank and the IMF it has taken a harder, market-oriented approach to 'land reform' that favors corporations and wealthy landowners. For more information, see: http://www.idrc.ca/en/ev-12011-201-1-DO_TOPIC.html

(ECUT), one of the supposed prerequisites for awards. Fray Bartolomé Las Casas—one of the municipalities where this process occurs at an accelerated rate—has even been declared a "Municipality in Process of Registering Property." This means that personnel, a technical team and financial investments are located in the Office of Property Registration Information; they work together to facilitate the tracking, locating, and registering land for the palm company. In fact, in early 2008, the manager of FONTIERRAS ordered that the regional office give priority to land requests from that company.[XII]

After the 1996 Peace Accords, land transfer by the Land Fund and other nongovernmental organizations who supported communities looking for legal titles to their land typically took about two-and-a-half years. Similar work recently for the palm company in Fray Bartolomé Las Casas took only six months.

The Reduction in Land used for Local Food Production

The expansion of agrofuel production is also leading to a considerable loss in the amount of land available for food cultivation. When agribusinesses acquire or lease old and preexisting estates and farms, the areas devoted to basic grains (rice, sorghum, maize, and beans), dairy products, and meat for local markets are no longer used for those purposes. Food production is falling in areas that have recently been registered by the Land Fund as small and medium-scale farmers have stopped producing food for their own sustenance and for local markets. Previously, these smallholder farmers used to rent parts of their land to landless families, or families that did not have enough land, so that they could produce basic grains. This loss of this subsistence peasant production also works against local production. On top of that, when peasant families lose land they simultaneously lose access to forest resources such as firewood, timber products, hunting, medicinal plants and other resources that they formerly used.

This has been the case in the Polochic Valley and in some farms in the Northern Transverse Strip. Small and medium farmers who lease their land to agrofuel producers have had to force workers to leave the farms, and deny them access to the small plots of land where they previously produced food. While some farmers succeed in preserving their *own* access to some land, most peasants can no longer farm for themselves.

XII. Interviews done in 2008.

POLOCHIC RIVER VALLEY, GUATEMALA

Land Use Changes and the Loss of Forests and Biodiversity

There have been dramatic land use changes in areas where agrofuel plantations are being established. Forests are being destroyed, swamps and lakes are being drained and dried, and water courses are being diverted—all for the production of monocultures. Land use changes are fragmenting or completely erasing entire ecosystems, and eliminating biodiversity.

Satellite images captured in March 2004—the year in which the largest number of fires burned in protected and natural heritage areas in the department of Petén—by the Evaluation and Monitoring Center of the National Commission for Protected Areas (CONAP) showed that the main heat source came from fires set to create palm plantations in the southern part of the department. In spite of this, neither the Environmental and Natural Resources Ministry (MARN) nor CONAP has demanded that agribusinesses conduct environmental impact studies, nor have they required these corporations to apply for land use change permits.[XIII] Superimposing a forest map from 2003 over a map of land

---

XIII. For the Polochic Valley case the Defenders of Nature Foundation was consulted, an environmental entity that co-administers the Sierra de las Minas and Refugio de Vida Silvestre Bocas of Polochic. In the case of African palm plantations in the north, the regional office of the National Forest Institute (INAB) was consulted. According to INAB, they only issue a request for change of land use in the municipality of Cobán. By June 2008, the company PADESA had

currently occupied by palm plantations reveals the tremendous loss of forests and biodiversity that is taking place in Guatemala. [XIV]

Conclusion

Encouraged by the rising global demand for agrofuels, biodiesel and ethanol production from African palm and sugarcane is leading to a concentration of land in Guatemala. This development is contrary to the spirit and letter of the 1996 Peace Accords, which called for the State to promote democratization of land ownership and access to land by peasants. The State and International Financial Institutions have actually facilitated peasants' loss of access to land. Simultaneously, the expansion of monoculture agrofuel production is leading to dramatic land use changes. Forests are being eliminated, rivers are diverted, wetlands are drying up, ecosystems are being fragmented or eliminated, and biodiversity is being lost.

In the past, peasants integrated their incomes with activities based in their landholdings (food production, stock breeding, handicraft work, and commercial and extractive activities), but when they lease or sell lands these opportunities are gone. The leasing of land represents an immediate, but limited, source of income for landed peasants. The consequences of dependency on this income will, in the long run, be diminishing returns due to the increase in prices of basic consumer products, the lowering of relative purchasing power, soil and water degradation on their property, the loss of access to other natural resources, and the limited number of low-salaried jobs with precarious working conditions. While land sellers and lessors often maintain some access to land, the situation is much worse for those who already had only tenuous access. A significant number of landless peasant families—families with small plots that could not have two annual harvests or those who used to have access to land by renting it from someone else—have lost all access to land and productive resources. The creation and expansion of agrofuel plantations is occurring at the expense of these families, putting nutritional and food security at risk and violating their fundamental Right to Food.

Photo and Image Credits:

1. Workers on a Palm Plantation, Fray Bartolomé Las Casas. Laura Hurtado, Food First.
2. Central America Map, Rick Jonasse, Food First. Cartographic Data: GeoCommunity

---

not negotiated any requests for a change of land use.

XIV. The study offers maps for the cases of the San Román farm and in the Parcelamiento Fray Bartolomé Las Casas, both in the Sayaxché municipality.

3. Guatemala Map: Rick Jonasse, Food First. Cartographic Data: GeoCommunity
4. Woman to be forced to leave her home. Laura Hurtado, Food First.
5. Polochic River Valley, Guatemala. Google Earth, accessed 04/15/2009

References:

1 Maluf, Renato S. Elevaçao nos preços dos alimentos e o sistema alimentar global. In: Observatorio de Políticas Públicas para a Agricultura. No. 18, abril 2008. www.ufrrj.br/cpda

2 World Food Programme. 2008. Alza de Precios, Mercados e Inseguridad Alimentaria y Nutricional en Centroamérica. Accessed 03/09/09: http://home.wfp.org/stellent/groups/public/documents/liaison_offices/wfp189554.pdf

3 Instituto Nacional de Estadística de la República de Guatemala (INE). 2003. Censo Nacional Agropecuario 2003 (CENAGRO). Accessed 03/09/09: http://www.ine.gob.gt/index.php/agricultura/45-agricultura/74-cenagro-2003

4 Instituto Nacional de Estadística de la República de Guatemala (INE). 2007. Encuesta Nacional Agropecuaria 2007 (ENA 2007). Accessed 03/09/09: http://www.ine.gob.gt/index.php/agricultura/45-agricultura/62-ena-2007

5 ibid.

6 Ortiz, A. 15/07/2008. Auge de biocombustibles dispara demanda de tierras. El Periodico. Accessed 03/09/09: (cached) http://209.85.173.132/search?q=cache:ZnUn0dp3NAIJ:www.elperiodico.com.gt/es/20080715/economia/61450/+%22el+periodico%22+2010+palma+africana+guatemala+15+julio+2008&cd=1&hl=en&ct=clnk&gl=us (URL)http://www.elperiodico.com.gt/es/20080715/economia/61450/

7 Rede Brasileira pela Integracao dos Povos (REBRIP). 2007. Agrocombustives e a Agricultura Familiar e Camponesa. Accessed 03/09/09: http://www.boell-latinoamerica.org/download_pt/Agrocombustiveis_e_a_agricultura_familiar.pdf

8 INE. 2003 Agricultural Census and 2007 Agricultural Survey.

9 Some Data From: Voegele, E. 2008, July, 01. Fondos estadounidenses realizan inversión en el agro guatemalteco. El Periodico Guatemala. Accessed 03/09/09: http://www.elperiodico.com.gt/es/20080701/economia/59513

10 Quinto, R. 2008, June, 23. Prevén Crecimiento del Cultivo de la Palma Africana en el País. El Periodico Guatemala. Accessed 03/09/09: http://www.elperiodico.com.gt/es/20070623/actualidad/40976/

11 Dardón, B. 2008/07/14. Abrirán una planta para procesar aceite de piñón. Prensa Libre de Guatemala. Accessed 03/09/09: http://www.prensalibre.com/pl/2008/julio/14/250104.html

12 El Periodico Guatemala. 2007, Feb. 05. Empresas centenarias: el Ingenio Pantaleón. Accessed: 03/09/09: http://www.elperiodico.com.gt/es/20070205/actualidad/36439/

13   International Relations and Security Network, Primary Resources in International Affairs
      (PRIA). 2006. Agreement on Social and Economic Aspects and Agrarian Situation.
      Accessed 03/09/09: http://se1.isn.ch/serviceengine/FileContent?serviceID=ISN&file
      id=7CCBF5C6-574E-6220-EC96-7CD0B6F02EC4&lng=en

14   Fradejas, A., Fernando Alonzo & Jochen Dürr. 2008. Caña de Azúcar y Palma
      Africana: Combustibles para un nuevo ciclo de acumulación y dominio en Guatemala.
      CONGCOOP. Accessed 03/09/09: http://centroamerica.ded.de/cipp/ded/
      lib/all/lob/return_download,ticket,g_u_e_s_t/bid,3752/no_mime_type,0/~/
      Ca%C3%B1a_palma_acumulacion_y_dominio_IDEAR_CONGCOOP.pdf

15   Hurtado Paz y Paz, Laura. 2008. Dinámicas Agrarias y Reproducción Campesina en la
      Globalización. Guatemala, F&G Editores.

16   ibid.

17   Samayoa, R. 2008. Guatemala: Lachuá, a Corner of the Jungle Resists. IPS. Accessed
      03/10/09: http://ipsnews.net/news.asp?idnews=44042

18   Hurtado Paz y Paz, Laura. 2008.

CHAPTER VII

THE ECOLOGICAL AND SOCIAL TRAGEDY OF CROP-BASED BIOFUELS IN THE AMERICAS

BY MIGUEL ALTIERI & ELIZABETH BRAVO

Shanna Riley

Biofuels in the U.S.: Extent and impacts

Ethanol Production

The Bush Administration is committed to significantly expanding biofuels to reduce its dependence upon foreign oil. (The U.S. imports 61% of the crude oil it consumes,[1] at a cost of $75 billion per year.) Although a range of prospects for biofuels exists, ethanol derived from corn and soy currently constitutes 99% of all biofuel use in the U.S., and its production is expected to exceed 2012 targets of 7.5 billion gallons per year.[2] The amount of corn grown to produce ethanol in the distilleries has tripled in the U.S. from 18 million tons in 2001 to 55 million in 2006.[3]

Dedicating all present U.S. corn and soybean production to biofuels would meet only 12% of the country's gasoline needs and 6% of diesel needs. Agricultural land area in the U.S. totals 625,000 square acres. At the present rate of consumption, meeting oil demand with biofuels would require planting 1.4 million square miles of corn for ethanol or 8.8 million square miles of soy for biodiesel.[4] South Dakota and Iowa already devote more than 50% of their corn to ethanol production, which has led to a diminishing supply of corn for animal feed and human consumption. Although one fifth of the U.S. corn harvest was dedicated to ethanol production in 2006, it met only 3% of the U.S.'s total fuel needs.[5]

The scale of production needed to yield the projected crop mass will encourage industrial methods of monoculture corn and soybean production with drastic environmental side effects. Corn production leads to more soil erosion than any other U.S. crop. Farmers throughout the Midwest have abandoned crop rotations to grow corn and soy exclusively, increasing average soil erosion from 2.7 tons per acre annually to 19.7 tons.[6] Lack of crop rotation has also increased vulnerability to pests, and therefore requires higher levels of pesticides than most crops (in the U.S., about 41% of all herbicides and 17% of all insecticides are applied to corn.[7] Specialization in corn production can be dangerous: in the early 1970s when uniform high-yielding maize hybrids constituted 70% of all corn grown, a leaf blight that affected these hybrids led to a 15% loss in corn yields throughout the decade.[8] This sort of crop vulnerability can be expected to grow in our increasingly volatile climate, causing ripple effects throughout the food supply. We should be considering the implications of tying our energy economy to that same fluctuating and volatile food system.

Corn cultivation generally involves use of the herbicide atrazine, a known endocrine disruptor. Low doses of endocrine disruptors can cause developmental harm by interfering with hormonal triggers at key points in the development of an organism. Studies show that atrazine can result in sexual abnormalities in frog populations, including hermaphrodism.[9]

Corn requires large amounts of chemical nitrogen fertilizer, a major contributor to the ground and river water pollution responsible for the "dead zone" in the Gulf of Mexico. Median rates of nitrate application on U.S. farmland range from 120 to 550 kg of N per hectare. Inefficient use of nitrogen fertilizers by crops leads to nitrogen-laden runoff, mostly in surface water or in groundwater. Aquifer contamination by nitrate is widespread and at dangerously high levels in many rural regions. In the U.S., it is estimated that more than 25% of drinking water wells contain nitrate levels above the 45 parts per million safety standard.[10] High nitrate levels are hazardous to human health, and studies have linked nitrate intake to metahemoglobinemia in children and gastric, and bladder and esophageal cancer in adults.[11]

Expansion of corn into drier areas, such as Kansas, requires irrigation, increasing pressure on already depleted underground sources such as the Ogallala aquifer in the Southwestern U.S. In parts of Arizona, groundwater is already being pumped at a rate ten times the natural recharge rate of these aquifers.[13]

Soy for Biodiesel
In the U.S., soy is currently the main fuel crop for the production of biodiesel. Between 2004 and 2005 biodiesel consumption increased by 50%. About 67 new refineries are under construction with investments from agribusiness

giants such as ADM and Cargill. About 1.5% of the U.S. soy harvest produces 68 million gallons of biodiesel, equivalent to less than 0.1% of consumption. Therefore, if the entire soybean harvest were dedicated to biodiesel production, it would meet only 6% of the nation's diesel needs.[13]

"ROUNDUP-READY" SOY

Most soy in the U.S. is transgenic, engineered by Monsanto to resist their proprietary herbicide, Roundup, which is made from the systemic chemical Glyphosate. In 2006, 30.3 million hectares of Roundup-Ready soy was grown in the U.S.;[14] more than 70% of the domestic crop. Reliance on herbicide-resistant soy leads to an increase in problems with weed resistance and natural vegetation loss. Given industry pressure to increase herbicide usage, increasing amounts of land will be treated with Roundup. Glyphosate resistance has already been documented in Australian populations of annual ryegrass, quackgrass, birdsfoot trefoil and Cirsium arvense.[15] In Iowa, populations of the weed Amaranthus rudis exhibited signs of delayed germination that enabled them to better adapt to earlier sprayings. The weed velvetleaf has also demonstrated glyphosate tolerance, and the presence of a Roundup-resistant strain of horseweed has been documented in Delaware. Even in areas where weed resistance has not been observed, scientists have noted increases in the presence of stronger weed species, such as Eastern Black Nightshade in Illinois and Water Hemp in Iowa.[16,17]

Data does not presently exist on levels of Roundup residues in corn and soy, as grain products are not included in conventional market surveys for pesticide residues. Nevertheless, it is known that as Glyphosate is a systemic herbicide (applied on about 12 million acres of farmland in the U.S.) that is carried into the harvested parts of plants and is not readily metabolized, thus accumulating in meristematic regions including roots and nodules.[18]

Further, information on the effects of this herbicide on soil quality is incomplete, yet research has demonstrated that glyphosate application is likely linked to the following effects:[19]

- A reduction in the ability of soybeans and clover to fix nitrogen by indirectly affecting symbiosis.

- A rendering of soy and wheat more vulnerable to disease, as evidenced by last year's increase in Fusarium wheat Head Blight in Canada.

- A decrease in the presence of soil microorganisms, which perform necessary regenerative functions including organic matter decomposition, nutrient release and cycling, and suppression of pathogenic organisms.

- Potential changes include altered soil microbial activity due to differences in the composition of root exudates, alteration of microbial populations, and toxicity in metabolic pathways that may prevent the normal growth of bacteria and fungi.

Glyphosate also has negative effects upon amphibian populations, especially that of the highly susceptible North American tadpole.[20]

Implications and Impacts in Latin America
Soybeans

The United States will not be able to produce sufficient biomass for biofuel domestically to satisfy its energy appetite. Instead, energy crops for the U.S. market will be cultivated in the Global South. Large sugarcane, oil palm, and soy plantations are already supplanting forests and grasslands in Brazil, Argentina, Colombia, Ecuador, and Paraguay. Soy cultivation has already resulted in the deforestation of 21 million hectares of forests in Brazil, 14 million hectares in Argentina, two million hectares in Paraguay and 600,000 hectares in Bolivia. In response to global market pressure, Brazil alone will likely clear an additional 60 million hectares of land in the near future.[21]

Since 1995, total land dedicated to soybean production in Brazil has increased 3.2 percent per year (320,000 hectares per year). Soybean—along with sugar cane—currently occupies the largest area of any crop in Brazil at 21 percent of the total cultivated land. The total land used for soybean cultivation has increased by a factor of 57 since 1961, and the volume of production has multiplied 138 times. Fifty-five percent of the soy crop, or 11.4 million hectares, is genetically modified. In Paraguay, soybeans occupy more than 25 percent of all agricultural land. Extensive land clearing has accompanied this expansion; for example; much of Paraguay's Atlantic forest has been cleared, in part for the soy production that comprises 29% of the country's agricultural land use.[22]

Particularly high rates of erosion accompany soy production, especially in areas where long cycles of crop rotation are not implemented. Soil cover loss averages 16 tons per hectare of soy in the U.S. Midwest. It is estimated that in Brazil and Argentina soil loss averages between 19 and 30 tons per hectare, depending on management practices, climate and incline. Herbicide tolerant soy varieties have increased the feasibility of soy production for farmers, many of whom have begun cultivation on fragile lands prone to erosion.[23]

Luis Argerich

INDUSTRIAL SOYBEAN PRODUCTION, ARGENTINA

In Argentina, intensive soybean cultivation has led to massive soil nutrient depletion. It is estimated that continuous soybean production has resulted in the loss of one million metric tons of nitrogen and 227,000 metric tons of phosphorous from soils nationwide. The cost of replenishing this nutrient loss with fertilizers is estimated to be U.S. $910 million. Increases in nitrogen and phosphorus in several river basins of Latin America is linked to the increase in soy production.[24]

Monoculture soy production in the Amazon Basin has rendered much of the soil infertile. Poor soils necessitate increased application of industrial fertilizers for competitive levels of productivity. In Bolivia, soybean production is expanding eastward, and areas in the east already suffer from compacted and degraded soils. One hundred thousand hectares of depleted former soy-growing lands have been abandoned to cattle-grazing, which leads to further degradation.[25] Biofuels are initiating a new cycle of expansion and devastation in the Cerrado and Amazon regions of Brazil. As Latin American countries increase their investment in soy cultivation for biofuel production, the associated ecological implications can be expected to intensify.

Sugarcane for Ethanol in Brazil

Brazil has produced sugar for ethanol fuel since 1975. As of 2005, there were 313 ethanol processing plants with a production capacity of 16 million cubic meters. Brazil is the largest producer of sugarcane in the world, and produces 60% of the world's total sugar ethanol with cane grown on 3 million hectares.[26] In 2005, production reached a record 16.5 billion liters, of which two billion were slated for export. Monocultures of sugarcane alone account for 13% of the nation's herbicide application. Studies conducted in 2002 by EMBRAPA (The Brazilian Agricultural Research Corporation) confirmed the presence of water contamination linked to pesticide use in the Guarani Aquifer, attributable primarily to cane growth in the State of Sao Paulo.

The U.S. is the largest importer of Brazilian ethanol, importing 58% of the nation's total production in 2006. This trade relation was reinforced by the Bush administration's 2007 ethanol agreement with Brazil. It would not be good news for Brazil if the U.S.'s Renewable Fuel Standards for ethanol proposed by the Bush administration were to be met by Brazilian sugarcane. Brazil would need to increase its production by an additional 135 billion liters per year. The planted area is rapidly expanding in the Cerrado region, whose natural vegetation cover is expected to disappear by 2030. Sixty percent of sugar-growing lands are managed by 340 large distilleries that control more than 60% of the sugarcane acreage.[27]

Given the new global energy context, Brazilian politicians and industry officials are formulating a new vision for the economic future of the country, centered on production of enough energy sources to displace 10% of world gasoline use in the next 20 years. This would require a five-fold increase in the land area devoted to sugar production, from 6 to 30 million hectares. This added cultivation will lead to land clearing in new areas, and deforestation comparable to that which occurred in the Pernambuco region, where only 2.5% of the original forest cover remains.[28]

SUGAR PLANTATION, SÃO PAOLO BRAZIL

Energy Efficiency and Economic Implications

Ethanol production is extremely energy intensive. To produce 10.6 billion liters of ethanol, the U.S. uses about 3.3 million hectares of land, which in turn requires massive energy inputs to fertilize, weed and harvest the corn.[29] These 10.6 billion liters of ethanol only provide 2% of the gasoline utilized by cars in the U.S. per year.

Despite the study of Shapouri, et. al., from the USDA[30] that reports a positive net energy return for ethanol production, Pimentel and Patzek, utilizing data from all 50 states and accounting for all energy inputs (including farm machinery manufacture and repair and fermentation-distillation equipment) conclude that ethanol production does not provide a net energy benefit. Rather, they claim that more fossil energy is required to produce ethanol than it provides. In their calculations, corn ethanol requires 1.29 gallons of fossil fuels per gallon of ethanol produced, and soy biodiesel requires 1.27 gallons of fossil energy per gallon of diesel produced. In addition, because of the relatively low energy density of ethanol, approximately three gallons of ethanol are needed to displace two gallons of gasoline.[31]

American ethanol production has benefited from $3 billion in federal and state subsidies annually ($0.54 per gallon), most of which accrues to agribusiness giants. In 1978 the U.S. introduced a tax on ethanol, but made an exception of 54 cents per gallon for that used for gasohol (gasoline with 10% ethanol). This resulted in subsidies to Archer Daniels Midland of 10 billion dollars from 1980 to 1997.[32] In 2003 more than 50% of the ethanol refineries in the U.S. were farmer owned. By 2007, over 90 percent of all new ethanol plants were absentee owned.[33]

Food Security and the Fate of Farmers

Proponents of biotechnology champion the expansion of soybean cultivation as a measure of the successful adoption of the transgenic technology by farmers. But this data conceals the fact that soybean expansion leads to extreme land and income concentration. In Brazil, soybean cultivation displaces eleven agricultural workers for every new worker it employs. This is not a new phenomenon. In the 1970s, 2.5 million people were displaced by soybean production in Parana, and 300,000 were displaced in Rio Grande do Sul. Many of these new landless people moved to the Amazon where they cleared pristine forests. In the Cerrado region, where transgenic soybean production is expanding, displacement has been relatively modest because the area is not densely populated.[34]

In Argentina, 60,000 farms foreclosed while areas planted to Roundup Ready soy nearly tripled. In 1998 there were 422,000 farms in Argentina, while in 2002 there were only 318,000; a decrease of 25 percent. In one decade, soybean area increased 126 percent at the expense of dairy, maize, wheat and fruit production. In the 2003/2004 growing season, 13.7 million hectares of soybean were planted, but there was a reduction of 2.9 million hectares in maize and 2.15 million hectares in sunflowers. For the biotech industry, huge increases in the soybean area cultivated and a doubling of yields per unit area are an economic and agronomic success. For Argentina, this means more imports of basic foods and a loss of food sovereignty, higher food prices and hunger.[35]

The advancement of the "agricultural frontier" for biofuels threatens the food sovereignty of developing nations as land for food production is increasingly devoted to feeding the cars of people in the North. Biofuel production also affects consumers directly by increasing the cost of food. Due to the fact that more than 70% of the corn grain in the U.S. is used for feedstock, doubling or tripling ethanol production can be expected to increase corn prices, and as a consequence, the price of meat. Demand for biofuels in the U.S. has been linked to a massive rise in the price of corn which led to a recent 400% increase in tortilla prices in Mexico.

Warren Rohner

Climate Change

One of the main arguments of biofuel advocates is that these new forms of energy will help mitigate climate change. But promoting large-scale mechanized monocultures that require agrochemical inputs and machinery will most likely result in an overall increase in CO_2 emissions. As carbon-capturing forests are felled to make way for biofuel crops, CO_2 emissions will increase rather than decrease.[36,37]

As countries in the Global South enter into biofuel production, development will rely primarily on exporting much of their production. Transporting this to other countries will greatly raise fuel use and gas emissions. Moreover, turning plant biomass into liquid fuels at the refineries produces immense quantities of greenhouse gas emissions.[38]

Global climate change will not be remedied by the use of industrial biofuels. There must be a fundamental shift in consumption patterns in the Global North. The only way to stop global warming is to transition away from large-scale, industrial farming toward small-scale and organic agriculture, and to decrease worldwide fuel consumption through conservation.

Conclusion

As governments are persuaded by the promises of the global biofuel market, they devise national biofuel plans that will lock their agro-systems into production based on large scale, fuel monocultures, dependent upon intensive use of herbicides and chemical fertilizers, thus diverting millions of hectares of valuable cropland from much needed food production. There is a great need for social analysis to anticipate the food security and environmental implications of the unfolding biofuel plans of small countries such as Ecuador. This country expects to expand sugarcane production by 50,000 hectares, and to clear 100,000 hectares of natural forests to give way to oil palm plantations. Oil palm plantations are already causing major environmental disaster in the Choco region of Colombia.[39]

Clearly, the ecosystems of areas in which biofuel crops are being produced are being rapidly degraded, and biofuel production is neither environmentally and socially sustainable now nor in the future.

There is no doubt that the conglomeration of petroleum and biotech capital will increasingly decide the fate of the rural landscapes of the Americas. Only strategic alliances and coordinated action of social movements (farmers' organizations, environmental and farm labor movements, NGOs, consumer lobbies, committed members of the academic sector, etc) can put pressure on governments and multinational companies to ensure that these trends are halted. More importantly, we need to work together to ensure that all countries retain the right to achieve food sovereignty via agroecologically-based, local food production systems, land reform, access to water, seeds and other resources and domestic farm and food policies that respond to the true needs of farmers and all consumers, especially the poor.

Photo and Image Credits:

1. Burning Sugar Cane: Shanna Riley, Creative Commons License (details: http://creativecommons.org/licenses/by-sa/2.0/deed.en) Photo URL: http://www.flickr.com/photos/skatoolaki/2308050201/

2. "Roundup Ready" Soy: Keith Weller, U.S. Department of Agriculture, Agricultural Research Service. Photo URL: http://www.ars.usda.gov/is/graphics/photos/k5197-3.htm

3. Industrial Soy, Argentina: Photo by Luis Argerich Creative Commons License (details: http://creativecommons.org/licenses/by/2.0/deed.en) Photo URL: http://www.flickr.com/photos/lrargerich/2362203548/

4. Sugarcane, São Paulo Fernando Stankuns, Creative Commons License (details: http://creativecommons.org/licenses/by-nc-sa/2.0/deed.en) Photo URL: http://www.flickr.com/photos/stankuns/2960142646/

5. Six Hummers!: Photo by Warren Rohner, Creative Commons License (details: http://creativecommons.org/licenses/by-sa/2.0/deed.en) Photo URL: http://www.flickr.com/photos/warrenski/2102684379/

References:

1 Gibson Consulting. 2009. Some Interesting Oil Industry Statistics - Imports/Exports. Accessed 02/09/09:http://www.gravmag.com/imports.shtml

2 Pimentel, David, Hugh Lehman. 1993. The Pesticide Question. New York: Chapman and Hall

3 Bravo, E. 2006. Biocombustibles, cutlivos energeticos y soberania alimentaria: encendiendo el debate sobre biocommustibles. Quito, Ecuador: Accion Ecologica.

4 Korten, David C. 2006. The Great Turning: From Empire to Earth Community. Berrett-Koehler Publishers.

5 Bravo, E. 2006.

6 Pimentel, D. et al. 1997. Water Resources: Agriculture, environment and society. BioScience 47: 97-106

7 Pimentel, David, Hugh Lehman. 1993. The Pesticide Question. Chapman and Hall, New York

8 Altieri, M.A. 2004. Genetic Engineering in Agriculture: The Myths, Environmental Risks and Alternatives. Oakland: Food Books.

9 Hayes, TB, A. Collins, M. Lee, M. Mendoza, N. Noriega, AA Stuart, and A. Vonk. 2002. Hermaphroditic, Demasculinized Frogs after Exposure to the Herbicide, Atrazine, at Low Ecologically Relevant Doses. Proceedings of the National Academy of Sciences (US) 99:5476-5480.

10 Conway, G.R. and J.N. Pretty. 1991. Unwelcome Harvest: Agriculture and pollution. London: Earthscan publications.

11 Dissanayake, C.B.,Weerasooriya,S.V.R. and Senarathne,A.1087. The heavy metal Pollution of the Kelani River in Sri Lanka. Aqua No.02;79-85pp,1985.

12 Pimentel, D. et al. 1997.

13 Pimentel, D and T.W. Patzek. 2005. Ethanol Production using Corn, Switchgrass, and Wood; Biodiesel Production using Soybean and Sunflower. Natural Resources Research 14: 65-76.

14 Dill, Gerald M, Claire CaJacob,Stephen R Padgette. 2008. Glyphosate-Resistant Crops: Adoption, use and future considerations. Pest Management Science, Volume 64, Number 4, April 2008 , pp. 326-331(6)

15 Altieri, Miguel. 2004. Genetic Engineering in Agriculture: The myths, environmental risks and alternatives. Oakland: Food First Books.

16 Ibid.

17 Certeira, A.L. and S.O. Duke. 2006. The Current Status and Environmental Impacts of Glyphosate-Resistant Crops.   Journal of Environmental Quality 35: 1633-1658

18 Duke, S.O., S.R.Baerson, A.M.Rimando. 2003.Herbicides: Glyphosate. Encyclopedia of Agrochemicals. HTTP://WWW.MRW.INTERSCIENCE.WILEY.COM/EOA/ ARTICLES/AGR119/FRAME.HTML

19 Motavalli*,P.P., R. J. Kremerb, M. Fanga & N. E. Meansa. 2004. Impact of genetically modified crops and their management on soil microbially mediated plant nutrient transformations," J. Environ. Qual. 33:816-824

20 Relyea, R.A. 2005. The Impact of Insecticides and Herbicides on the Biodiversity and Productivity of Aquatic Communities. Ecological Applications 15 : 618-627

21 Bravo, E. 2006.

22 Altieri, Miguel and Walter Pengue. 2006. GM Soybean: Latin America's new colonizer. Grain.org. Seedling: January 2006. Accessed 02/09/09: http://www.grain.org/seedling/ index.cfm?id=421#_14

23 Jason, C. 2004. World Agriculture and the Environment. Washington: Island Press.

24 Pimentel, D. 2003. Ethanol Fuels: Energy balance, economics and environmental impacts are negative. Natural Resources Research 12: 127-134

25 Fearnside, P.M. 2001. Soybean Cultivation as a Threat to the Environment in Brazil. Environmental Conservation 28: 23.

26 Jason, C. 2004.

27 Bravo, E. 2006.

28 Fearnside, P.M. 2001.

29 Pimentel, D. 2003.

30 Shapouri, Hosein, James Duffield, Andrew McAloon. 2004. The 2001 Net Energy Balance of Corn Ethanol. U.S. Department of Agriculture.Accessed 02/09/09: http://www. ethanol-gec.org/netenergy/NEYShapouri.htm

31 Pimentel, D and T.W. Patzek. 2005. Ethanol Production using Corn, Switchgrass, and Wood; Biodiesel Production using Soybean and Sunflower. Natural Resources Research 14: 65-76

32 Bravo, E. 2006.

33 Morris, David. 2008. Cellulosic Biofuels: Another Opportunity for Washington to Marry Agriculture and Energy Goals. Institute for Local Self-Reliance. Accessed 02/09/09: http://www.ilsr.org/columns/2008/05-2008ethanoltoday.pdf

34 Altieri, Miguel and Walter Pengue. 2006.

35 Pengue, Walter. 2005. Transgenic Crops in Argentina: The ecological and social debt. Bulletin of Science, Technology and Society 25: 314-322.
36 Bravo, E. 2006.
37 Donald, P.F. 2004, Biodiversity Impacts of Some Agricultural Commodity Production Systems. Conservation Biology18:17-37.
38 Pimentel, D. and T.W. Patzek. 2005.
39 Bravo, E. 2006.

PART THREE

The Future: "Next
Generation" Agrofuels and the
Transformation of Life

THE AGROFUELS TROJAN HORSE: BIOTECHNOLOGY AND THE CORPORATE DOMINATION OF AGRICULTURE

BY ANNIE SHATTUCK

SOYBEANS

Biotechnology is poised to strike at our agricultural system on a scale never before imagined. Ten years after the launch of biotech in agriculture, the debate rages on. Consumers, farmer's organizations, social movements and environmental advocates all fiercely oppose biotechnology in agriculture, while the industry has continued to expand its presence in the developing world, often through undemocratic means. But resistance, and effectively all public debate on biotech, may well be put to rest for good by the world's growing dependence on agrofuels. The sunny glow of alternative fuels helps lend biotech the public credibility it has lacked since its market debut. While new traits for agrofuels are already helping corporations amass unprecedented market power, a pipeline of new fuel crops stands waiting in the wings. The new pipeline will have much the same effect as previous biotech offerings: contamination of public genetic resources and even further industry consolidation. Agrofuels are the perfect Trojan Horse, promising not only whole new markets for biotech products, but the irreversible entrenchment of genetically modified crops throughout the world.

Background: The Birth of an Oligopoly

How did we get here? A brief look at the history of consolidation in the biotech industry paints a disturbing picture of what is to come.

Riding the waves of the Green Revolution in the 1960's and '70s, large agricultural chemical corporations that formerly specialized in chemical weapons began buying up small seed companies to compliment their nascent agricultural chemicals businesses. In the eighties, when agricultural biotechnology was being developed, these companies were the first to jump on board. Over the last decade, with the global spread of biotechnology, the hybrid seed-chemical-biotechnology industry (from here on biotech) consolidated. In 1998, the top ten seed companies controlled 30% of the global market. Now, that same market share is controlled by only two companies.[1,2] This latest round of consolidation was fueled by biotechnology itself. Genetic modification (GM) has been used to vertically integrate market power, allowing the same companies that sell seed to also sell the herbicides and other inputs these GM crops require.

Shubert Ciencia

BT (BACILLUS THURINGIENSIS) CORN

The pattern of technological development in GM is to develop traits that increase dependence of farmers on the biotech industry. The first and most widely planted products are the "Roundup Ready" or herbicide-tolerant products; crop species like corn, soy, and cotton that are resistant to the herbicide glyphosate. Monsanto, Syngenta, and DuPont all sell glyphosate resistant seeds as well as the herbicide itself, often in a package. This technology has not only dramatically boosted the sales of glyphosate, but it has become so widespread as to undercut farmers' use of non-chemical alternatives and integrated weed management systems, fostering farmers' dependence on both the patented seed and the herbicide.[3] The much discussed "terminator gene," another early biotech trait, would have served to ensure farmers' dependence on licensed products by physically preventing farmers from saving seed, had the technology gained regulatory approval (the industry is still pushing for this). Even Bt corn, a variety that produces a natural pesticide in the stem of corn plants, increases the share of the seed market subject to strong-arm patent laws and licensing fees, while eroding the effectiveness of Bt as part of a more holistic integrated pest management system.[4] The economic function of these foreign genetic traits is not to decrease chemical use, but to increase market dominance and control over the agro-input industry by the corporations holding the patents.

Integrating agrochemical sales with patented seed has worked extremely well for big biotech. In 2006, Monsanto alone controlled 20% of the global seed market, worth nearly $4.5 billion annually. The top three seed companies now control nearly 40% of the global market.[5] All this investment and market dominance has fueled the quest for even more control. In the past ten years the pace of mergers and acquisitions between former chemical companies, smaller biotechnology firms, and the big seed sellers has outstripped all expectations. In a span of eight weeks in 1998, Monsanto absorbed four major agricultural biotechnology firms, including two of the top ten seed sellers in the world at the time.[6] This pattern of swallowing up smaller biotechnology and seed companies continues apace.

Consumer Rejection Threatens Markets

Biotechnology wasn't always so good to Monsanto however. In 2002 alone, Monsanto lost a staggering $1.7 billion. Monsanto invests 80% of their research and development budget on ag-biotechnology,[7] producing foods being met with staunch consumer rejection in Europe and parts of North America. After 2002's stunning losses, the company's future, and the future of biotechnology in agriculture itself looked grim. Public campaigns by major environmental groups including Greenpeace labeled GM food as unhealthy and dangerous "Frankenfoods." Prospects for market growth were limited because of the difficulty of gaining regulatory approval for GM plantings outside of the U.S., Canada, and Argentina. In fact, because the controversy generated by GM food was so strong, the Monsanto and the biotech industry it pioneered faced the very serious threat of losing a market for their investments.[8]

Then miraculously, Monsanto experienced a turnaround. Brazil, once dead set against the cultivation of GM crops within their borders, opened the country

INDUSTRIAL SOYBEAN PLANTATIONS, MATO GROSSO, BRAZIL

to both GM soybeans (for which they are the second largest exporter behind the U. S.) and Monsanto's best selling herbicide, Roundup. GM soy was pushed through the Brazilian legislature as fait acompli. Farmers in southern Brazil were already planting Monsanto's Roundup Ready soy, and Monsanto argued Brazil was impeding their legal right to collect royalties on their intellectual property,[9, 10] a position that would leave Brazil vulnerable in international trade proceedings. However, according to Terra de Direitos (Land of Rights), a civil society organization based in Curitiba, Brazil, Monsanto was actually encouraging farmers to plant illegally imported Roundup Ready soybeans from Argentina much before this supposed "seed piracy" was used to push through legalization.[11,12] GM soy was legalized in 2003. In 2004, a congressman from southern Brazil, pushed through a series of federal amendments legalizing the herbicide glyphosate, or Roundup, the necessary partner to Monsanto's soy. The Brazilian government is currently investigating the congressman for corruption after he purchased a large farm from Monsanto at one third the market price.[13] Monsanto's sales of Roundup went up 30% after the corrupt Brazilian land deal.[14]

The fact that Monsanto was forced to use illegal tactics to enter the Brazilian market illustrates the strength of public resistance to their products. Even in the U. S., where 50% of corn, 90% of soy, and 80% of cotton are genetically modified, consumers are still resistant to GM foods. A 2004 survey done by the Food Policy Institute at Rutgers University indicated that 41% of Americans disapproved of the technology.[15] The level of awareness of GM foods however is low. The Rutgers study indicates that only 31% of American consumers believe they have ever consumed a GM product (nearly all processed foods sold in the

U.S. contain GM ingredients), and 89% said they think GM products should be labeled.[16] After labels were required on all food products that contain GM ingredients in Europe, GM food virtually disappeared from European shelves.[17] Rejection of GM technology is strongest in the European Union, where, according to a recent WTO ruling, the reticence of EU regulators to approve new GM varieties constitutes an illegal trade barrier.[18] From small nations like Sri Lanka, whose government only withdrew plans for a popular GM ban when threatened with WTO lawsuits,[19] to powerful social movements like Brazil's Landless Worker's Movement, which demands a ban on all forms of genetic use restriction,[20] the global tide of public opinion is turning against transgenic food.

Monsanto may have saved their business (and perhaps the biotech industry) in the short run by strong-arming their way into the Brazilian market, but they cannot force consumers to want their products. The biotech industry is constantly faced with the threat of market contraction and consumer rejection. This leaves the industry two options: either quickly recycle their capital, as they did in the 1970's when chemical companies switched from producing warfare-related chemicals like Agent Orange to producing agricultural inputs, or somehow turn global public opinion in their favor. *With the onset of the agrofuels boom, the biotech industry hopes to do both.*

Corn Ethanol: Harbinger of the New Ag-Economy

With the signing of the 2007 Energy Bill, President Bush committed the nation to a Renewable Fuels Standard which will, according to Republican Senator Pete Dominici, "use ethanol and a new generation of advanced biofuels to displace oil."[21] The standard pushes an already growing market for liquid biofuels, to 36 billion gallons a year by 2022. While 36 billion gallons represents only a fraction of the U. S.'s total fuel consumption, it opens a bonanza of investment and even further consolidation in the agricultural industry, what many have dubbed the "Agrofuels Boom." The Renewable Fuels Standards (RFS) in Europe and the U.S. mandate the use of more corn ethanol than is physically possible for either region to produce, driving the transformation of corn for food to GM "dedicated energy crops." While language in both RFS suggest an eventual move to alternate feedstocks, the biotech industry's foray into fuel corn gives us a picture of what future markets for agrofuel feedstocks might look like.

Both Monsanto and Syngenta have recently come out with genetically modified varieties specifically for processing into ethanol. According to industry, increased processing efficiency and higher yield of ethanol per bushel for these varieties will benefit both the ethanol refiners and farmers. However, farmer's marketing options are much more limited with these newly-patented energy crops. In an indication of what is to come, Monsanto and agribusiness giant Cargill have recently launched a joint venture called Renessen, a whole new corporation with an initial investment of $450 million dollars. Renessen is the sole provider of the first commercially available GM dedicated energy crop, "Mavera High-Value Corn." Mavera corn is stacked with foreign genetic material coding for increased oil content and production of the amino acid lysine, along with Monsanto's standard Bt pesticide and its Roundup Ready gene. The genius of this operation, and the danger to farmers, is that farmers must sell their crop of Mavera corn to a Renessen-owned processing plant to recoup the "higher value" of the crop (for which they paid a premium on the seed). Cargill's agricultural processing division has created a plant that only processes their brand of corn. Further, due to the genetically engineered presence of lysine, an amino acid lacking in the standard feedlot diet, they can sell the waste stream as a high priced cattle feed. Renessen has achieved for Monsanto and Cargill nearly perfect vertical integration. Renessen sets the price of seed, Monsanto sells the chemical inputs, Renessen sets the price at which to buy back the finished crop, Renessen sells the fuel, and farmers are left to absorb the risk. This system robs small farmers of choices and market power, while ensuring maximum monopoly profits for Renessen/Monsanto/Cargill.

Resistance to corn ethanol however, is strong among farmer's movements and environmental groups. Even in official policy circles corn ethanol is seen as a temporary step towards "second generation" fuel crops. U.S. federal subsidies to corn ethanol are politically unsustainable, and numerous studies have questioned its energy efficiency, claiming ethanol yields less energy than it eats up in production.[22, 23, 24] Civil society groups have also accused ethanol of robbing food from the mouths of the poor. This food vs. fuel debate has been the most damaging for the image of agrofuels. Agrofuels were blamed as one of the reasons the price of tortillas in Mexico shot up 400%, leading to widespread protests and an eventual government cap on prices.[25] The recent spike in global food prices has sparked food revolts in Italy, Morocco, Mauritania, Senegal, Indonesia, Burkina Faso, Cameroon, and Yemen. In Egypt and Haiti over a dozen protesters were killed in food-related protests. While the ethanol industry's champions proudly claim "We drink the best and drive the rest!"[26] For many people burning food in a world with 824 million hungry people is clearly immoral.

While sales of GM corn and soy for agrofuels climb steadily, these crops do little to solve the biotech industry's PR problem. Advanced energy crops, like cellulosic ethanol, promise to open new markets for biotech products and put to bed the issue of consumer rejection once and for all.

Second Generation Energy Crops: Power and Profit Painted Green

The biotech industry promises to develop a "second generation" of new cellulose-based energy crops that can grow on land unusable for modern agriculture, eliminating the food vs. fuel debate currently plaguing the agrofuels industry. They promise to use environmentally friendly native plants like switchgrass, to produce carbon-neutral fuels, and to reduce chemical inputs on these new green energy plantations by engineering plants to grow in resource poor areas. Greater efficiency, opportunities for small farmers, and nothing less than the complete revitalization of rural economies are all supposed to come down the magic biotechnology pipeline in the form of cellulosic energy crops. Cellulosics are inedible but little understood, making all the mythology surrounding them easier for the public to swallow. Perhaps best of all for the biotech industry, second generation ethanol, like cellulosic, promises to open brand new proprietary markets for the biotechnology products being rejected by consumers worldwide.

Cellulosic energy crops can conceivably be produced from any plant material: corn stalks, trees, sugar cane biomass, or grasses. One might ask, with so many possibilities for feedstock, why biotechnology stands to play such a large role. Biotechnology addresses two key factors: processing efficiency and yield. For example, "Energycane," a new product in the pipeline at Ceres, Inc., in which Monsanto is a key equity shareholder, is merely sugarcane with genetic coding for increased biomass and decreased sugar content, i.e. a higher yield of cellulose. Other biotech traits aim at faster growth, shorter time until maturity, increased oil content, and frost or drought tolerance, all traits that attempt to conform nature to an industrial model.

Like first generation biotech traits, many of the energy traits being developed are designed for opening and dominating markets. In fact, many of these traits will create markets from scratch, augment the already lucrative markets for chemical inputs, and deliver the full control of these markets to the tightly packed corporations of the biotech industry. What do these new traits look like?

- *Range expansion, drought/freeze tolerance, growth on marginal land* – Some of the most highly advertised traits being developed allow a plant to escape its own physiological limitations to grow on poor soils, in water scarce regions, and to withstand freezing temperatures. In other words, these traits aim to make industrial monocrops grow where they otherwise could not. Expanding the range of energy crops will expand the acreage under industrial agriculture worldwide, and with it, a dramatic expansion in the market for seed, fertilizers, pesticides, and other inputs, conveniently sold by the same group developing this technology. Mendel Biotechnology, a privately controlled firm with heavy investments by Monsanto and British Petroleum, has already identified and isolated genes for these new traits.

- *Increased biomass and faster growth* – The biotech industry is working on code for faster growing plants that put more energy into producing biomass, or overall material, than specific products like sugars, nuts, oils, and tubers. What fast growing really means, though, is high nitrogen consuming. Nitrogen, in the form of nitrates and ammonium, is the primary limiting factor in plant growth. Plants that are good at using nitrogen and can use a lot of it quickly, will grow faster, and produce more biomass. This is all well, except that in industrial agriculture the pressure of high-density, high-nitrogen using plants rapidly depletes soil nutrients, making the system more dependent on chemical fertilizers. Increased biomass is also a physiological trade-off. Plants like the GE sorghum being developed by Ceres Incorporated (a small biotech firm with significant equity investment from Monsanto), trade their ability to produce a food product for increased biomass. Farmers growing this crop in the future will have to accept the price offered by the nearest ethanol refinery, instead of having diverse local and international food markets to fall back on when commodity prices inevitably fluctuate.

- *Reduced lignin content in trees* – Lignin is the woody compound in the cell wall that gives trees both their structural integrity and their resistance to pests. Lignin is also what makes it difficult to pulp trees into paper and unlock cellulose in wood to produce ethanol. ArborGen, a biotechnology firm with heavy investments from the industrial forestry industry, is developing trees with 20% reduced lignin content. This development could necessitate the use of pesticides in plantation forests, because some of the natural pest resistance will have been engineered out of the trees. Because genetic modification of tree species is a relatively new field, only a few companies have invested in GM trees. This means that competition in the field will be next to nothing, ensuring a global monopoly. The CEO of Rubicon, an industrial forestry company and one of three owners of ArborGen, notes "the annual unit sales of forestry seedlings are well into the billions, recur every year, and span the globe. ...there are no global competitors to ArborGen."[27]

- *Proprietary GM Enzymes, Bacteria and Catalysts* – Processing cellulose into sugars is the largest hurdle in making cellulosic ethanol practical. At its current stage, processing is vastly inefficient. Much disagreement exists as to when and if cellulosic processing will be efficient. Some reports say it will arrive within the next two years, others claim it will never come. Regardless of doubts about the technology, the engineering of new enzymes and bacteria that can break down cellulose is a multi-million dollar race. Large ag-biotech corporations and oil companies are partnering with smaller startup biotech firms to control the keys to unlocking the potential of cellulosic ethanol. Codexis, one of the leading developers of GE enzymes is partnering with Syngenta and Shell Oil Corporation for its research and development, while Iogen Corporation is funded by the major venture-capital firm Goldman-Sachs as well as Shell. Some enzyme biotechnology firms also own ethanol processing plants, like the Kholsa Ventures funded company, Range Fuels. Patents on this technology will essentially put a stranglehold on the cellulosic ethanol market. Whoever controls the most efficient catalysts will have a virtual monopoly on processing fuel, meaning that feedstock prices paid at the farm gate will be set by the processor, robbing farmers of market power yet again.

The Cellulosic Halo

After ten years of controversy, the biotech industry is basking in the rosy halo of second generation energy crops. None of these crops are destined for our food supply; a fact that the industry hopes will ease public distaste for biotechnology. Investors have poured untold billions into cellulosic energy crops, counting on them to simultaneously clear up biotech's nasty public image and create whole new markets for its products. The potential value of these new markets is not to be underestimated. Some of the largest venture capital firms in the U.S., Kholsa Ventures, Goldman-Sachs, Warburg-Pincus, and Soros Fund Management, to name a few, have invested hundreds of millions of dollars in dedicated energy crops and cellulase enzymes. With plenty of capital and political clout, competition between industries seems to be minimal, with corporate partnerships the norm. British Petroleum has partnered with Monsanto and Mendel Biotechnology, Royal Dutch Shell with Cargill, and Syngenta, and DuPont with British Petroleum.[28]

But cellulosic ethanol is not just a matter of making an existing technology market-ready. Rather, much like the dream of nuclear fusion, it will depend on major breakthroughs in our understanding and manipulation of plant physiology. Investors claim the second generation agrofuels revolution will be bigger and more lucrative than the IT revolution. Because the stakes are so high (and because the world is experiencing a glut of venture and finance capital), big bets are being placed by big players. In second-generation roulette, whoever cracks the cellulose code will likely win the controlling share in the world's food *and* fuel systems.

But regardless of whether cellulosics are ever commercialized on a grand scale, these investments are already improving the image of both agrofuels and GE. Proponents say that the first generation agrofuels are merely building infrastructure for the second, cleaner round of fuels, and that without corn and sugarcane, switchgrass could never be viable. Belief in cellulosics as a gasoline substitute is blind faith that technology can liberate us from the constraints of finite resources. The very idea that cellulosics will ever be viable gives them a futuristic halo, transforming biotechnology from a very real environmental threat to our collective savior.

Investing in second generation agrofuels politically legitimizes the current astronomical profits and market control being swallowed by the biotech industry. Monsanto posted over $689 million in profits in 2007. Syngenta netted $1.1 billion. Global production of agrofuels has tripled over the past three years, as have Monsanto and Syngenta's stock prices. The link is no coincidence: the companies themselves credit the rise in profits to agrofuels. A recent article in Business Weekly outlined the connection even more explicitly: Monsanto's stock prices are more closely correlated with the price of oil than Exxon

Mobil's.[29] Over the past year, the price of a barrel of crude tracked Monsanto's stock prices at a correlation of 0.94 (the highest possible correlation value is 1.0). The price of corn, Monsanto's most important product, barely correlates to Monsanto's stock prices at all, coming in at a scant 0.17.[30] What we are seeing, between the heavy investment in fuel traits and biotech's soaring profit margins, is a growing dependence on ethanol. With profits this high during a powerful recession, it doesn't matter if cellulosic takes ten or twenty years to reach even a scant percentage of the public. The profits are being made now. The mere *dream* of second generation ethanol is breaking down the gates to biotechnology in agriculture.

Roberto Vincinio

LANDLESS WORKERS OCCUPY A MONSANTO GM EUCALYPTUS PLANTATION IN BRAZIL

If The Horse Enters the Gates...

Once in the field, there is no way to prevent GM fuel crops from contaminating their food-crop cousins. Cases of genetic contamination are commonplace. In the past 2 years alone, there were at least 73 publicly documented cases of genetic contamination.[31] Proving contamination can be difficult, making the actual amount of genetic pollution hard to judge, but likely much higher than reported. GM corn traits were even found in native corn varieties in the mountains of Oaxaca, Mexico, where GM corn was never legally grown.[32] In fact, every commercial fuel crop so far is under consideration or has been approved for human consumption in the U.S. without long term independent testing. This includes Syngenta's fuel corn with traits from a deep sea bacteria that has never come in contact with humans, much less entered our food chain.[33, 34] The danger of an agronomically flat, GMO world is that it leaves our food systems vulnerable to climate change events and pest and disease outbreaks. Agrofuels based on GMOs and controlled by a handful of corporate giants do not lessen our vulnerability, they worsen it. Once GM agrofuels have entered the agricultural gates they will soon escape into the wild, contaminating food crops across the globe. Nothing short of a sustained, coordinated (and expensive) international eradication campaign will rein them in.

While big biotech corporations claiming to have the future answer to the energy crisis are raking in profits, the debate on genetic engineering in agriculture rages on. Consumer acceptance of GM food has not grown in the past ten years, but by taking the back door left open by agrofuels, biotechnology in agriculture is about to become the standard.

The Food Bait and Switch Crisis

The fact that agrofuels have exacerbated the vulnerabilities in our food systems, leading to rampant food price inflation and food rebellions across the globe reveals an evil irony. In a sleight of hand that draws our attention away from the fact that they created the crisis in the first place, big grain, seed and chemical companies now claim that in order to solve the crisis we need more GMOs. Their message is clear; "Don't worry about the displacement of food crops by agrofuels, or the contamination of our genetic diversity, just buy more crop-based fuel and more GM seeds and we will consume our way out of the food and fuel crises."

We don't need agrofuel plantations to solve our energy problems. Neither do we need GMOs to overcome food price inflation or to combat hunger. In the words of many activists, "We need to turn the industrial food system on its head." The vision for a new food system is well reflected in the growing movement for food sovereignty, "the right of all people to healthy and culturally appropriate food produced through ecologically sound and sustainable methods, and their right to define their own food and agriculture systems." This means dismantling the control companies like ADM, Cargill, Bunge, Monsanto, Syngenta and DuPont exercise over our food systems—control that is held in place both by regulations—like the renewable fuel standards—that force us to consume

DIVERSE AGRICULTURAL PRODUCTION, BOLIVIA

their products, and the GM technologies that limit our options to one: theirs. We need to support movements for food sovereignty that promote policies and technologies for local rather than international markets; for keeping people on the land, rather than driving them off; and for bringing genetic diversity back into agriculture, rather than reducing it to the GMO patents held by a few corporate oligopolies.

The international farmers' movement La Via Campesina sees seeds as the "heritage of mankind for the good of all humanity." The movement offers a drastically different vision of agriculture from the industrial model being pushed through the agrofuels boom, a model based on family agriculture, locally cultivated seeds, and food sovereignty. Increasingly, they are being joined by movements for community food security and neighborhood food systems throughout the industrial North. As farmers and consumers of the global North and South come together on food sovereignty—in policy and in practice— we will find ways to take back our food systems. Rolling back the industrial onslaught of GMOs is key to establishing food systems that serve the needs of the majority. Stopping the agrofuels boom, with its attendant corporate-owned GMOs, is an essential step in this challenge.

Photo and Image Credits:

1. Soybeans: Photo by Ken Colwell Creative Commons License (details: http://creativecommons.org/licenses/by-nc-sa/2.0/deed.en) Photo URL: http://www.flickr.com/photos/kcolwell/2886767927/
2. Bacillus Thuringiencis Corn: Photo by Shubert Ciencia Creative Commons License (details: http://creativecommons.org/licenses/by/2.0/deed.en) Photo URL: http://www.flickr.com/photos/bigberto/2838972365/
3. Soybean Farm Mato Grosso, Brazil: Photo by Leonardo F. Freitas Creative Commons License (Details: http://creativecommons.org/licenses/by-nc-sa/2.0/deed.en) Photo URL: http://www.flickr.com/photos/leoffreitas/790063686/
4. MST Protesters: Photo by Roberto Vinicius/ Creative Commons License (details: http://creativecommons.org/licenses/by-nc-nd/2.0/deed.en) Photo URL: http://www.flickr.com/photos/robvini/498862842
5. Diverse Agriculture, Bolivia: Photo by Sam Beebe, Ecotrust Creative Commons License (details: http://www.flickr.com/photos/sbeebe/3274210237/) Photo URL: http://www.flickr.com/photos/sbeebe/3274210237/

References:

1   ETC Group 2007. "The World's Top Ten Seed Companies 2006" October 2007. http://www.etcgroup.org/en/materials/publications.html?pub_id=615
2   RAFI Rural Advancement Foundation International. 1998. "Seed Industry Consolidation: Who Owns Whom?" *Communique.* July/August 1998.
3   Benbrook, Charles. 2003. "Principles Governing the Long-Run Risks, Benefits, and Costs of Agricultural Biotechnology. paper presented at Conference on Biodiversity, Biotechnology and the Protection of Traditional Knowledge. April 3, 2003. http://www.biotech-info.net/biod_biotech.pdf
4   ibid.
5   ETC Group 2007a. "The World's Top Ten Seed Companies 2006" October 2007. http://www.etcgroup.org/en/materials/publications.html?pub_id=615
6   RAFI Rural Advancement Foundation International. 1998. "Seed Industry Consolidation: Who Owns Whom?" *Communique.* July/August 1998.
7   Schonfeld, Erick. 2005. Betting the Farm. *CNNMoney.* September 1, 2005. http://money.cnn.com/magazines/business2/business2 archive/2005/09/01/8356513/index.htm
8   ibid.
9   ibid.
10 Kenfield, Isabella. 2006. "Monsanto's Seeds of Corruption in Brazil." *NACLANews.* North American Congress on Latin America. 16 October 2006. http://news.nacla.org/2006/10/16/monsantos-seeds-of-corruption-in-brazil/
11 ibid.
12 Lee, Rennie. 2007. "Allied with Brazilian Agribusiness, Syngenta Resists Governor's Decree to Expropriate Site" Americas Program, Center for International Policy. May 17, 2007 http://americas.irc-online.org/am/4239

13 ibid.

14 Kenfield, Isabella. 2006. "Monsanto's Seeds of Corruption in Brazil."
    NACLANews. North American Congress on Latin America. 16 October 2006.
    http://news.nacla.org/2006/10/16/monsantos-seeds-of-corruption-in-brazil/

15 Hallman, W. K., Hebden, W. C., Cuite, C. L., Aquino, H. L., and Lang, J. T.
    2004. Americans and GM Food: Knowledge, Opinion and Interest in 2004.
    (Publication number RR-1104-007). New Brunswick, New Jersey; Food Policy
    Institute, Cook College, Rutgers - The State University of New Jersey.
    http://www.foodpolicyinstitute.org

16 ibid.

17 Holbach, Martina and Lindsay Keenan. 2005. "EU Markets: No Market
    for GM Labelled Food in Europe." Greenpeace International. Amsterdam,
    Netherlands. January 2005. http://www.greenpeace.org/eu-unit/press-centre/
    reports/no-market-for-gm-labelled-food

18 Kanter, James. 2007. "WTO gives EU more time on genetically modified foods."
    International Herald Tribune. November 22, 2007.

19 Lopez, Juan, Ann Doherty, Niccolo Sarno, and Larry Bohlen. 2005 "Genetically
    Modified Food: A decade of failure (1994-2004)" Friends of the Earth
    International. February 2005. http://www.foei.org/en/publications/pdfs/gm_
    decade.pdf

20 MST. 2007 "Small Scale Sustainable Farmers are Cooling Down the Earth" *MST
    Informa*. Movimento dos Trabalhadores Rurais Sem Terra. N. 145 November 30,
    2007. http://www.mstbrazil.org/?q=node/552

21 Letourneau, Matthew. 2007. "President Bush Signs Energy Bill Into Law" Press
    Release, United States Senate Committee on Energy and Natural Resources.
    December 19, 2007.

22 Pimentel, David. 2005. "Weighing in on Renewable Energy" *Geotimes*. 50 (18).

23 Crutzen, P.J., A.R. Mosier, K.A. Smith, and W. Winiwarter. "Nitrous oxide release
    from agro-biofuel production negates global warming reduction by replacing fossil
    fuels" *Atmospheric Chemistry and Physics*. Disucss ., 7 11191-11205, 2007

24 Searchinger et al. 2008. "Use of U.S. Croplands for Biofuels Increases Greenhouse
    Gases Through Emissions from Land Use Change." *Science*. 319 (1238).

25 BBC News. "Mexicans Stage Tortilla Protest." BBC News MMVIII. February 1,
    2007. http://news.bbc.co.uk/2/hi/americas/6319093.stm

26 BIOWA Director Michael Ott

27 Langelle, Orin and Anne Petermann. 2006. "Plantations, GM trees and indigenous
    rights." *Seedling*. GRAIN. July 2006.

28 ETC Group. 2007. "Peak Oil + Peak Soil = Peak Spoils" *Communique*. N. 96,
    November/December 2007.

29 Hindo, Brian. 2008. "Monsanto's Rich Harvest." *BusinessWeek*. January 4, 2008.

30 ibid.

31 GM Contamination Register. GeneWatch UK and Greenpeace International.
    www.gmcontaminationregister.org, accessed on 8 April 2008.

32 Quist, David and Ignacio H. Chapela. "Trasgenic DNA introgressed into
    traditional maize landraces in Oaxaca, Mexico" *Nature*. Vol. 414 November 2001

33 Bonnette, Richard E. 2007. "Biotechnology Consultation Note to the File BNF
    No. 000095" Center for Food Safety and Applied Nutrition, Office of Food
    Additive Safety. U.S. Food and Drug Administration. August 7, 2007. http://www.
    cfsan.fda.gov/~rdb/bnfm095.html

34 African Centre for Biosafety. 2006. "Comments on Syngenta's Application for
    Commodity Clearance of Genetically Modified Maize, Event 3272." 29 May
    2006. http://www.biosafetyafrica.net/

CHAPTER VIII

MAGICAL, MYTH-ILLOGICAL BIOLOGICAL FUELS?
BY RACHEL SMOLKER & BRIAN TOKAR

CORN STOVER

"First generation" Biofuels; made from sugar cane, corn, wheat, cassava, vegetable oils and other edible food crops have resulted in a host of problems. These include (but are not limited to) rapid food price increases caused in significant part by the diversion of food crops and agricultural resources into fuel production, greenhouse gas emissions resulting from land use change when biodiverse and carbon rich forest and grassland ecosystems are converted to agriculture, greenhouse gas emissions and ecosystem damage from the excessive use of nitrogen and other fertilizers, depletion and contamination of dwindling freshwater resources, displacement of smallholder farming for local food consumption and loss of agricultural diversity, human rights abuses; and rural and indigenous populations kicked off their traditional lands as a result of land grabs by corporate producers

The food crisis of 2007-2008 served as a catalyst to reevaluate the wisdom of diverting food into fuel production. While the urgency of the food crisis is indeed critical, the fixation on that issue to the exclusion of the other problems has allowed "second generation" advocates to claim that corn ethanol and other first generation technologies are merely a "stepping stone" towards new and improved "advanced" agrofuel technologies that will avoid the food versus fuel pitfalls and lead us to salvation.

Specifically, they claim that second generation fuels will 1) be available very soon, and 2) will not compete with food production because they will 3) utilize abundantly available, inedible plant material, including wastes and residues and energy crops that can be 4) grown on widely available "marginal" and "idle"

155

lands, 5) providing opportunities for the poor, and 6) achieve improved energy and greenhouse gas balances.

But are these claims valid? A cautious and comprehensive analysis is not only prudent, but absolutely critical given the crises of climate change and political instability which these fuels are intended to address. The rapid escalation of problems created by the "first generation" of biofuels and the fact that little margin for error in addressing climate change remains means that we simply cannot afford to be mistaken on this matter.

Yet proponents, including the new U.S. Obama administration, seem ready and eager, (perhaps even desperate) to blindly leap from the corn and cane ethanol bandwagon straight onto the grass, wood-chip and "wastes and residues" bandwagon, apparently having learned little about precaution from their first wild ride!

What follows is an assessment of the "6 myths" of second generation agrofuels that points out why they will not only fail to resolve the problems encountered with the first generation, but will in fact worsen them and introduce some additional risks and problems.

What are Second Generation Agrofuels?

Second generation agrofuels are fuels derived from plant material. But unlike ethanol made from starches and sugars in edible plant parts, second generation fuels make use of the inedible "woody" parts of grasses, wood, straw, corn stover, rice hulls etc. They also use other forms of biomass such as municipal solid waste, construction waste, used tires and plastics, agricultural waste, animal manure, meat-packing waste, food processing waste, spent pulping liquor, cooking oil, paper mill residue, and wastewater treatment sludge. The terms "cellulosic" fuels and "advanced biofuels" are also used, but the distinctions among different fuel technologies and their intended end uses are not so clear cut. The ultimate "vision" advanced by the U.S. Department of Energy (DOE) and others is one of "integrated biorefineries" wherein large amounts of feedstocks are converted not only into liquid transportation fuel; but also into heat and electricity, chemicals and various co-products.

On the horizon are emerging new technologies that convert plant matter directly into hydrocarbons identical to those in petroleum. These have the advantage that the fuel can be transported through existing infrastructure and burned in existing engines, (unlike ethanol which is too corrosive) and may be favored once they are more fully developed. Therefore the term "cellulosic ethanol" is not altogether satisfactory at this point, and the broader term "second generation" is preferable.

Converting plant matter into fuels has proven more difficult than expected. Woody biomass is composed of cellulose, hemicellulose and lignin (a structural material). Cellulose makes up more than half of the total organic carbon in the biosphere. Highly resistant to biological degradation, it is the major structural component of plant cell walls.[1] The stems of woody plants contain about 50 percent cellulose and about 25 percent lignin.[2] Lignin provides trees with resistance to decay and disease, and is even more resistant to biological digestion than cellulose. In nature, it is only broken down by specialized species of bacteria, fungi, and cows and termites that retain cellulose digesting microbes in their digestive tracts. This should come as no surprise since plants have evolved over millions of years to protect their energy stores. If the sugars in cellulose were readily accessible, naturally voracious animals and microbes would quickly strip the earth bare.

Numerous technologies are being explored, but for the most part they rely on either thermal processes (gasification and pyrolysis), microbial enzymes that can break down, digest and ferment cellulose, or chemical treatments (transesterification of fats, and pretreatments using acid hydrolysis, for example).[3]

In many cases these processes result in intermediate products, gases and oils for example, which can then be further refined into more usable forms, as well as "coproducts" for which further uses and markets are sought. In general, thermal processes require considerable amounts of energy input, but can handle more diverse feedstocks. Processes that use microbial enzymes would require less energy input, but more homogenous feedstocks. Biotechnology companies such as Verenium and Genencor in the U.S., and Novozymes in Denmark, are working to simplify production of enzymes that digest cellulose, for example by modifying the enzymes used by termites to break down woody material.[4] Others are investigating microbes that live in extreme environments, from volcanoes to insects' digestive tracts, hoping to find organisms with unique digestive properties. Companies like Virent, Amyris and LS9 are using synthetic biology to create novel, human-made fuel-producing organisms (discussed in detail below).[5]

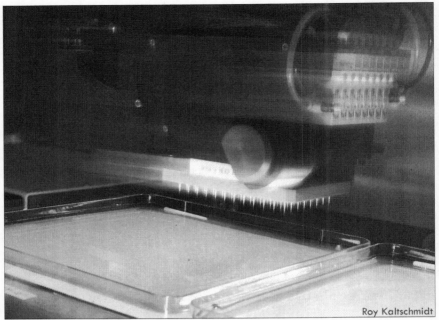

GENETIX "QPIX" COLONY PICKER ON A DNA SEQUENCING
PRODUCTION LINE AT LAWRENCE BERKELEY NATIONAL LABORATORY

In spite of the steep technological hurdles, advocates continue to claim that breakthroughs are imminent, that commercial scale production will be possible "soon"…"within 5-10 years."[6] But not all are so optimistic. According to the International Energy Agency: "The transition to an integrated 1st and 2nd generation biofuel landscape is … most likely to encompass the next one to two decades," and "it could be argued that in reality the first commercial plants are unlikely to be widely deployed before 2015-2020."[7] Economic modeling studies indicate that "once the opportunity cost of land is taken into account, rational farmers will not grow switchgrass or soybeans for biofuel production, and rational investors will not build these plants."[8]

Even with all this uncertainty, the 2007 Energy Independence and Security Act mandated an increasing quantity of second generation "advanced" transport fuels before the technologies were proven to be viable or the quantities feasible. Currently in the U.S. there are about 55 pilot and demonstration scale refineries, most still in planning stages.

Generous subsidies and massive research and development funding are financing the race to develop these technologies. Since February 2007, the U.S. DOE has invested over a billion dollars in research and development. Ethanol accounted for three-quarters of tax benefits and two-thirds of all federal subsidies provided for renewable energy sources in 2007. This amounted to $3 billion in tax credits in 2007, more than four times that which was made available to companies trying to expand all other forms of renewable energy, including solar, wind and geothermal power.[9]

The Global Subsidies Initiative estimates that "the biofuels industry will, in aggregate, benefit from support worth over $ 92 billion within the 2006 - 2012 time-frame."[10] Currently we spend only about $5 billion a year on all U.S. Department of Agriculture conservation programs to protect soil, water and wildlife habitat.[11]

In spite of the difficulties, and in spite of the growing awareness that corn ethanol has contributed to pushing large numbers of people into starvation, we are told it is a "necessary stepping stone," establishing a precedent and promoting the infrastructure changes needed for the eventual transition to "better" agrofuels. Since they are made from inedible plant parts (or wastes and residues), we are told, they will not compete with food production; and until they are commercially viable we should simply accept that many more people will starve, even as we continue to pay enormous subsidies to the industry.

Exactly What Feedstocks are being Considered and what are the Impacts of Producing them?

Grasses:
One of the most often cited feedstock for cellulosic fuel are grasses, particularly varieties of switchgrass (*Panicum virgatum*). Highly diverse grasslands, with healthy populations of leguminous plants, have been shown to be far more productive and far better at sequestering carbon dioxide than monocultures,[12] but using mixed feedstocks in any industrial process adds complexity to the enterprise. Grass monocultures are highly dependent on nitrogen fertilizers.[13] U.S. advocates for grass-based agrofuels have suggested that suitable species could be harvested from grasslands now allocated to the Agriculture Department's Conservation Reserve Program (CRP). This program pays farmers not to farm on lands that have high biodiversity, are vulnerable to erosion or are essential to waterway protection. Conservationists have highlighted the reserve program's remarkable success in reducing soil erosion and preserving wetlands. CRP lands have already been returned to production as pressures to grow corn for ethanol

have mounted. The predicted loss of Reserve Program lands in just three states in the U.S. alone will result in emissions equivalent to an adding 15 million cars on the road.[14] Harvesting grasses from remaining CRP lands will undermine their value for biodiversity protection, including essential pollinators.[15]

Tim Lindenbaum
BIODIVERSE NACHUSA GRASSLANDS

(The EU, under pressure to expand cultivation of energy crops has completely abolished a "set aside" land protection program analogous to the U.S. CRP program.)

Advocates for grass-based fuels also claim that harvesting grasslands could simulate the periodic fire disturbances that are necessary for the sustenance of prairie ecosystem, but this type of harvesting, (unlike fires) returns few nutrients to the soil, and harvesting equipment may prove far more disruptive to wildlife habitat than the spread of wildfire.

Many of the grass species being considered, like switchgrass and miscanthus, are invasive, lack known pests or diseases, and grow very rapidly; therefore outcompeting other (native) plants.[16, 17] One species, Giant Reed (*Arundo donax*), is listed among the world's most chronically invasive species—hazardous to riparian habitat on three continents. Efforts to develop faster-growing genetically engineered varieties of these grasses raise even greater alarm.[18] For example, the biotech company Ceres is currently engineering various prairie grasses to increase yields, resist drought and be more easily "digested" for fuel production.[19]

While grasses have the potential to increase soil carbon in some places where soils have been depleted, they generally require consistent water supplies, and are more productive with fertilizer application. Hence they will grow best in the same places that food crops grow best, namely prime agricultural land. If the price is right, farmers will switch from growing food to growing fuel crop grasses. Grasses also require a lot of space to produce enough volume. A recent modeling study showed that grasses, as well as short rotation woody crops would increase food-fuel competition even beyond that which is occurring with corn ethanol.[20] In short; the specific crop grown is less important than the amount, the incentives, or the type of land required.

Agricultural Residues:
Agricultural residues have been promoted specifically because they do not require additional land, but rather make use of the inedible portions of food crop plants. Unfortunately, those inedible plant parts are an essential source of organic soil matter when farmers leave them on fields. Removing them depletes soil nutrients, therefore necessitating increased use of fertilizers and agro-chemicals. Nitrous oxide emissions resulting from fertilizer use are a major source of greenhouse gases. They also contaminate waterways and are disrupting natural nutrient cycles on a global scale. Producing synthetic fertilizers depends upon the use of fossil fuels (natural gas).

Removal of crop residues also exposes soils to greater erosion, compaction and reduced water retention. The collection of residues requires more frequent use of redesigned, probably heavier combines, adding to costs and logistical problems for farmers and worsening soil compaction.[21] Nonetheless, some optimistically estimate that as much as 30% of crop residues could be removed.[22] These estimates, however, consider only erosion and do not consider soil nutrient impacts.[23]

The logistics of collecting, transporting and storing large quantities of feedstocks, are a huge obstacle. Refineries require massive and continuous feedstock supplies close at hand. For example, a corn stover-based refinery converting 25 tons per hour and running 24 hours/day would require 600 tons per day or 220,000 tons per year of stover delivery. Since the harvest season for stover is only about

5 weeks long, the entire annual supply would have to be harvested and stored during that time frame. This would require running about 57 harvesters capable of harvesting about 11 tons per hour each operating 10 hour days over those 5 weeks. Storing the stover for later use presents yet another challenge.[24]

These logistical problems are a recipe for perpetuating and expanding the industrial monoculture model of agriculture with all of its inherently destructive impacts. A small handful of large multinational corporations (Monsanto, Cargill, Bunge, Syngenta, ADM and others) profit enormously from this model and view second generation fuels as an opportunity to further consolidate their control and profits.

D'arcy Norman

MUNICIPAL WASTE

Wastes:

Some second generation agrofuel processes use wastes such as construction debris, paper refuse, used pallets, even old tires and plastics. These are promoted on the basis that they do not require agricultural lands, and "make use" of materials that would otherwise be wasted and decompose in landfills.

However, these wastes are the by-products of unsustainable and polluting practices. Creating a market for wastes only provides incentive to maintain the waste stream. An example is the diversion of organic matter, which could be composted, into landfills to maintain methane gas production for facilities that produce electricity from landfill gas.

Another major issue with waste technologies is that they consist of a mixture of materials, including painted, treated wood, inks and dyes etc. The toxic emissions that result when these materials are heated (including volatile organic compounds, heavy metals, dioxins, mercury, hydrocholoric acid, furans sulphur dioxide etc.) are poorly regulated and a matter of great concern, especially for the lower economic status communities where these facilities are often sited.

Wood:

Trees contain massive quantities of cellulose, can be grown in many different environments and can be harvested year-round. Wood is also extremely versatile; it can be burned to produce heat and electricity, refined into liquid transport fuel or used as raw material for chemicals and manufacturing processes. It therefore fits well in the "integrated biorefinery" concept where enormous facilities produce power, chemicals, fuels and more, from biomass.

By-products and residues from the pulp industry (black liquor, sawdust, limbs and thinnings etc.) as well as "purpose grown" trees can be used. Proponents claim that trees are a "renewable resource;" that using trees (or other biomass) is "carbon neutral" and that trees can be "sustainably harvested." But these terms are conveniently vague.

We can nonetheless cut through the fog by looking at the existing pulp and paper industry, which is based on the same 'green, renewable and sustainably managed' resource. The pulp industry is a leading cause of deforestation and pollution. It operates by first heavily logging or clear-cutting native forests, then replanting with industrial tree monocultures. Tree monocultures for pulp are often exotic species (i.e. fast growing eucalyptus, native to Australia, planted in Brazil or South Africa). Tree plantations bear no resemblance to forests, they sequester only a small portion of the carbon that primary forests are capable of sequestering and provide little or no habitat for biodiversity. They also displace people and are a major cause of waterway depletion and contamination. Lack of distinction between natural forests and monocultures has resulted in "reforesting" or "afforesting" land with industrial tree monocultures. These are little different than other industrial agricultural crops except that, because trees take longer to grow, they eliminate any possibility of natural forest regeneration, or the application of other less destructive land uses.

New research has shown that undisturbed old growth forests store FAR more carbon than disturbed forests.[25] This means that a much larger portion of the current atmospheric greenhouse gases have been generated by deforestation and degradation than previously estimated. It is increasingly clear that if we fail to protect remaining forests and do not permit natural forest cover to regenerate, we will not have a livable planet in the not too distant future. Given this state of

FOREST BIOMASS

affairs, it does not make sense to burn (or otherwise convert) trees for fuel.

Proponents often claim that only "thinnings" and "residues" will be removed, thereby "improving forest health." For example, researchers at Pennsylvania State University have proposed the harvesting of "small diameter trees that are overcrowded, underutilized, and inhibit the opportunity for professional management." They estimate that some 500 million tons of such trees could be harvested from 16 million acres of forestland in the state of Pennsylvania alone. [26] But, as in all ecosystems, (or a home garden, for that matter), forests function as closed systems: sustained removal cannot continue without depletion. Deadwood on forest floors is critical to much biodiversity, including lichens, fungi, birds and mammals;[27] as well as to the regeneration of forest soils and controlling water runoff.

The tired mantra that we need to remove wood and thin forests to "protect them" (from fire, pests and diseases) is misleadingly referred to as "forest restoration." For those who have followed the history of forestry practices and policies, such terms are no more than a thinly-veiled cover for destructive and unsustainable cutting that degrades and disrupts forest ecosystems to the point where they are indeed vulnerable. This leaves little basis for the notion that yet further "maintenance and restoration" will in fact be beneficial.

At a recent industry conference, Ron Barmore, the CEO of Range Fuels enthused that "We will see changes in how forest stands are managed: thinned quicker and cut sooner. We will see purpose grown trees and energy crops and other enhancements that will be valuable for companies like us."[28]

Because wood is expensive to harvest and transport, economics dictate that as much as possible be harvested as close as possible to facilities. A recent report on the practices of "residue removal" from forests in Germany (for biomass electricity facilities) described how storm damaged trees were gathered. The damaged trees were removed first, followed by the removal of virtually every scrap and twig. Afterwards heavy machinery was brought in and the stumps and roots were pulled up and dragged out. Following that, the land was completely emptied and soil damaged to the extent that no future tree growth was deemed possible.[29] Such poor practices are driven by short-sighted economics, not ecology.

A recent major forest products industry research report from Resource Information Systems Inc. (RISI) points out that there is already increasing competition between the pulp and paper industry and the bioenergy industry, and that there simply is not enough "waste and residue" to sustain the level of demand that is entailed in operating large biorefineries.[30] This does not seem to be dampening enthusiasm however, and the consequences for forests, biodiversity and climate are likely to be severe.

Companies like Arborgen; a partnership between International Paper, Mead-Westvaco and New Zealand-based Rubicon; claim that the solution is to develop genetically engineered trees that produce "more trees on less land." Toward this end; with the backing of the U.S. DOE; research is underway to engineer fast-growing species like eucalyptus and poplar for characteristics such as even faster growth, reduced lignin, tolerance to drought, pests and diseases, and freeze tolerance.[31, 32] These are intended to be of use to both the timber industry and to fuel producers.[33, 34]

Industrial tree plantations are not forests and are in fact extremely destructive, as has been well documented by the World Rainforest Movement. This is clearly evident, for example, in the southeastern U.S.; where more than 13 million hectares of natural forests have been converted to industrial pine monocultures. The prospect of large plantations of genetically engineered eucalyptus, poplar or pine raises the risk that native forests will be contaminated. The consequences of this are unknown, potentially severe and irreversible.

In spite of the various problems with feedstocks, claims are made that there is plenty of "marginal" and "idle" land available on which large quantities of feedstocks could be grown. At least an estimated 17 to 44% increase in the amount of land in agricultural production would be needed globally by 2020.[35] At the same time agriculture must feed an expanding and more affluent (meat eating) population, using soil and water resources that are in serious decline from poor management and from the impacts of climate change. The global scramble for access and ownership of good land is heating up. In a recent report, the Rights and Resources Initiative estimates that an additional 515 million hectares of land will be needed to grow crops and trees by 2030, which can only be achieved by cutting into the remaining intact forests. The author states that: "we are on the verge of a last great global land grab... that will mean more deforestation, more conflict, more carbon emissions, more climate change and less prosperity for everyone."

The idea that large quantities of "marginal" or "idle" lands are available is a dangerous myth that fails to consider the importance of biodiversity or to acknowledge the rights of pastoralists, smallholder farmers and indigenous peoples who rely upon these lands for their livelihoods. These terms are deliberately vague, and their misuse is facilitating massive land grabs that are destroying what remains of biodiverse ecosystems, and displacing people from their traditional lands. The magnitude of these land grabs is staggering and proceeding very rapidly throughout Africa, Asia and the Pacific and Latin America.[36] Unfortunately, the claim that there are massive quantities of "marginal and idle lands" is false. With powerful incentives in place, the conversion of biodiverse ecosystems and lands that are the basis of survival for many peoples, will continue to be converted to energy crops to fuel automobiles and produce other forms of energy.

"Second Generation Agrofuels Will be Good for the Poor"

As is already clear from the above, demand for food crops and energy crops, is stimulating a massive new demand for land. The U.S. farming and forestry communities view this as a boon to local economies, often with little attention paid to the ecological consequences or to the underlying causes of economic decline.

As large mandates for agrofuels in industrialized countries come into play, companies are eagerly buying up land with an eye to servicing these captive markets. This is hardly translating into an "opportunity" for the poor who are increasingly displaced and do not have the means to compete with large corporate agribusinesses. Companies seek access to the best land they can find, and local inhabitants are pushed aside. In some cases people are being violently kicked off their traditional lands and conflicts are increasingly frequent and bloody. In other cases, people are coerced, often with the complicity of their own national governments (see also Mendonça, Hurtado, this volume).

Expansion of oil palm plantations has led to particularly bloody conflicts in Colombia.[37] Loss of biodiversity and the displacement of millions of indigenous peoples has occurred in the wake of oil palm expansion throughout Indonesia and Malaysia.[38] The cultivation of palm oil in the Amazon is likely to expand in the near future.[39]

Jatropha is often touted as an energy crop ideally suited to "marginal" or degraded lands. Proponents claim it is a "wonder plant," capable of growing on poor soils, providing enormous quantities of valuable oil, and requiring little water or chemical inputs. Jatropha is native to Central America, where research on large scale cultivation is underway.[40]

India already has plans to put 14 million hectares of land under jatropha. Some of these lands are communal lands essential to local peoples for livestock grazing and subsistence farming. China similarly has plans for large scale jatropha cultivation, as do other countries. Unfortunately, the claims for jatropha have proven false: yields decline steeply on poor, infertile and dry soils, the seeds are highly toxic and the plant is invasive.[41] Meanwhile, huge investments have been made, and projects are already underway. Farmers who have been displaced or have agreed to contracts to cultivate jatropha are now facing dire consequences and expressing regrets.[I]

I. November 2008. Starving and Penniless, Ethiopian Farmers Rue Biofuel Choice.

YOUNG WORKERS AT AN EXPORT (EU) CASTOR
BEAN BIODIESEL PLANTATION IN TANZANIA

It is common for companies to represent their projects as providing development opportunities, and to offer false promises in exchange for land access. For example: foreign companies were granted access to nearly 641,170 hectares of land for biofuel production in Tanzania. According to the director of the Dar es Salaam-based Land Research and Resources Institute "most of the companies got the land directly from villagers in one-sided negotiations and contracts, given the little capacity of village officials to handle negotiations and correctly interpret the country's land use laws and regulations."[42]

In Ethiopia, Sun Biofuels (UK) was granted 3000 hectares of land on which they are cultivating castor bean for agrofuel feedstock. Local inhabitants in this densely populated and very poor area were coerced into participation with promises of payments, and assurances that only the "marginal" land would be used. Instead, the best agricultural areas were taken over, and the company has reneged on payments plunging the area further into poverty and hunger.

http://afp.google.com/article/ALeqM5gQXrMBu7K_4zYNu3ndLzilvHHDbw

With considerable freshwater resources and large amounts of land that are not currently in use for agriculture (though they are nonetheless vital to the livelihoods of people), Mozambique is being targeted for foreign investment. According to recent reports, there is a long line of massive biofuel projects backed by investors ranging from local speculators to multinational corporations like BP. As of 2007, biofuel investors had applied for rights to use about 12 million acres, nearly one-seventh of the country's 89 million acres of arable land; unofficial tallies are double that."[43]

Similar stories are flowing in daily from all corners; especially Africa, Asia and Latin America, where global assessments of land availability claim there are large amounts of "marginal land." These assessments are based on the assumption that large scale industrial farming in service of export markets is the only valuable "use" of land, and completely ignore the welfare of those currently living off these lands.

The "Bioeconomy"

Less recognized than the push for liquid transportation fuels is the larger trend towards a "bioeconomy," which would entail replacing virtually anything currently produced with fossil fuels with a plant biomass substitute. This includes not only powering transportation, but also burning biomass for electricity and heat, powering industrial processes, manufacturing everything from construction materials to carpeting to fabrics, making chemicals and plastics, and more.

Under pressure to reduce greenhouse gases, enormous quantities of plant matter (wood chips, wood pellets, grasses, vegetable oils, etc.) are being consumed by a growing armada of biomass powered electricity and heat generation facilities. While there are major technological hurdles involved in converting plant biomass into liquid fuels, there are few barriers to burning it. In the EU, a large proportion of facilities are already cofiring biomass with coal or burning biomass (including vegetable oils) alone. In the U.S. a similar transition is occurring, albeit a bit more slowly.

This enormous transition to biomass as a substitute for fossil fuels sets the stage for a wave of genetic engineering, corporate patenting, and privatization of plant resources that is deeply troubling. Plants like sugar cane, sugar beet, corn and other food crops are already being engineered for easy conversion to fuel. What will the implications be if/when cross pollination with food crops occurs?

Resistance to genetically engineered (GE) crops has been strong in the EU, Africa, Latin America and elsewhere, based largely on concerns about health impacts of consuming GE crops. Since fuel crops are not intended for human consumption, the biotechnology industry is seizing the opportunity to sidestep those concerns and break down barriers to markets in those regions.

The development of synthetic microbes for accessing and fermenting the sugars in cellulosic biomass are also troubling. Unlike more established 'transgenic' genetic engineering, where already existing genes are identified in nature and then transferred between organisms, the practice of synthetic biology allows engineers to invent entirely new genetic sequences that may never have existed before and to combine them into new sets of genetic instructions. These synthetic DNA instructions are then engineered into yeast, bacteria and other microbes which in turn are transformed into microbial production units for churning out drugs, chemicals, plastics and of course fuels. Companies developing synthetic microbes include DuPont, Solazymes, BP, Chevron, Shell, Cargill, LS9, Virent, Amyris, Virgin Fuels, and others.

If genetic modification has raised biosafety concerns, those pale in comparison to the safety and ecological risks of synthetic organisms. The same technology that allows synthetic biologists to build designer DNA for agrofuels has already been used to build working versions of dangerous bioweapons.[44] Like genetically modified organisms (GMOs), synthetic organisms are alive, meaning they can reproduce, mutate and escape but unlike earlier genetic engineering where genes are sourced form existing organisms, synthetic DNA sequences may have no known analogue in nature. This makes any biosafety assessment a shot in the dark since these organisms are in no way 'substantially equivalent' to anything we know. Much of synthetic biology involves adding not one genetic trait but a whole 'pathway' of genetic mechanisms, so the potential for disruption and unanticipated side effects is much higher. Furthermore synthetic biologists tend to treat the task of building novel life-forms as a hard information technology or engineering discipline, even though practitioners are increasingly finding that the wet and living materials they are working with are far less predictable than electronic circuits or computer code.

In spite of the risks—an absence of biosafety regulations, and very poor understanding of microbial communities and ecology—the synthetic biology industry envisions thousands of biorefineries dotting the landscape efficiently turning plant matter into plastics, fuels and drugs. In such a scenario environmental escape of synthetic microorganisms through waste streams or human error is inevitable, with largely unpredictable consequences.

Conclusions

No matter what choices we make about feedstocks for agrofuels, and no matter what plant parts we use; arable land, soils, water and fertilizers are all in limited supply. At the same time we are faced with a rapidly expanding human population to feed, and a rapidly warming planet in which agricultural production and biodiversity are declining. Against this background, it does not make sense to add an enormous new demand for plant biomass.

The U.S. uses more than 140 billion gallons of gasoline and almost 40 billion gallons of diesel fuel annually. The 2005 Energy Independence and Security Act mandated that 250 million gallons of ethanol be obtained from cellulose materials by 2012. The Obama administration is considering expanding this further and it will also likely be increased by adoption of a Low Carbon Fuel Standard, first in California and then at federal level. Current ethanol yields from agricultural residues (corn stover, etc.) are about 65 gallons per dry ton.[45]

For a moderate sized refinery producing around 65 million gallons per year of ethanol from corn stover, about a million dry tons of feedstock would be needed. Depending on what percentage of stover was removed, this would entail harvesting from at least approximately 500,000 acres of surrounding land.

The USDA estimates that 1.3 **billion** tons of biomass could be harvested "sustainably," but this estimate is based on removing most agricultural residues from all U.S. farmland, planting 55 million hectares under perennial crops like switchgrass, putting all U.S. farmland under "no-till" agriculture, harvesting from Conservation Reserve Program lands, *and* greatly increasing fertilizer use. A recent analysis by Pimentel concludes that total biomass production in the U.S. amounts to about 2 billion tons. Thus, the idea that 1.3 billion could be utilized for fuel production would require using most of the grass, trees, agricultural crops produced, leaving the country virtually denuded (and hungry).[46]

For another (more international) perspective: the highest yielding bioenergy process, sugar cane ethanol in Brazil, currently accounts for 0.4 EJ of gross energy from cane harvested on 3.6 million hectares. This translates into about 0.11 EJ per one million hectares. Assuming that Brazilian sugar cane ethanol achieves an energy balance of 8.3 (an optimistic assessment from Machedo[47]), that would mean 0.097EJ net energy is gained from one million hectares of sugar cane: a rather small contribution given that, according to the Intergovernmental Panel on Climate Change (IPCC), global transport energy use is 77 EJ.[48]

To extrapolate, 794 million hectares of land would be required to supply transport energy at the current rate of consumption. To put this amount of land in perspective, consider that the U.S. has, in total, about 384 million hectares (950 mil acres) of farmland,[II] (and this is using overly optimistic figures for sugar cane growing in humid tropics, which could not be replicated in many parts of the world).

Humans already use between a quarter and 40 percent of the earth's net primary productivity for feed, fiber, food, and fuel. As the 2005 Millennium Ecosystem Assessment demonstrated, this degree of appropriation has already compromised essential ecosystem functions such as water and nitrogen cycling.[49] According to Energy historian Vaclav Smil, proposals to increase the use of biomass used to 1-2 gigatonnes (as in the U.S. 'billion ton' vision) would likely push human appropriation of plant matter above 50%—a deeply unsustainable prospect.[50]

Proponents of cellulosic fuels fundamentally lack a realistic appraisal of how much biomass exists, how much energy can be derived from it, and what the ecological consequences of biomass removal on such a large scale, will be. This "disconnect" with reality is leading us down the wrong path at the wrong time! We cannot simply substitute biomass for fossil fuels without stripping the planet bare and burning up every available scrap of plant matter.

Fossil fuels are derived from a process in which the energy in organic matter was concentrated over millions of years. Living plants store a much smaller amount of energy, limited to the efficiency of their photosynthetic processes. We are faced with dwindling soils and water resources, an expanding population, and the dire consequences of climate change; all of which demand that we protect and enhance ecosystems, including forests, grasslands and oceans that regulate climate and water cycles; not burn them up to fuel our completely unsustainable appetite for energy.

II. USDA Economic Research Service http://www.ers.usda.gov/StateFacts/US.htm

Corporate greed, along with a failure to recognize—or the deliberate obfuscation of—these limitations have led to huge financial and other investments in biomass technologies. They have distracted us from the fundamental restructuring of lifestyles and infrastructures that are desperately needed: a dramatic decrease in consumption by wealthy countries, re-localization of food production and distribution, efficient public transportation systems, stewardship of biodiversity and reigning in of corporate control over all aspects of life. We would do well to reallocate the funds currently committed to second generation agrofuels, towards these necessary ends.

Photo and Image Credits:

1. Corn Stover: Photo by Wally Wilhelm, U.S. Department of Agriculture.
2. Colony Picker Robot: Photo by Roy Kaltschmidt, Lawrence Berkeley National Laboratory. Creative Commons License (details: http://creativecommons.org/licenses/by-nc-nd/2.0/deed.en) Photo URL: http://www.flickr.com/photos/berkeleylab/3523095147
3. Diverse Nachusa Grasslands: Tim Lindenbaum, Creative Commons License (details: http://creativecommons.org/licenses/by-nc-nd/2.0/deed.en) Photo URL: http://www.flickr.com/photos/lindenbaum/3504378251/
4. Municipal Waste: D'arcy Norman, Creative Commons license (details: http://creativecommons.org/licenses/by/2.0/deed.en) Photo URL: http://www.flickr.com/photos/dnorman/3590135801/
5. Wood Biomass: Photo by Asea_ Creative Commons License (details: http://creativecommons.org/licenses/by-nc-sa/2.0/deed.en) Photo URL: http://www.flickr.com/photos/asea/2843890318/
6. Castor Bean Biodiesel Plantation, Tanzania: Photo by Ilan Sharif, Creative Commons License (details: http://creativecommons.org/licenses/by-nc/2.0/deed.en) Photo URL: http://www.flickr.com/photos/ilans1/669318292

References:

1   Albert L. Lehninger, Biochemistry, New York: Worth Publishers, 1970, p. 231.
2   ibid., pp. 231-232.
3   EPA Biomass Conversion Matrix
4   Food and Water Watch. 2007. The Rush to Ethanol: Not all biofuels are created equal. p. 55. Food & Water Watch and Network for New Energy Choices In collaboration with Institute for Energy and the Environment at Vermont Law School. http://www.foodandwaterwatch.org/food/pubs/reports/rush-to-ethanol/download?id=pdf
5   Agrofuels: Towards a reality check, pp. 14-15; Nicholas Wade, "Scientists Transplant Genome of Bacteria," New York Times, June 29, 2007.
6   Allen Baker and Steven Zahniser, "Ethanol Reshapes the Corn Market," Amber Waves, Vol. 4, No. 2, Washington, DC: USDA, April 2006, p. 35.

7   Sims, R., Taylor, M., Saddler, J. and Mabee, W. 2008. From 1st to 2nd Generation
     Biofuel Technologies. IEA/OECD

8   Crop-Based Biofuel Production under Acreage Constraints and Uncertainty, by Mindy
     L. Baker, Dermot J. Hayes, and Bruce A. Babcock; Working Paper 08-WP 460, February
     2008; Center for Agricultural and Rural Development, Iowa State University. Ames, Iowa.

9   Environmental Working Group. 2009. Ethanol's Federal Subsidy Grab Leaves Little
     for Solar, Wind and Geothermal Energy. Accessed 03/27/09: http://www.ewg.org/
     node/27498

10   Koplow, Doug.. 2007. Biofuels-at what Cost? Government support for ethanol and
     biodiesel in the United States: 2007 Update. The Global Subsidies Initiative (GSI).
     Accessed 03/21/09: http://www.globalsubsidies.org/files/assets/Brochure_-_US_
     Update.pdf

11   Ethanol's Federal Subsidy Grab Leaves Little for Solar, Wind and Geothermal Energy.
     Environmental Working Group. January 8th, 2009http://www.ewg.org/book/export/
     html/27498

12   David Tilman, et al., "Carbon-Negative Biofuels from Low-Input High-Diversity Grassland
     Biomass," Science Vol. 314, December 8, 2006, p. 1598.

13   Kenneth P. Vogel, et al., "Switchgrass Biomass Production in Midwest USA: Harvest and
     Nitrogen Management," Agronomy Journal, Vol. 94, 2002, pp. 413-420.

14   Carbon, Conservation Reserve Program and Native Prairie. Ducks Unlimited.
     April 2008

15   Izaak Walton League, et al., Letter to Congress, June 14, 2006. http://www.iwla.
     org/index.php?id=325.

16   Raghu, S, R. C. Anderson, C. C. Daehler, A. S. Davis, R. N. Wiedenmann, D. Simberloff,
     & R. N. Mack. 2006. "Adding Biofuels to the Invasive Species Fire?" Science Vol. 313,
     September 22, 2006, p. 1742.

17   Andrew Pollack, "Redesigning Crops to Harvest Fuel," New York Times,
     September 8, 2006, p. C1.

18   ibid.

19   Crop-Based Biofuel Production under Acreage Constraints and Uncertainty, by Mindy
     L. Baker, Dermot J. Hayes, and Bruce A. Babcock; Working Paper 08-WP 460, February
     2008; Center for Agricultural and Rural Development, Iowa State University. Ames, Iowa,
     http://www.card.iastate.edu/publications/DBS/PDFFiles/08wp460.pdf

20   Rachel Barron, "Q&A: Harvesting Cellulosic Ethanol," Greentech Media,
     September 21, 2007, at http://www.greentechmedia.com/articles/harvesting-
     cellulosic-ethanol-097.html.

21   Food & Water Watch. 2007. The Rush to Ethanol: Not all biofuels are created equal,
     analysis and recommendations for U.S. biofuels policy. Food & Water Watch and Network
     for New Energy Choices In collaboration with Institute for Energy and the Environment at
     Vermont Law School. p. 57. http://www.newenergychoices.org/uploads/RushToEthanol-
     rep.pdf

22   American Society of Agronomy. 2007. November 29). Limited Biofuel Feedstock
     Supply?. Science Daily. Retrieved March 25, 2008, from http://www.sciencedaily.com /

releases/2007/11/071128163240.htm

23 Cundiff, John. 2008. Biomass South 2008 Conference, Panel Discussion: "How will the Southeast Contribute to the Renewable Fuels Standard?" Raleigh, North Carolina, September 21-23, 2008.

24 Green Carbon: The role of natural forests in carbon storage_Part 1. A green carbon account of Australia's south-eastern Eucalypt forests, and policy implications. Brendan G. Mackey, Heather Keith, Sandra L. Berry and David B. Lindenmayer 2008 http://epress. anu.edu.au/green_carbon_citation.html

25 David Pacchioli, "Researchers at the new Biomass Energy Center are Honing in on Future Fuels," Penn State University, September 24, 2007, at http://www. rps.psu.edu/indepth/bioeneergy1.html.

27 Paul, Helena & Almuth Ernsting. 2007. Second Generation Biofuels: An Unproven Future Technology with Unknown Risks. World Rainforest Movement. http://www.wrm.org. uy/subjects/agrofuels/Secon_Generation_Biofuels.pdf

28 Ron Barmore at "Biomass South", Sept 21-23, 2008, Raleigh, North Carolina

29 Odenwald, Michael. 2008. Biomasse: Modernes Waldsterben. Online Focus. http://www. focus.de/wissen/wissenschaft/klima/tid-12399/biomasse-modernes-waldsterben_ aid_345106.html

30 Resource Information Systems Inc. 2008. Market Report dispels myth of ' overabundant waste wood' myth.   http://www.risiinfo.com/technologyarchives/ risi-wood-biomass-market-report-woodfiber-supply.html

31 U.S. Animal and Plant Health Inspection Service. 2007. "of No Significant Impact and Decision Notice. USDA Docket No. APHIS-2007-0027, August 17, 2007.

32 Gunther, Mark. 2007. Super trees: The latest in genetic engineering. Fortune, August 27, 2007. http://money.cnn.com/2007/07/31/technology/pluggedin_ gunther_supertrees.fortune/index.htm

33 Zeman, Nicholas. 2007. Growing Forests of Fuel. Ethanol Producer, April 2007.

34 Marc Gunther, "Super trees: The latest in genetic engineering," Fortune, August 2007, at http://money.cnn.com/2007/07/31/technology/pluggedin_gunther_ supertrees.fortune/index.htm.

35 July 2008. The Gallagher Review of the Indirect Effects of Biofuel Production. Renewable Fuels Agency. UK

36 GRAIN. 2008. Seized: The 2008 land grab for food and financial security. Accessed 03/09/09: http://www.grain.org/briefings_files/landgrab-2008-en.pdf

37 Monahan, Jane. 2008. Afro-Colombians fight biodiesel producers. BBC News. Accessed 03/21/09: http://news.bbc.co.uk/2/hi/business/7784117.stm

38 Ernsting, Almuth. 2007. Agrofuels in Asia: Fuelling poverty, conflict, deforestation and climate change. Grain. Accessed 09/11/08: http://www.grain.org/seedling_files/seed-07-07-4-en.pdf

39 Butler, Rhett, and W. Laurance. 2009. Is Oil Palm the Next Emerging Threat to the Amazon? Tropical Conservation Science Vol. 2(1): 1-10 2009

40 Syngenta. 2008. Jatropha Biofuel in Central America. Accessed 03/21/09:
    http://www.syngentafoundation.org/index.cfm?pageID=554

41 Jonschaap, R.E.E. 2007. Position Paper on Jatropha curcas. European Commission
    meeting in Brussels, December, 7, 2007.

42 The Citizen (Dar es Salaam). 23 July 2008. Government On the Spot Over Biofuel
    Production. http://allafrica.com/stories/200807240051.html

43 Welz, Adam 2009. Ethanol's African Land Grab: Mozambique has survived colonialism,
    and civil war, but can it survive the ethanol industry? Mother Jones, March/April issue.

44 ETC Group. 2007. Extreme Genetic Engineering: An introduction to synthetic biology.
    www.etcgroup.org/upload/publication/pdf_file/602

45 U.S. Department of Energy. 2006. Breaking the Biological Barriers to Cellulosic
    Ethanol: A Joint Research Agenda. June 2006, DOE/SC-0095. http://74.125.93.104/
    search?q=cache:ZA0s48MhnXQJ:www.biomatnet.org/secure/Other/S2098.htm+Break
    ing+the+Biological+Barriers+to+Cellulosic+Ethanol:+A+Joint+Research+Agenda&cd=6
    &hl=en&ct=clnk&gl=us

46 Pimentel, D. Marklein, A, Toth, M.A., Karpoff, M.N., Paul, G.S., McCormack,
    R., Kyriazis, J. and Krueger, T. 2009. Food Versus Biofuels: Environmental and
    Economic Costs. Human Ecology. 37: 1-12

47 Macedo, Isaias de Carvalho. 2005, Sugar Cane's Energy. Twelve studies on
    Brazilian sugar cane agribusiness and its sustainability. UNICA

48 Ernsting, Almuth, and Deepak Rughani. 2008. Climate Geo-engineering with 'Carbon
    Negative' Bioenergy: Climate saviour or climate endgame? Biofuel Watch: Accessed
    03/21/09: http://www.biofuelwatch.org.uk/docs/cnbe/climate_geoengineering_
    web221208.pdf

49 Millenium Ecosystem Assessment. 2005. Ecosystems and Human Well-being: Biodiversity
    Synthesis. Washington D.C., World Resources Institute.

50 Smil, Vaclav. 2003. The Earth's Biosphere: Evolution, Dynamics, and Change.
    Cambridge, MIT Press.

About Food First

Food First, also known as the Institute for Food and Development Policy, is a nonprofit research and education-for-action center dedicated to investigating and exposing the root causes of hunger in a world of plenty. It was founded in 1975 by Frances Moore Lappe, author of the bestseller Diet for a Small Planet, and food policy analyst, Dr. Joseph Collins. Food First research has revealed that hunger is created by concentrated economic and political power, not by scarcity. Resources and decision making are in the hands of a wealthy few, depriving the majority of land and jobs, and therefore of food.

Hailed by The New York Times as "one of the most established food think tanks in the country," Food First has grown to profoundly shape the debate about hunger and development.

But Food First is more than a think tank. Through books, reports, videos, media, and public speaking, Food First experts not only reveal the often hidden roots of hunger, they show how individuals can get involved in bringing an end to hunger. Food First inspires action by bringing to light the efforts of people and their organizations around the world who are creating farming and food systems that truly meet people's needs.

More Books From Food First

NEW FROM FOOD FIRST:

Food Rebellions: *Crisis and the Hunger for Justice*
Eric Holt-Gimenez and Raj Patel

'In this very timely book, two of the world's most prominent critics of the global food system, Eric Holt-Giménez and Raj Patel, dissect the causes of hunger and the food price crisis, locating them in a political economy of capitalist industrial production dominated by corporations and driven by the search for profits for the few instead of the welfare of the many. The picture that emerges is a political economy of global production that is failing badly in terms of feeding the world and is itself contributing to the spread of inequalities that promote hunger.'

Walden Bello, president of the Freedom from Debt Coalition and professor of sociology at the University of the Philippines

Food Rebellions! takes a deep look at the world food crisis and its impact on the Global South and under-served communities in the industrial North. While most governments and multilateral organisations offer short-term solutions based on proximate causes, authors Eric Holt-Giménez and Raj Patel unpack the planet's environmentally and economically vulnerable food systems to reveal the root causes of the crisis. By tracking the political and economic evolution of the industrial agri-foods complex, Food Rebellions! shows us how the steady erosion of local and national control over their food systems has made African nations dependent on a volatile global market and subject to the short-term interests of a handful of transnational agri-food monopolies

Beyond the Fence: *A journey to the roots of the migration crisis*
Dori Stone

Inspiring stories of Mexico's farmer to farmer movements restoring degraded hillsides and watersheds, reclaiming old methods of seed saving and seed exchange, and incorporating the latest agroecological techniques developed by other farmers and agroecology scientists and practitioners.

Beyond the Fence explores aspects of migration largely unnoticed by the public and mainstream media. These are the root causes and complex realities, the stories and surprising possibilities that get lost in a debate over fences. They are the tales of people's desperation and irretrievable loss, but also of their growing visions for hope. They are the stories of farmers, politicians and activists on both sides of the border.

"Dori Stone travels with an open mind and open heart to investigate the deeper meaning of Mexican migration to the United States, and in her traveling asks dozens of good questions, and often comes up with excellent answers that will be of interest to a wide readership. Many will be inspired to want to take a similar trip, whether by actually repeating her steps, or intellectually, by further investigating the amazing array of urgent issues she explores. The combination of first-hand observation with serious research works beautifully. She not only travels far into Mexico for the issues, but she travels profoundly and always with a good spirit. The book is ideally suited for students, but I can think of few people who would not benefit from reading it."

Angus Wright, author of The Death of Ramon Gonzalez: The Modern Agricultural Dilemma (University of Texas Press, 2005)

Paperback, $16.95

OTHER BOOKS FROM FOOD FIRST:

◆*Alternatives to the Peace Corps: A guide to global volunteer opportunities, Twelfth Edition*
Edited by Caitlin Hachmeyer
Newly expanded and updated, this easy-to-use guidebook is the original resource for finding community-based, grassroots volunteer work—the kind of work that changes the world, one person at a time.
Paperback, $11.95

◆*Campesino a Campesino: Voices from Latin America's farmer to farmer movement for sustainable agriculture*
Eric Holt-Gimenez
The voices and stories of dozens of farmers are captured in this first written history of the farmer-to-farmer movement, which describes the social, political, economic, and environmental circumstances that shape it.
Paperback, $19.95

◆*Promised Land: Competing visions of agrarian reform*

179

Edited by Peter Rosset, Raj Patel, and Michael Courville
Agrarian reform is back at the center of the national and rural development debate. The essays in this volume critically analyze a wide range of competing visions of land reform.
Paperback, $21.95

•*Sustainable Agriculture and Resistance: Transforming food production in Cuba*
Edited by Fernando Funes, Luis Garcia, Martin Bourque, Nilda Perez, and Peter Rosset
Unable to import food or farm chemicals and machines in the wake of the Soviet bloc's collapse and a tightening US embargo, Cuba turned toward sustainable agriculture, organic farming, urban gardens, and other techniques to secure its food supply. This book gives details of that remarkable achievement.
Paperback, $18.95

•*The Future in the Balance: Essays on globalization and resistance*
Walden Bello. Edited with a preface by Anuradha Mittal
A collection of essays by global south activist and scholar Walden Bello on the myths of development as prescribed by the World Trade Organization and other institutions, and the possibility of another world based on fairness and justice. Paperback, $13.95

•*Views from the South: The effects of globalization and the WTO on Third World Countries*
Foreword by Jerry Mander. Afterword by Anuradha Mittal Edited by Sarah Anderson
This rare collection of essays by activists and scholars from the Global South describes, in pointed detail, the effects of the WTO and other Bretton Woods institutions.
Paperback, $12.95

•*Basta! Land and the Zapatista rebellion in Chiapas, Third Edition*
George A. Collier with Elizabeth Lowery-Quaratiello
Foreword by Peter Rosset
The classic on the Zapatistas in its third edition, including a preface by Rodolfo Stavenhagen.
Paperback, $16.95

♦*America Needs Human Rights*
Edited by Anuradha Mittal and Peter Rosset
This anthology includes writings on understanding human rights, poverty and welfare reform in America.
Paperback, $13.95

♦*The Paradox of Plenty:* Hunger in a bountiful world
Edited by Douglas H. Boucher
Excerpts from Food First's best writings on world hunger and what we can do to change it.
Paperback, $18.95

We encourage you to buy Food First Books from your local independent bookseller; if they don't have them in stock, they can usually order them for you fast. To find an independent bookseller in your area, go to www.booksense.com.

Food First books are also available through major online booksellers (Powell's, Amazon, and Barnes and Noble), and through the Food First website, www.foodfirst.org. You can also order direct from our distributor, Perseus Distribution, at (800) 343-4499. If you have trouble locating a Food First title, write, call, or e-mail us:

Food First
398 60th Street
Oakland, CA 94618-1212 USA
Tel: (510) 654-4400
Fax: (510) 654-4551
E-mail: foodfirst@foodfirst.org
Web: www.foodfirst.org

If you are a bookseller or other reseller, contact our distributor, Perseus Distribution, at (800) 343-4499, to order.

Films from Food First

◆ *The Greening of Cuba*
Jaime Kibben
A profiling of Cuban farmers and scientists working to reinvent a sustainable agriculture based on ecological prinCiples and local knowledge.
DVD (In Spanish with English subtitles), $35.00

◆ *America Needs Human Rights*
A film told in the voices of welfare mothers, homeless men and women, low-wage workers, seniors, veterans, and health care workers.
DVD, $19.95

◆ *Caminos:* The immigrants' trail
Juan Carlos Zaldivar
Stories of Mexican farmers who were driven off their land, foced to leave their families and risk their lives to seek work in the U.S.
DVD and Study Guide: $20.00

How to Become a Member or Intern of Food First

Join Food First

Private contributions and membership gifts fund the core of Food First/Institute for Food and Development Policy's work. Each member strengthens Food First's efforts to change a hungry world. We invite you to join Food First. As a member you will receive a 20 percent discount on all Food First books. You will also receive our quarterly publications, Food First News and Views and Backgrounders, providing information for action on current food and hunger crises in the United States and around the world. If you want to subscribe to our Internet newsletter, People Putting Food First, send us an e-mail at foodfirst@foodfirst.org. All contributions are tax deductible.

You are also invited to give a gift membership to others interested in the fight to end hunger www.foodfirst.org.

Become an Intern for Food First

There are opportunities for interns in research, advocacy, campaigning,

182

publishing, computers, media, and publicity at Food First. Our interns come from around the world. They are a vital part of the organization and make the work possible.

To become a member or apply to become an intern, just call, visit our website, or clip and return the attached coupon to:
Food First
398 60th Street
Oakland, CA 94618-1212 USA
Tel. 510/654-4400
www.foodfirst.org

◆*Education for Action:* *Undergraduate and graduate programs that focus on social change, Fourth Edition*
   Edited by Joan Powell
   An updated authoritative and easy-to-use guidebook that provides information on progressive programs in a wide variety of fields.
   Paperback, $12.95

JOINING FOOD FIRST

☐ I want to join Food First and receive a 20% discount on this and all subsequent orders. Enclosed is my tax-deductible contribution of:

☐ $25 Low Income ☐ $50 Member ☐ $100 Sustainer
☐ $1,000 Major Donor ☐ OTHER

NAME: _____

ADDRESS:_____

CITY/STATE/ZIP

_____

DAYTIME PHONE (____)_____

EMAIL_____

ORDERING FOOD FIRST MATERIALS

ITEM DESCRIPTION	QTY	UNIT COST	TOTAL

PAYMENT METHOD:
(PAYABLE TO
FOOD FIRST)

☐ CHECK

☐ MONEY ORDER

☐ MASTERCARD

☐VISA

☐ AMERICAN EXPRESS

MEMBER DISCOUNT 20%_____
CA SALES TAX 9.75%_____
SUBTOTAL_____

SHIPPING DOMESTIC ORDERS:
$5.00 FOR THE FIRST BOOK_____
$2.50 FOR EACH ADDITIONAL BOOK_____
MEMBERSHIP(S)_____
ANNUAL CONTRIBUTION_____
TOTAL ENCLOSED_____

NAME ON CARD _____
CARD NUMBER _____ EXP. DATE _____
SIGNATURE _____

FOOD FIRST ▪ 398 60TH STREET, OAKLAND, CA 94618 - 1212

For gift memberships and mailings, please see coupon on next page

FOOD FIRST GIFT BOOKS
Please send a gift book to (order form on previous page):

NAME _____

ADDRESS _____

CITY/STATE/ZIP _____

FROM _____

FOOD FIRST PUBLICATIONS CATALOGS
Please send a publication catalogue to:

NAME _____

ADDRESS _____

CITY/STATE/ZIP _____

FROM _____

NAME _____

ADDRESS _____

CITY/STATE/ZIP _____

NAME _____

ADDRESS _____

CITY/STATE/ZIP _____

FOOD FIRST GIFT MEMBERSHIPS
☐ Enclosed is my tax-deductible contribution of:

☐ $50 ☐ $100 ☐ $1,000 ☐ OTHER

Please send a Food First membership to:

NAME _____

ADDRESS _____

CITY/STATE/ZIP _____

FROM _____

...